汇中外　语通世界

我的「成电梦」

WODE CHENGDIANMENG

——电子科技大学外语专业本科生论文习作

（第二辑）

主　编　冯文坤　楚军

执行主编　李杰　周劲松

　　　　　姚连兵　罗旋

　　　　　俞博

电子科技大学出版社

University of Electronic Science and Technology of China Press

·成都·

图书在版编目(CIP)数据

我的"成电梦":电子科技大学外语专业本科生论文
习作.第二辑 / 冯文坤,楚军主编. —成都:电子科技
大学出版社,2018.3

ISBN 978-7-5647-5877-6

Ⅰ.①我… Ⅱ.①冯…②楚… Ⅲ.①英语-毕业论
文-写作-高等学校-教材 Ⅳ.①G642.477②H315

中国版本图书馆 CIP 数据核字(2018)第 051567 号

我的"成电梦"——电子科技大学外语专业本科生论文习作(第二辑)

主　　编　冯文坤　楚　军
执行主编　李　杰　周劲松　姚连兵　罗　旋　俞　博

策划编辑　谢应成
责任编辑　谢应成

出版发行　电子科技大学出版社
　　　　　成都市一环路东一段 159 号电子信息产业大厦九楼　邮编　610051
主　　页　www.uestcp.com.cn
服务电话　028-83203399
邮购电话　028-83201495

印　　刷　成都市火炬印务有限公司
成品尺寸　185 mm×260 mm
印　　张　12.5
字　　数　290 千字
版　　次　2018 年 3 月第 1 版
印　　次　2018 年 3 月第 1 次印刷
书　　号　ISBN 978-7-5647-5877-6
定　　价　48.00 元

树立精英意识·优化育人环节·培养精英人才

电子科技大学外语学院　冯文坤

　　学生主动选择一所大学，意味着他们认同了一所大学的价值，意味着他们对"我将成为什么样的人"有了一种期待，尽管这种期待在一个大学生那里还十分朦胧，但他们却从此接受了这所大学对他们未来的一种承诺。"我是谁？从哪里来？到哪里去？"这是古希腊哲学家苏格拉底提出的问题。古希腊哲人认为，人活着就是为了弄清楚这三个问题。"我是谁？""从哪里来？到哪里去？"这三问不仅是哲学中询问"人"的意义的问题，也可以是一所大学应该首先思考"培养什么人"和"如何培养人"的问题，因为大学是青年人自我塑型和自我形成的地方，是向社会许下未来和承诺美好价值的地方，因此，大学责无旁贷，应率先帮助学生去思考"我从哪里来""我是谁""我将到哪里去"这三个问题，并在教育过程中回答学生对人生的建构。

　　两年前，言荣校长在"关于我校本科人才培养的思考"的报告中，全面总结了学校人才培养所取得的成绩、存在的问题和今后人才培养的目标与实现路径，至今令人振奋，发人深思，催人改进和革新，尤其是言荣校长直逼大学"要培养什么人"和"如何培养人"的发问，并立足电子科技大学，提出了未来电子科技大学精英人才培养目标定位，体现了言荣校长枕于忧患、着眼于未来的教育战略思维和一位教育家的人才培养观，更体现了秉持科大"追求卓越，大气大为"之校训精神的办学理念自信、发展自信和责任自信。精英培养，引领大众，服务于社会是大学的崇高使命，更是对电子科技大学几代人崇高使命的继承和发扬。根据校长讲话，结合外语学院办学实际，围绕精英人才培养定位谈几点愚见和忧思。

一、创新人才培养模式，蕴育精英人才成长

　　要成就精英人才之办学目标，要明确人才培养的模式定位，要使学生明确知道"我成为谁""我要到哪里去"，要以学生成才或培养效果或标准为终极目标。也就是说，效果或标准重于环节，环节推动人才成长，要把有效教学、有效学习和有效评估统一起来。今天，我们的教学管理过程，学习管理过程，似乎每个环节都做到了，有的环节还非常严苛，我们的精力都用来应付这些环节，形式大于内容，学生成长实际效果如何，却没有给予充分重视，因为对人才终端之效果如何担责的问题十分模糊，也是十分复杂，但背后折射出的却是大学之全体责任。法不责众，更何况是一个庞大之机构。生产线上的不合格产品可以退回，可人不同于物。拿外语人才培养来说，一个学生通过 4 年学习，他是不是实现了当初选择的专业人才愿望，是不是达到该专业人才所应有的要求，如外语交际能力、外语写作能力、系统的学科知识以及认知能力等，还是仅仅入了大学，遵循了每个环节，蹲满了学分，最后成为"毕了业的人才"。就我个人愚见，大众教育重通识，精英教育更重研究能力和创新思维。大众教育造就学生"成人"，精英教育造就学生"成为杰出的人"或成为具有精英意识的人。

二、创新课程体系，适应精英人才培养

要培养精英外语人才，就要遵循外语学科的系统性和人文人才培养规律，要实现语言的人文性和工具性的高度统一，要实现中国情怀和国际视野在一个外语人才身上的结合，要在把握语言工具性的过程中含化人文教育，要实实在在把语言转化为学科性学习和向外拓展的工具理性。由此，应该反思我们现有的外语课程内容体系：缺乏学科系统性、内容片段化、破碎化和随意性；操作性、技能训练占到接近 80%、内容倒转为技能服务；课程体系性不衔接，课程层级不分明，课程目标不清楚；特色原本是学科体系中的特色，却一言以蔽之，外语加特色，其结果是特色性遮蔽专业学科属性，不伦不类。

由此产生三大后果、引发三大整改：外语人才学科定位不清楚，专业兴趣游移，效果不明确，标准不清楚，不利于杰出专业人才成长，因此应强化学科专业定位和人才培养目标的课程体系建设；仅仅为技能而设计的课程体系就如有"矛"无"盾"，有驾照无车开，开花不结果，因此应将操作性、技能性训练溶于内容系统性传达、素养含化和学科培养目标之中；目前课程体系只具有指标意义，如专业基础课、专业核心课和专业选修课，它们在多大程度上是服务于外语学科专业人才"成才"是值得我们思考的，因此应以人才效果和标准为鹄的，加强以"人才培养为中心，以成才为目标"的专业课程体系建设，应推进课程内容调整，建设由 How to Speak English 向 What to Speak with English 转变的课程内容体系。

今天，略举一例，一个十分怪异的事实是：外语文学专业的学生少有读完一本英文原著，一个较长时间从事文学课教学的老师却鲜见他或她读完读透几本原文著作。我一直觉得由体系性课程教学推动学科性研究，进而推动学科人才培养和学科平台建设是自然而然的。可事实则是，一批教师应急而上课，且续且止，留下许多僵死课程，到头来，科研与教学二元对立，元音与辅音永远靠不近。作为学院派的外语学科教学，我们不能让外语教学内容在浅层次上循环，我们的教师不能在浅层次上经年循环，最后自我矮化，语言用语格式化。我们虽然不能教会学生像奥巴马那样讲英语，但我们可以培养像奥巴马那样运用思维的人。总之，精英人才有各样的，但精英人才一定是有内涵的。大学中的外语专业应该培养"精通外语的精英人才"，不是培养"没有内涵的外语人才"。这是大学院系外语学科人才培养体制与新东方语言培训方式的本质区别。

三、创新人才培养评估体系，适应精英人才成长效果评估

要培养精英人才，反思和调整现有评估机制非常迫切。"以人才培养为中心，以学生成才为目标"，重在成才效果，重在学生"成为谁""到哪里去"。这一目标对学校、教师要求特别高，心理压力特别大，因为这意味教与学之间无间隙的接触，无间隙的全员投入、无间隙的关怀。这不仅仅是一个规定教授每周在指定时间与学生面谈所能完成的，或循规蹈矩，完成教学各环节，因此做到无教学事故了事。"以学生成才为目标"，把老师的日常意识变成日常责任，时时牵挂，萦于心际，教师就如参加大赛的领队，直到最后一刻，方才身心委地。优化生源，减少师生比，小班授课是完成学生成才的路径，同时还要有若干系统路径，如创新目前的评估体系：建立以学生成才为依据的有效学习路径体系与有效教学综合效果指标体系，如课程内容体系、教／学环节（硬性与灵活结合）、资源体系、学科教学团队；建立以学生成才为目标的"一体两翼"的培养机制和评估机制（学生选、育、评一体化），教

师个体（遴选、考核、评价）和教学团队（团队考核个人）；采取内部和外部相结合的评价和测试办法——内部评估指学科体系评估、教、学评估、课程和课程内容评估；外部评估指学生外语水平认证评估、行业用人评估、国际化水平评估等。

四、建立全程导师制，落实全员育人

建立全程导师制，形成贯穿四年的学业指导、科研训练、成人成才"三位一体"的引导学生全面发展的指导制度；形成教师团队与学生班级相融合的团队式教与学模式；形成学生（思想工作）与教学一体化的学业、成长、成才体系。从2013年开始，外语学院在全体本科生中落实导师制，对学生的学业过程、学业规划发展、成人成长等进行指导。接下来，学院将实施班级教授导师制，专业教学团队责任制（探索中），基于"基础、提高和发展"的大学外教学团队责任制，以及已经实施并取得显著效果的指导各类外语大赛的"外语实践教育团队"等。

五、学、研、训一体化，在思辨与运思中成长

建立贯穿学生培养全过程的研究方法论课程群、学期论文、学年论文、科研训练等一体化研训机制，培养具有方法论的思维模式与批判性思维能力；根据本科学生毕业走向（直接就业或继续深造），进行差异化的论文或毕业环节训练等；实施"外语写作课程"贯穿四年不下课，培养学生规范写作，独立思考，考量心理变化历程。

今天的大学生似乎并不缺乏知识，一键网络天下，大数据时代的一个重要特征是我们只需要知道"what it is"，而不需要知道"why it is"，可这恰恰指出了我们大学在当今的使命：更应该去培养学生的判断能力、逻辑思维能力，从相似性、类似性、联想性和模糊性中，去培养学生的选择能力和判断能力。

据观察，大多数具有创新思维能力的人都具有类似性思维、联想性思维和关联性思维等特征，能从两件表面上毫无联系的事情上发现其关联性，一般被人戏称"发散思维"，其实是他们省略了线性逻辑，而直接地领悟到其内隐逻辑。人们常说，有些人无学历却能干大事，如知名企业家，而那些搞量化经济学的却并非能够对市场做出准确的预测，也没有成为企业家。问题的关键是，做出的固化数学建模尽管来源于经验观察所取得的数据分析，却永远也取代不了直观洞察力、类似性思维、关联性思维以及想象力，后者的所有者就是创新性人才。

六、"学科内培养，学科外发展"

人们常讲，育人者应"授人以渔"，要育人者授人可以临深渊而渔之的本领。"授人以渔"与"授人以鱼"是对操作型人才和社会适应性人才的暗喻式诠释。言荣校长讲，当今社会发展，产业更新，变化快于规划，今日就业明日失业，我们的教育应为学生的第二次转岗打下基础，这话讲得简单却深刻，说出了一个教育家"道术合一"的崇高信念和面向未来、与时俱进的责任感和发展观。大学既要培养满足社会行业阶段性需要的应用性人才，又要使学生具有应对变化挑战、掌控变化以及人生变化的适应性人才。前者是学科内培养，后者需要通过培养学生的综合人文素质，厚基础、宽口径，以培养学生的持续再生产能力。前者是培养学科专业精英，后者是造就具有精英意识的商界精英、政治精英和社会贤达。一言以蔽之，培养精英人才，以造就学科领域大师、专业方向领军和行业界翘楚，而培养具有精英意

识的大学生，则惠及全体学生之终生和全社会之发展，这或许就是我们对大众中的精英教育的最好诠释。

学院组织和推动研究生和本科生文集出版，这是一种记载和书写学生成长中的记忆。湖泊中的涟漪总是由振荡而来，微风过林，七窍玲珑心。我相信这里记录的是同学们的认知自信、成长自信。

前　言

　　岁月荏苒。每逢 9 月，寒窗苦读的莘莘学子带着新鲜好奇的眼神，怀揣美好的人生梦想，来到美丽的成电校园，加入温馨浪漫的外院大家庭；学在成电，度过丰富多彩的四年大学生活，在成电校园里留下难以忘怀的、深深的成长足迹；再插上"成电梦"的翅膀，扬起人生的风帆，充满自信地朝着成功的彼岸遨游！

　　《我的"成电梦"》——电子科技大学外语专业本科生论文习作（第二辑）展现在大家面前的就是同学们学在成电的脚踏实地的学业足印：有对英语国家社会文化的领悟与思考，有对语言文学话题的志趣与研讨，有翻译理论与实践的分析与探索。

　　本书包括文化、语言文学和翻译三个部分。

　　"文化篇"收录课程论文 5 篇。李畅、邓慧元、汤滢滢、严曾芮等在民族认同视野下探讨了北爱尔兰问题；邓雪纯、张娣、谭帮雁、刘雪妍等分析研讨了 20 世纪 70—80 年代的英国状况；周霜、王蓉、张秋思、芦吉强等论述了美国历史上西进运动对美国民族精神的影响；易薇、张新璐、蒋天庆等对美国宪法第十九条修正案进行了研究；董虹宇尝试性地探析了百家争鸣与西汉独尊儒术之间的关联。

　　"语言文学篇"收录相关课程论文 13 篇。魏钰芬分析了中英网络词汇的构成差异；张蕊对《红字》中的主人公 Hester Prynne 的人物形象进行了剖析；秦佳音以叙事心理学视角对《宠儿》中黑人女性的主体意识建构进行了探讨；朱珈璇从原型批评视角对《宠儿》中主人公塞丝身上的树状伤疤进行了较为深入的剖析；彭诗祎对文学中的哥特元素进行了初步的分析；冯静对《理智与情感》中的次要人物形象亨利·达什伍德太太进行了阐释；谢倩倩对《简·爱》中的女性主义做了解读；李娜比较研究了《爱玛》和《傲慢与偏见》中的反讽现象；李盈吟和刘英子分别从女性主义和心理分析解读了《弗兰肯斯坦》；刘文佳从人物性格出发分析了《理智与情感》中的婚姻观；冯雨雪和胡希雅以女性主义角色分别对《黑暗的心》和《欢乐之家》进行了尝试性的识解。

　　"翻译篇"收录了习作 6 篇。沈安天对明清时期耶稣会士的翻译方法和思想策略进行了概括梳理；郭萌对彼得·纽马克的翻译理论及其应用进行了初步研讨；齐翔从修辞角度对《荷塘月色》的四个英译本中的结构美与意境美进行了比较研究。本部分最后收录了迟姗姗和李金慧分别对作品《母鸡》和《红鬃马》的英译习作。

　　目前，学校推进"双一流大学"建设，实施本科精英人才培养战略，着力提升同学们的"新四会"能力，培养学术精英、行业精英和创业精英，学院切实采取各项外语专业本科人才培养举措，以增强同学们的学业自信和成长自信，本书的出版也可视为诸类措施的具体体现。

　　由于时间仓促，加之本书中的作品都是出自外语专业在校本科同学之手，文中错误和不当之处在所难免，诚望读者批评斧正！

　　《我的"成电梦"》（第二辑）学生习作得以出版，感谢电子科技大学本科人才培养"特区建设"项目"外国语学院菁英人才工程计划"的资助，感谢冯文坤教授、邹涛教授、李杰老师、罗旋老师、俞博老师以及翻译系和英语系两位主任周劲松副教授和姚连兵副教授的悉心指导和辛勤付出，感谢电子科技大学出版社编辑们的辛勤劳动。

编　者
2018 年 3 月

目　录

文　化　篇

语言文学篇

翻　译　篇

文化篇

民族认同视野下的北爱尔兰问题研究

李 畅 邓慧元 汤滢滢 严曾芮

摘 要：12 世纪英国对爱尔兰进行殖民统治，对其实行民族歧视，宗教压迫，引发了新教和天主教的矛盾，导致两大教派难解的历史恩怨，形成互相敌视的民族认同和国家认同，分化瓦解了爱尔兰的社会，致使爱尔兰共和国独立以及北爱尔兰地区归属英国。本篇论文中，笔者对北爱尔兰冲突的历史进行研究，以历史发展过程中英国对爱尔兰采取的政策和天主教与新教的发展和矛盾为基础，探讨冲突双方的政治及民族认同冲突，最终发现导致北爱尔兰民族冲突的根源和本质。从民族认同感的角度分析北爱问题，分别从其民族认同感存在的巨大差异以及分歧的原因研究民族认同感在北爱尔兰民族运动中所扮演的重要角色。考察北爱尔兰历史上的民族冲突发展脉络，为当代的民族冲突分析提供思想源泉和历史基础。分析北爱尔兰冲突双方通过谈判和妥协之道，最终签订了北爱尔兰和平协定，实现了权利转移，并建立起权力共享的政府。通过对北爱尔兰的和平进程的分析，探讨实现民族冲突的化解之道。

关键词：爱尔兰；北爱尔兰；天主教；新教；民族认同

Abstracts: In the twelfth century, British colonized Ireland. The ethnic discrimination and religious oppression rouse the antagonism between Protestants and Catholics, generate complicated historical grievances develop hostile national identity and divided Irish society, finally forming the Republic of Ireland and Northern Ireland. In this paper, we study the history of conflicts in Northern Ireland that is underpinned by British over Irish colonial policies and contradiction between Protestants and Catholics. We also explore their politics and conflicts of national identity. Finally, we discover the origin and essence of conflicts in Northern Ireland. This article analyzes the Irish issue by national identity through the tremendous differences and the reasons of divergence to study the national identity that plays a critical role of Irish liberation movements. We investigate the development of conflicts in Northern Ireland and provide contemporary ethnic conflict for the source of thoughts and historical foundations. Analyzing conflicts in Northern Ireland, both of them sign 'The Good Friday Agreement' through negotiation and compromise and realize transfer of power. And then they establish a power-sharing government. So we probe into implementation of the road to resolve ethnic conflicts through the analysis of the peace process in Northern Ireland.

Key Words: Ireland, Northern Ireland, Catholicism, Protestantism, National identity

第一章 民族认同的定义以及体现

1.1 本论文的研究意义

当今世界可谓是风云变幻，而由民族主义运动引发的民族冲突更是风起云涌，成为诱导国际、国内冲突最重要的因素之一。如备受瞩目的巴以冲突等民族问题都与民族间存在差异的认同有着密不可分的关系。

首先，民族问题具有普遍性。从全球来看，当今世界是一个多民族的世界，而民族问题又广泛地存在于资本主义国家、社会主义国家，存在于发达国家、发展中国家。其次，民族问题具有长期性。长期性主要是指解决民族问题是一个长期的历史过程。如果只是一味地强制同化、采用暴力或行政手段，不可能使一个民族的精神消亡，反而会使民族问题变得更加尖锐，导致更加激烈的冲突。在面对民族间存在的差异时，要顺应其自然发展，才能有自觉的融合，在此基础上才有自然的消亡。最后，民族问题具有复杂性。这主要表现为：民族问题与宗教问题、历史问题、现实问题、政治问题、社会问题、国际问题、国内问题、物质贫困与精神贫困、优秀的传统文化、落后的生活方式、合法的民族宗教活动以及非法的民族宗教活动等交织在一起，涉及政治、经济、文化以及国际关系等社会生活的方方面面，纵横交错、相互渗透，不能轻而易举地解决。民族问题的这些特性充分地表现了它的重要性，所以对于一个多民族国家来说，民族问题就显得尤为重要：它不仅关系国家主权、领土完整、社会稳定、边疆巩固、经济发展，也关系国内各民族的团结。因此，民族问题十分重要但却相当难以化解，是实现世界和平的一大阻碍，众所周知，民族认同却正是一个诱发民族问题的重要因素。

一直以来，各国的政治学家都被民族认同所引发的民族问题如何和平解决所困扰，20 世纪 90 年代以来，学术界也对民族主义和民族认同进行了持续、激烈的辩论，充分表明众多学者已经把民族问题作为一种重要的政治现象在进行理论研究。

英国的北爱尔兰问题最早是由于殖民统治而带来的民族问题，经历了从殖民统治、自治运动、冲突的持续激化到通过谈判来化解冲突的过程。这些因素使得北爱尔兰民族问题及其化解成为研究民族问题的极佳题材。鉴于此，从爱尔兰岛不同的民族认同的角度来深入探究北爱尔兰问题的根源是一个极具现实意义的论题。希望可以通过本论题的研究讨论，吸取解决民族问题的教训并从中探寻良好的解决方式。此为本论文的主要研究目的。

1.2 爱尔兰与北爱尔兰的民族认同及分歧

1.2.1 爱尔兰的民族认同

爱尔兰民族问题的发生有其独特的历史根源。在爱尔兰的历史发展过程中，各个民族之间交往频繁，不断地碰撞和融合，其中凯尔特爱尔兰人的影响和作用是特别突出的。

爱尔兰之所以有其独特的历史与文化，是因为它是世界上仅存的凯尔特人（Celts 或盖尔人 the Gael）①后裔建立的民族国家。爱尔兰天主教徒的祖先主要是来自欧洲大陆的古凯尔特人（Celts）。公元前 350 年左右，凯尔特人中的一支自法国南部与西班牙北部一带渡海而来，征服了爱尔兰，带来了凯尔特的文化。进入爱尔兰的凯尔特人主要属盖尔部落，还有一部分比利其、布立吞部落的凯尔特人也陆续来到了爱尔兰。这些进入爱尔兰的古代凯尔特人有着自己独特的宗教、社会生活和政治结构。

公元 208—211 年，罗马军团征服了不列颠。在公元 4 世纪末，作为罗马帝国国教的基督教也由一些教士传到爱尔兰，并建立了很多凯尔特人的教会，基督教在爱尔兰逐步得到发展。凯尔特人原来信奉的教派自基督教传入之后，渐趋沉寂，退出了社会生活，基督教便在一个

---

① "Celts"也被译成"克尔特人""塞尔特人""居尔特人"，现在一般通用"凯尔特人"。

相对较短的时间内成为爱尔兰社会的主流宗教。基督教在爱尔兰的繁荣发展得益于一批圣徒不懈的努力，其中最负盛名的是圣·帕特里克（St.Patrick）。他是爱尔兰基督教布道团中的领袖人物之一，被尊称为"爱尔兰的圣徒"（the Apostle of Ireland)。圣帕特里克对爱尔兰基督教的发展产生了重要的影响，在他的努力下，爱尔兰教会稳固地建立起来并在发展过程中形成了自己鲜明的民族特色。

大约公元 800 年，凯尔特人已经在爱尔兰创造出了高度的文化，可以是爱尔兰凯尔特文明的"黄金时代"。凯尔特人虽然在爱尔兰发展出高度文化，但是在政治结构上是非常脆弱的。因为在政治上始终缺乏强有力的中央王权来整合全国，导致政治结构非常的脆弱，所以他们注定难以抵抗外敌的侵袭。

从 8 世纪末开始，凯尔特爱尔兰人开始遭到外患侵袭。这些外来侵袭不仅对爱尔兰政治结构造成了冲击，也在爱尔兰的民族成分中又进一步增添了新的元素。12 世纪英国入侵，在爱尔兰强行推行新教教义，但遭到爱尔兰人的强烈反对，随后英国对爱尔兰本地的凯尔特人和信仰天主教的英格兰老移民进行压迫与剥削，长期受压迫的他们渴望统一与独立便逐步形成了支持爱尔兰统一与独立的民族认同。

1.2.2 北爱尔兰的民族认同

1169 年，英格兰王国的亨利二世（Herry II，1154—1189）率领大军横渡海峡进入爱尔兰，不久征服爱尔兰全境。从此，爱尔兰便长期处于英格兰的管辖之下，这一局面直到 1921 年为止。英格兰诺曼王朝在 12 世纪中叶的入侵是爱尔兰历史的重要转折点，因为它结束了爱尔兰的民族独立。

1529 年英国王亨利八世实行宗教改革，创立英国国教（即新教），宣布英国教会不再受罗马天主教会管辖。英国王室欲将宗教改革推行到爱尔兰，但是爱尔兰人笃信天主教，这些做法遭到爱尔兰教会的强烈反对。为了强化对爱尔兰的统治，亨利八世下令关闭爱尔兰的天主教修道院，没收其土地归英王所有，大力推广"英国国教"。英格兰人入侵爱尔兰以后，虽然英国统治者企图通过强制的手段来实现英格兰化，但凯尔特文化以其包容力和影响力，使得英格兰化依然无法动摇爱尔兰民族与文化的凯尔特基本性质，反而使得这些早期到达爱尔兰的英国人逐渐爱尔兰化了。但是到了斯图亚特王朝时期，英国对爱尔兰实行全面的殖民政策，是要以一个全新的新教徒占优势的社会取代原以阿尔斯特（阿尔斯特是爱尔兰古代省份之一。包括今爱尔兰共和国的阿尔斯特省和北爱尔兰的 6 个郡）天主教徒为主的社会，致使该地区信奉天主教的爱尔兰人与信奉新教的英国人之间的矛盾冲突一直延续不断。面对无休止的矛盾与冲突，新教徒为了消除矛盾冲突带来的恐惧感，维护自己在爱尔兰的优越地位，他们认识到必须争取英国政府的支持与信任，从而使信仰新教的人民逐渐形成了归属于英国的民族认同。

正是在爱尔兰岛复杂多变的民族文化大背景下，爱尔兰逐步形成了以下两大存在差异的民族认同。

天主教徒大多形成了支持北爱尔兰与爱尔兰共和国统一的认同。他们的这种政治立场被称为"爱尔兰民族主义者"（Nationalist）。因为爱尔兰本地的凯尔特人和信仰天主教的英格兰老移民在英国殖民过程中受到压迫与剥削，渴望统一与独立，希望所有爱尔兰人能够生活在同一疆界中，并确保能够享有自决与自治的权利。

而绝大多数的北爱尔兰民族主义者（新教徒）却支持英国的民族认同。他们认为自己是英国人或阿尔斯特人，认可英国在北爱尔兰统治的合法性，主张与英国实行宪政上的联合以及对英王和英国效忠。这种历史渊源来自他们曾经被天主教徒包围的恐惧感。为了消除恐惧感，维护自己在爱尔兰的优越地位，北爱尔兰民族主义者认识到必须得到英国政府的支持，而这又要以对英国的忠诚为前提，因此他们渐渐形成了支持英国的民族认同。

虽然两种认同存在巨大的差异，但无论是何种民族认同，都饱含爱尔兰历史发展的辛酸。爱尔兰多彩的传统文化以及多样的宗教信仰为爱尔兰的崎岖发展埋下了伏笔，而英国等外来侵入势力则掀开了爱尔兰的这段辛酸历史的大幕。

1.3　关键术语的论述

1.3.1　民族

民族和民族主义到底是什么，为何它能够在爱尔兰引起一场巨大的民族风暴？

Nation（民族）一词来自拉丁文 natio、nationis，意为：人们在历史上形成的一个有共同语言、共同地域、共同经济生活以及表现于共同文化上的共同心理素质的稳定的共同体。

但是，时代更迭，风云变幻，经过数百年历史尘埃的积淀，我们已经很难给民族下一个标准的定义，因此关于民族的概念众说纷纭。英国政治学家恩斯特·巴克尔（Ernst Barker）认为：民族是一个为着不同目的自愿组成的社会共同体的基本形式，而国家则是建立在这个社会共同体之上的政治上层建筑。因为这种定义更多地停留在民族的客观特征上，是通过对各民族特征的分析所得出的概念，所以具有一定的抽象性。

而安德森却为"民族"提出了一个充满创意的定义：它是一种想象的政治共同体，并且，它是被想象为本质上是有限的，同时也享有主权的共同体。这个定义回避了一般为民族下定义时所看重的客观特征，转而面向一种认知过程。民族在历史演变中是不断变化的，因此在不同的时代，民族就会有不同的客观特征，而在民族发展中不断形成的认知却是一种内化在人民心里的思想，用它来定义民族与民族主义更有助于深入理解民族的内涵。

在安德森看来：即使再大的民族，其边界也是可变的，所以还是有限的；与此同时，民族又是向往自由的，而衡量这个自由的尺度就是主权国家。民族被想象成一个共同体，所以尽管在每个民族内部都可能存在不平等与剥削，但民族总是被想象成一种深刻的同志爱。这种同志爱是没有边界的，是可以为了心中的自由而努力拼搏的，是可以为了消除民族中的不平等与剥削而浴血奋战的。最终，正是这种友爱驱使数以百万计的人们甘愿为民族去屠杀或从容赴死。这就是在民族发展中形成的认知的巨大力量，而这样的一个共同体才是真正的民族，一个可以生存下去的强大民族。

1.3.2　民族主义

民族主义是指一种以自我民族的利益为基础的思想，是一种意识形态。

美国学者汉斯·科恩认为："民族主义首先而且最重要的是应该被看成是一种思想状态。"英国学者爱德华·卡尔认为："民族主义通常被用来表示个人、群体和一个民族内部成员的一种意识，或者是增进自我民族的力量、自由或财富的一种愿望。"

民族主义在民族发展中起到了至关重要的作用。民族主义思想会促使人民形成一种强大的、具有驱动力的认知，这种认知其实就是一种民族认同。在共同体的建构过程中，认同具有非常重要的作用，直接关系共同体的形成和巩固。一个多民族国家发生民族冲突的核心原因就是冲突各方对民族国家没有一个共同的认知。

1.3.3 民族认同

民族认同是指人们对于自己归属于自己宗教、文化、血统和语言等的认知和感情依附，偏重于"种族上的亲族认同"。

格罗斯认为民族认同是通过族裔纽带联系起来的，而族裔纽带又是建立在共同文化基础之上的，所以共同的文化会形成共同的认知，共同的认知会催发人们向着同一个目标不断进发。

而费孝通先生则把民族认同意识（民族认同性）看成是"同一民族的人感觉到大家是同属于一个人们共同体的自己人的一种心理"。在大家看来，这种看法更为接近"民族是一种想象的共同体"的理论。同一民族的人民对同属于一个共同体的人民的同志爱促进了民族认同的形成。

民族认同意识需要通过某种特质来作为标志。这些用来指示民族成员身份的显性因素，就称为民族象征（symbolic ethnicity），或称为民族标志（ethnic boundary markers）。人们通常是选择文化中的一些特殊层面作为界定民族的特征，一般来说民族标志包括集体名称、共同血统、语言、宗教、体质外表、或特定文化特质，甚至包括团结感、与特定领土的联系等，其中，语言和宗教是民族标志中最常见的，所以由宗教、文化等引起的民族认同的分歧成为导致民族冲突的主要根源，而北爱尔兰民族问题正是由这类民族认同所引起的冲突的典型。

1.3.4 凯尔特人及其文化

关于凯尔特人的起源，至今没有定论，一般认为他们操印欧语系的凯尔特语，属于古印欧人的西欧分支。凯尔特人身材高大、红色头发，他们的语言比较接近拉丁文。

凯尔特人早期尚且相当强盛，他们曾经建立横跨中欧的帝国，但后来被东边的日耳曼人、南边的罗马人驱赶到高卢地区与北西班牙，而爱尔兰是他们最后的征服之地。凯尔特人有着自己独特的宗教、社会生活和政治结构。在进入爱尔兰岛的时候也带来了他们的宗教——德鲁伊特教（Druid），因其祭司而得名。德鲁伊特享有尊贵的地位，并且具备丰富的学识，如同贵族一样通常担任祭祀、教师和法官等重要职务。中世纪早期，基督教开始传入爱尔兰并得到了蓬勃发展，凯尔特人原来信奉的宗教渐趋沉寂，退出了社会生活。

第二章 爱尔兰与北爱尔兰的民族认同分歧造成的原因

在了解了第一章中关于民族认同的概述和爱尔兰及北爱尔兰的各自不同的民族认同感的状况之后，笔者下面将对造成不同民族认同的原因进行分析。第一点是宗教原因，爱尔兰和北爱尔兰的宗教与民族关系夹杂在一起，密不可分。第二点就是英国侵略爱尔兰后的殖民干预。这两大根源使得爱尔兰和北爱尔兰的原本统一的民族认同出现分化。

2.1 爱尔兰与北爱尔兰的民族认同感分歧的宗教原因

爱尔兰与北爱尔兰问题上，宗教与民族关系密不可分。宗教作为一种强而有力的凝聚力，与民族认同相互结合，为民族的独立起到了精神支撑与动员本国人民的作用。所以宗教原因是造成爱尔兰和北爱尔兰民族认同分歧中十分重要的因素，提到爱尔兰与北爱尔兰的民族就一定会牵扯他们的宗教——天主教与新教。

从第一章中我们知道了：作为古代凯尔特后裔的爱尔兰人之所以在 6 世纪时已基本全部接受了罗马的天主教，是得益于圣·帕特里克对罗马文化和基督教的传播。此后，英国在殖民爱尔兰后推行的国教和一系列宗教歧视政策引起了爱尔兰人强烈的宗教敌对情绪，导致英爱之间的矛盾冲突逐渐增多。英国有计划地向爱尔兰移民，本土爱尔兰人与新移民之间不断爆发冲突，使得爱尔兰人对居于统治地位的英国人的仇恨已经铸成，并深深地植根于爱尔兰人的意识之中。1649 年，克伦威尔渡海征战爱尔兰，战争中其军队的残暴行径大大推动了爱尔兰人分化成两个民族：天主教民族和新教民族。正如美国罗耀拉大学历史系教授麦卡弗里所言："Religious reform delimit the huge gap of Britain and Ireland. In the 16th century to the 17th century competition for survival between the local Gaelic culture and the invading British culture, religion became an important element. Catholicism became the symbol of a closed lifestyle, Protestantism is a foreign force, and is the part of the conquest and imperialism."换言之，从 16—17 世纪英国爱尔兰推行的宗教改革成为英国与爱尔兰两大政治实体在政治、宗教、文化上彼此对立的历史根源，天主教成了爱尔兰人农业社会的象征，新教则成为工业社会的标志。麦卡弗里在《爱尔兰民族主义与爱尔兰天主教》一文中进一步指出："Irish religious reforms internally generated two community — Protestant and Catholic, the conqueror and the conquered, slave owners and slaves. Religion became the natural marks of whether owned powerful and property."宗教改革使爱尔兰岛上形成了天主教共同体（主要在南部）和新教共同体（主要在北部，尤其是厄尔斯特地区），新教意味着权力、财富与特权，而天主教则意味着贫穷、愚昧与奴隶，由此两大民族——新教民族和天主教民族之间的分野便形成了。新教徒认为天主教徒头脑简单、盲目崇拜。而天主教徒则认为新教徒没有真正的信仰。宗教信仰的不同，思想认识的差异，使得他们的关系水火不容，彼此视对方为异教徒，更进一步加深了他们的裂痕，由此加强了爱尔兰的民族意识和宗教的分歧。

2.1.1　天主教与爱尔兰民族认同的结合及原因

从17世纪末到18世纪，凯尔特文化一直充当着将苏格兰启蒙思想传递到爱尔兰的重要载体。凯尔特人也一直与欧洲大陆，尤其是与天主教国家保持密切的军事、文化和经济联系，爱尔兰的天主教一直是其主流宗教。但后来由于英国的新教政策，爱尔兰天主教失去了统治地位，英国新教徒在爱尔兰肆无忌惮地推行他们的国教和歧视天主教徒的"惩戒法"，许多天主教精英被迫逃往欧洲大陆，因此，天主教在爱尔兰从"主流宗教"沦为"民间宗教"。而同时在这期间受英国的盎格鲁—撒克逊文化冲击，凯尔特文化也被其边缘化，于是遭到破坏的凯尔特文化与受排挤的天主教更加紧密地结合在一起并进一步得到发展。于是，以凯尔特语为基础的天主教凯尔特民族认同便在这一宗教和文化冲突中逐渐成熟起来。

从一些爱尔兰的史书中关于爱尔兰的天主教凯尔特民族我们可以清楚地得到这样的评价：金塞儿战役后（金塞儿为爱尔兰的海边城镇，1601年英国与西班牙爱尔兰联军在此进行鏖战，西班牙远征军几乎被全灭，至此西班牙失去进攻英国的能力，爱尔兰此后被英国完全占领），爱尔兰进入一个新的历史阶段——爱尔兰被英国完全占领成为殖民地。因此爱尔兰民族出现新的特征，在宗教信仰方面属于天主教，在种族方面是英国人和凯尔特人的混合体，其上层阶级越来越广泛地使用英语。虽然在普通人里面看到的是一个混合民族，可是他们却具有典型的爱尔兰人特征：即对自己的国家爱尔兰怀有不可动摇的深情热爱，相互之间有着共同的历史（凯尔特文化下的）和共同的信仰（天主教）。此时的爱尔兰民族正如这句话所说："不管自己的祖先是爱尔兰人还是老一代英国人，是丹麦人还是诺曼人，他们都接受爱尔兰的传说，而不接受英国的传说。"

1775 年英格兰与北美殖民地的战争也促进了爱尔兰天主教和其民族认同感，正因为 1776—1780 年英军在美洲节节败退，英国政府在此时已经看到了将天主教徒争取到自己一边来的必要性，于是它开始考虑对天主教徒的宽容问题。同时爱尔兰人民也不断通过宗教解放运动来争取权利和减轻天主教徒的宗教压迫；蓬勃发展的宗教解放运动中，爱尔兰人民不断争取制定自己国家法律的权利掌握，也争取到了一定的独立的外交权力。这些都不得不说是宗教解放运动所带来的福音。如：19 世纪爱尔兰民族主义运动代表之一——丹尼尔·奥康内尔（Daniel O'Connell）。他作为一个天主教者，1828 年在广大的农民支持下击败其他新教候选人当选了议员，但违反了英国制定的天主教徒不能当选议员的规定，这个规定激起了爱尔兰人强烈的民族情绪，内战一触即发。迫于形势，当时英国的威灵顿政府不得不于 1829 年通过"天主教解放法案"，使得数百万天主教徒获得平等的公民权利。所以爱尔兰人民政治权利的获得是离不开宗教解放运动的，其天主教运动和追求政治独立相互促进。

而 1771 年在爱尔兰通过了"沼泽地法案"，这也使得爱尔兰天主教唤起了自身继续反抗的民族意识。"使天主教徒可以租种 50 英亩以内的瘦田，租期为 61 年，头七年不用交纳租税"。这种让步虽说可怜，然而它毕竟打破长期以来不准当地天主教徒自由耕种自己土地的不合理现象。"沼泽地法案"的颁布也是从法律上肯定了天主教徒对土地的使用权。虽然也有一些苛刻的前提与时间的限制，但是这对于天主教徒来说也是莫大的收获。我们都知道爱尔兰是一个宗教性国家，天主教徒利益的获得其实也就意味着爱尔兰大多数人民获得了利益。所以通过宗教解放运动谋利益其实为大多数爱尔兰人民在谋利益。爱尔兰人民有了自主发展经济的权利，虽然权利的范围有限，但不管怎样都是一种进步。在宗教解放运动中，这样的经济权利其实是可以扩散到整个爱尔兰的。通过宗教解放运动，爱尔兰人民得到了一定的自由贸易与自主发展经济的权利。在得到这些权利的时候，他们对爱尔兰的独立的国家身份又有了进一步的认识：一个独立的国家应该拥有独立自主的经济发展权利，爱尔兰的天主教运动应与其追求独立经济的民族认同感相结合。

就如艾德蒙·斯宾塞在《爱尔兰现状一瞥》里的这段文字里所描写出的爱尔兰天主教与新教的特点，我们能更好地体会到其天主教深入爱尔兰民众人心如此根深蒂固的现实原因："在这方面，人们惊奇地发现，天主教神父和国教牧师所表现的热忱有着天壤之别，他们之间悬殊简直令人惊奇。天主教神父不远千里，历尽艰险，从西班牙或罗马来到这里。他们一不畏死，二不为利，只是一心规劝人们皈依天主教会。我们有些懒惰的国教牧师坐享国家的俸禄，不劳而获，不担风险。然而他们对上帝却缺乏同等程度的热爱，或者根本不热爱，对宗教也毫无热忱，哪怕上帝的庄稼早待开镰，田野早已一片金黄，他们也不愿走出自己的安乐窝而去看望一下。"正因为他们不同的热忱与国教徒的懒惰故步自封而使爱尔兰对其没有好感，这种感情上的差异使得爱尔兰民族与天主教密不可分。

2.1.2 新教与北爱尔兰民族认同的结合及原因

17 世纪，新教集团虽然取得统治地位，但却一直处于孤立境地。"他们不但与天主教民众之间存在巨大的宗教鸿沟，而且与阿尔特斯的大批长老会众也格格不入"。尽管他们曾用复辟的方式将新的认同与爱尔兰传统联系在一起千方百计证明自己是爱尔兰人，可是根据天主教凯尔特人的民族标准出生地和居住地不说明任何问题只有"凯尔特传统文明的共同意识才是爱尔兰民族的根本标志"。而受到天主教凯尔特人和长老会苏格兰人的"歧视"的新教徒们，在英国的扶植下，工业发展较快，与英国联系紧密。于是，在这种复杂环境中形成了他们独特的认同——新教英爱民族认同。在北爱尔兰，尤其是厄尔斯特地区，居民绝大多数是新教徒。"1911年，贝尔法斯特93%的造船工人、76%的居民是新教徒"爱尔兰新教徒认为自治将使他们变成人口中的少数，落在天主教统治之下，并且使落后的南方统治先进的北方，为此他们宁愿留在一个统一的英国议会中，而不愿看到爱尔兰出现一个民族议会。

在思想上，新教中对天主教有排他性，表现为新教从民族起源中排除罗马天主教的因素。新教认为罗马天主教是腐败的代表，是反基督的化身。新教与罗马天主教的斗争是正义与邪恶的斗争，是建立人间天国的必经之路。这种"排他"的思想倾向早在英国宗教改革之前即已出现。在1265年的《格洛斯特编年史》中，作者对人物与史迹的描述开始出现本土化、民族化的趋势。有研究者认为此书所描述的布鲁图斯与巨人斗争而征服整个英国的传说不仅表明了殖民主义的思想，还表明了抵抗外来者的含义。总之，新教思想家试图在族源和教会起源两个方面排除罗马的影响，形成了英爱的历史定位与身份认同。北爱尔兰地区所主导的新教在思想上更贴近于英国，正如这句话所描述的那样："新教的统治集团代表18世纪辉格党的观点，他们赞成洛克的思想，认为一个国家的特殊功能就是保护人民财产不受侵犯，这是自然权利。国家存在在于保护市民社会，如果国家没有尽到这一职责就等于破坏了社会契约，就该被推翻。"这种思想上对英国的认同和归属感，分化了爱尔兰民族，形成了北爱尔兰民族与新教的相结合。

爱尔兰和英国在经济的差距，使得北爱尔兰的资本主义经济受英国很大影响，北爱尔兰地区，尤其是厄尔斯特，在英国的统治之下比较繁荣发达，当地居民深受其惠，不愿分割。新教徒和教会在当地经济良好的状况下，教会的资金和土地问题小，新教徒和资本家的矛盾不大，之间的经济冲突也不足为道，这使得爱尔兰新教徒和雇主可能建立联盟。因此北爱尔兰该地区的大部分爱尔兰人不主张与英国分离，以免影响其稳定的经济发展状况和利益。

而北爱尔兰也想受到英国的保护和援助。北爱尔兰愿意和英国一样进行议会制度，想与其合并成为一个国家。这种不愿与英国分离的主张，从描述北爱尔兰的一位被册封为克累尔伯爵十分能干的人物——约翰·菲茨吉的话中，可以更好地体现出来："He is a realist in politics, he despised persons who is a chatter about natural rights and national powers such gushing platitudes that only the oppressed Irish who have underlying grievances are the real grievance of Irish. He believes that top priority is to maintain relationship between Britain and Ireland and keep the control of Irish. Secondly we must make all sacrifices to maintain the Protestant Constitution, because Anglo Irish are the guard England."他认为头等大事是要维持不列颠跟爱尔兰的关系和对爱尔兰的控制，其次是必须不惜一切代价地去维护新教宪法，因为英裔爱尔兰人是"英格兰的警卫队"。假如这些英裔爱尔兰人自身难保，那唯一的办法就是合并，把他们投入大不列颠的怀抱。

2.2 爱尔兰与北爱尔兰的民族认同分歧的殖民原因

由于爱尔兰历来缺乏中央集权传统，这就形成了易被"入侵"的特点。历史上爱尔兰多次被入侵，但影响最深的是Gaelic people（盖尔人）和British people（英国人）。岛上的盖尔人不断与当地人融合，后来成为爱尔兰民族主体，而英国人却在这里进行殖民统治。英国高压的殖民方式（如同在印度的殖民一样）以及内部殖民主义（Internal Colonialism指在同一个社会内部的不同地区和种族社群之间存在着经济、社会、政治等方面的不平等，甚至是压迫性关系）使爱尔兰民族认同感一分为二。

英国对爱尔兰居民的高压统治也激起了爱尔兰人内部的民族意识，尤其引起爱尔兰天主教徒的激烈反抗。但由于天主教和新教各自的利益需求不同，其民族认同也相异。

2.2.1 英国的政治殖民

11 世纪末，英国与爱尔兰基本属于两个并行发展的独立的历史单位。但自 12 世纪下半叶起，英王（实际上是征服英国的诺曼人）凭借强大的军事武装和罗马教廷的支持，在封建法理上成为爱尔兰的最高宗主（The Lord of Ireland）。此后，这些从欧洲大陆来的诺曼人大量进入爱尔兰，这些诺曼人与爱尔兰人通婚，放弃诺曼式法语，采用爱尔兰式生活方式、法律制度，随后不少英格兰人也移民爱尔兰，其中不少人变得 "more Irish than Irish themselves"。1366 年，爱德华三世颁布《基尔肯尼法》（Statutes of Kilkenny），禁止 "在爱尔兰人出生的英格兰人穿着爱尔兰服装、蓄留爱尔兰发式、说爱尔兰语、使用爱尔兰法律等"。All the good intentions of the English(well, if they were good intentions) floundered, as we'll see, because the Irish just didn't like being told what to do. 当时英国人认为，"爱尔兰人像畜生一样的生活"，"他们的习俗和举止比已知世界的任何地方都更加不文明、不洁净和不开化。" 从此，英国开始了改造爱尔兰之旅。

但英国的努力基本付之东流。As the English in Ireland adopted Irish ways, they steadily became more distant from their old home. They even started referring to themselves as the middle nation: effectively loyal to England, but thinking of themselves as Irish.

英国的伊丽莎白时期，世界发现的时代开始，英国也在这个 "邻国" 进行殖民。英国采取的对爱尔兰的看法与同时期西班牙殖民者对南美洲的看法大同小异。当时的英国掌权贵族秉着 "蛮夷之邦必须先以战争破之，然后才能实施良政" 的想法对爱尔兰进行多次战争。战场上，英国对爱尔兰人的方式十分残暴："这些不称职的军官和士兵，不论军民，统统格杀勿论，甚至包括从未拿过武器的耕地农民。并且不论年纪，从摇篮里的婴儿到风烛残年的老人一概不能幸免。" 这样残酷的杀戮第一次在爱尔兰人民心中留下永恒的烙印——"到伊丽莎白女王在位末期，爱尔兰第一次处于英国政府的有效统治之下。但当时还有另一种共识：爱尔兰的共识。在伊丽莎白时代，爱尔兰人对统治地位的英国人的仇恨已经铸成，并将深深地根植于爱尔兰人的意识当中。" 至此，爱尔兰的民族认同以及民族的归属感开始形成。

与此同时，全欧洲的宗教改革正如火如荼地进行着，但英国在爱尔兰的宗教改革及推行失败，其结果使仅有极少数爱尔兰人为取得更高的社会地位而改宗，而大多数的天主教徒，相反地更加团结。

为巩固对爱尔兰的统治，英国在 1608—1610 年有计划地安排更大规模地、有计划地苏格兰、英格兰新教徒移居多尼戈尔、蒂龙、德里、阿马、卡文、弗马纳六郡，称为厄尔斯特殖民（Ulster colonial），直到 1622 年，移民人数大约有 13 000 多人。这些安置移民的土地都是没收的逃亡贵族的土地或者百姓的土地。信奉天主教的爱尔兰人面对分配的土地怒气冲天，因为他们认为这些土地原本就是自己的。而新教徒因为人数较少，也并未占有支配地位，整天处于爱尔兰人的包围之中，安全感十分缺乏，安全成为万分紧要之事。英国的大规模移民使移民者对自身安全的担忧不久成为现实。1641 年，大规模的爱尔兰天主教徒暴动开始，他们希望夺回自己的土地。新教人民在这场暴动中惨遭杀戮，人们相互传说有上百万人，但这个人数远远超出整个爱尔兰岛上的人口，综合各种证据，历史学家更倾向于新教遇害人数约为 12 000 多人（包括直接遇害或者挨冻受饿而亡）。

虽然此时的爱尔兰两大团体矛盾重重，但将爱尔兰人完全打造成拥有不同民族认同的、几乎是两个民族的却是奥利弗·克伦威尔（Oliver·Cromwell）。1649 年，克伦威尔因在爱尔兰受阻击便下令不准赦免城里任何拿武器的人，于是所有的天主教教士都被杀了，新教彻底激怒了天主教，爱尔兰社会真正分裂了。

到了 18 世纪初威廉三世，英国颁布了更为严厉的、针对天主教爱尔兰人的法案：天主教徒不得担任公职、进入议会、没有选举权、不可参加军队、不可从事法律工作，更重要的是不得买卖土地。英国苛刻的、富有歧视性的政策使爱尔兰社会死气沉沉，人民的生活困苦，民族认同的分化更加严重。

2.2.2 英国的经济殖民

英国除了对爱尔兰采取高压的政治统治之外，还采取了极力控制爱尔兰的经济政策（让爱尔兰继续成为其原料产地），尤其从爱尔兰人占有土地方面可以窥见一斑。

"厄尔斯特殖民"之后，天主教爱尔兰人拥有的土地减少了许多，因为移民的土地就是不公平地重新分配逃亡贵族和普通百姓的土地。1641 年大暴动后，天主教爱尔兰人拥有土地的比例比发动大暴动前减少至 59%；而克伦威尔变更土地权之后，天主教爱尔兰人的土地比例又下降至 22%。天主教爱尔兰人在接下来的重大事件中备受剥削，拥有的土地百分比比 1695 年减少到 14%，而到了 1714 年就只剩下 7%。到了 18 世纪中后期，天主教爱尔兰人竟然只拥有 5% 的土地。这些爱尔兰人在被剥夺了各种经济权利之后，政治地位下降，合法权利得不到保障，处于深重的苦难之中，过着极端贫困的生活。

在英国殖民政策的压迫和剥削下，天主教爱尔兰人的生活状况越来越差。爱尔兰的天主教农民几乎都被迫沦为没有任何保障的租佃者，他们主要靠着马铃薯过活。作为雇工，他们的工资一天不到 1 先令。他们普遍贫穷，即使是收成不错的日子，也只能勉强持家和缴纳佃租。他们要向爱尔兰国教缴纳 11 税，还要向外来的地主缴纳沉重的租税。他们无法享受优惠的租地权，不能以合理的租金租种设备较好的田庄，也不能享有土地，大部分的爱尔兰人民处于无土地、穷困、不安定的生活边缘。

与爱尔兰人艰苦的生活形成鲜明对比的是，英格兰人及新教徒居住在建筑坚固的城堡中，或居住在爱尔兰豪华的庄园别墅中，过着奢侈的生活，控制当地行政、司法、警察，向广大的爱尔兰佃户收取租佃。

1801 年，《合并法案》（爱尔兰与英国合并）正式生效，当时新教徒站在爱尔兰爱国主义的立场上反对，而天主教徒为希望获得众多英国新教徒的宗教宽容的立场上支持。两个王国合并后，在理论上，英国政府应该对爱尔兰投入与英国其他地区同样多的关注，可实际上，并非如此。

19 世纪中期，英国进入全面繁荣的黄金时期—Victoria era（维多利亚时代）。"1820 年，英国已占了世界工业总产额的一半，其中采煤总量占世界 75%，生铁产量占世界的 40%。到 40 年代，英国成了'世界工厂'，完全处于世界工业和贸易的'垄断'地位。"如此强盛的英国却对爱尔兰 1845—1849 年的大饥荒"束手无策"。

除东北地区之外的，占爱尔兰多数人口的天主教徒生活在新教国家中，很大程度上依赖农业为生。于是 1845 年大饥荒发生时，绝大多数天主教徒缺衣少食。时任英国首相皮尔爵士 1845 年对爱尔兰输入些粮食及兴建公共工程，但英国国内，由于当时社会自由主义思想的盛行，占多数的、拥有自由市场经济思想的人主张停止这些有可能"损害"经济的援助。1847 年，大饥荒两年之后，政府才首次发售少量玉米。下一届政府财政大臣查尔斯·伍德爵士更加直言不讳地说："我们根本没有为爱尔兰人进口粮食的打算。"1849 年 2 月，都柏林《公民报》撰文质疑英国政府的统治。大饥荒的后果就是从 1841—1851 年，爱尔兰人比预期人口少了 100 多万，锐减至 400 多万，至今爱尔兰人口也只有 600 多万，不曾恢复到饥荒前的水平。这样使得爱尔兰人，尤其是天主教徒脱离英国的愿望更加强烈。

英国对爱尔兰普遍的经济限制和饥荒时的放任不管让移民来的英格兰人寒心，并表现出对母国的厌倦。

2.2.3 爱尔兰民族主义的觉醒

英格兰人、诺曼人移民爱尔兰不久后就与爱尔兰人拥有相差不大的民族认同，在面对英国的统治时，他们曾共同联合苏格兰人对英作战。The combined armies of Scotland and Ireland were hugely successful. They attacked English settlers in eastern Ulster, laid siege to and attacked the towns of Ardee and Dundalk in Country Louth (and burnt them to the ground), and defeated the English army that was sent to fight them.

虽然现今北爱尔兰人民希望能继续留在英国的统治下，但实际上，现代爱尔兰民族主义的第一个版本是新教人民提出的。这是移民来的殖民者表达的对母国的厌烦情绪。英国议会对爱尔兰的经济压制使得爱尔兰发展缓慢，殖民者出现了情感不满和政治困扰。就连都柏林圣帕特里克大教堂的新教教长乔纳斯·斯威夫特号召除了英国煤外，烧掉英国的所有东西。他还提出立法权只能属于爱尔兰议会。北爱尔兰主义者与爱尔兰联合主义者"一拍即合"，决定合作发起暴动。

但是 18 世纪末期，联合爱尔兰人协会的暴动组织涣散、合作不密切，暗示了爱尔兰岛屿已经由两个分离的社会组成。特别经历了 1798 年的惊恐之后（天主教围堵新教，不少新教徒被杀害），原本的北爱尔兰民族主义者开始考虑成为高人一等的阶层，而不是爱尔兰的统一和独立。北爱尔兰与爱尔兰的分歧逐渐显露。在 1968 年，北爱尔兰民权协会（NICRA）的游行中暴动与骚乱此起彼伏。开始时，北爱尔兰总理特伦斯·奥尼尔对这场看来温和的运动赞赏有加，保证对北爱尔兰进行改革。但是他遭到许多联合主义强硬派分子的强烈反对，其中包括威廉·克雷格与伊恩·佩斯理，后者指责他是"叛徒"（sell out）。

英爱合并后，大多数新教徒逐渐转变了想法，保持他们权贵地位的最佳方式就是保持英爱合并；而天主教徒也认识到，废除英爱合并是推动他们利益的最佳途径。至此，由爱尔兰新教徒首创的、希望独立的现代爱尔兰民族主义被爱尔兰天主教徒接受，据为己有。这个历史遗留问题最终成为 20 世纪中后期的暴力流血事件。而 1970—1972 年北爱尔兰政治暴力活动井喷，不少普通平民丧生。

1875 年，帕内尔在下院讲道："不久之前我听到前任财政大臣说爱尔兰只不过是英格兰的地理碎片，依据何在？爱尔兰不是一枚地理碎片，而是一个民族。"

罗伯特·埃米特临刑前发表的最后演讲："当我的祖国自立于世界民族之林时，到那个时候，而且只有到那个时候，请写我的墓志铭吧。"

现在暴力已经被双方摒弃，但解决之路依然漫长。爱尔兰共和军仍未为罗伯特书写墓碑，但成功就在路上。北爱尔兰民族主义者（新教徒）与爱尔兰联合主义者（天主教徒）经过上百年的冲突，终于在 1993 年迎来英爱共同发表的"唐宁街宣言"。英国表示，在得到北爱尔兰大多数人统一的前提下将尊重并支持爱尔兰统一的要求；爱尔兰共和国政府也尊重认可北爱尔兰多数人的选择，并表示如果北爱尔兰问题能全面得到解决，它将修改宪法中关于拥有北爱尔兰主权的条款。至此，北爱尔兰归属问题的最终解决将掌握在爱尔兰岛上的人民手中。

1998 年，经过南北双方人民的投票以及政府间的斡旋，终于签订了《贝尔法斯特协定》，真正的和平指日可待。

2.3 北爱尔兰问题下民族认同感的发展

在世人印象中，北爱尔兰总是和暴力与恐怖联系在一起。在过去的 20 年里这块只有 14 000 多平方千米和 160 万人口的土地上发生了各类枪击事件 30 000 多起，各种爆炸事件 12 000 多起。因此有人称北爱尔兰为英国的"黎巴嫩"。那在北爱尔问题下其民族认同感的发展造成的分歧到底是如何的呢？

2.3.1 民族认同感激化北爱尔兰问题的原因

爱尔兰独立出去后，英国继续统治着北爱尔兰，这使得爱尔兰两大民族之间隔阂与分裂越来越深。而英国政府暴力与歧视的做法也使得两派之间的民族宗教矛盾不断发展，流血事件层出不穷，严重影响了南北爱尔兰的经济发展和社会稳定。从 20 世纪 60 年代，北爱尔兰各大城市暴力冲突加剧，1969 年 8 月，英国军队奉命进驻北爱尔兰，并在 1971 年制定"特别权利法"，逮捕数百名恐怖活动嫌疑分子，其中绝大部分是天主教徒。这种明显对新教徒的偏袒引起了天主教徒的强烈不满，最终酿成了 1972 年 1 月 30 日在德里举行的 15 000 人反对政府大游行。由此我们可以看到北爱尔兰的民族和宗教矛盾在其认同感的不同的激化下变得长期化和复杂化，不仅影响了南北爱尔兰经济发展的社会稳定，而且也深深震撼了英国社会并影响英国的国际形象与地位。历史的积怨加上现实的对立使两大族群间形成了所谓的"沉默"文化。在这种氛围中，两大族群民众接触有限，工作、教育等也常以族群为界，通婚现象更为少见。这种氛围又加剧了两大族群民众对对方的误读与妖魔化，造成了两大族群的进一步疏离与对立。"对北爱尔兰民众而言，长期的血腥仇杀导致新教徒和天主教徒之间根深蒂固的偏见和防范心理，要想让长期敌对的双方在短期内抛开宿怨，做到相互信任绝非易事。"（刘金源，2005）新教徒害怕与天主教徒和解会失掉自身所处的优势地位，失掉自己的身份认同，更怕北爱尔兰与爱尔兰实现合并。对于天主教徒而言，由于历史上遭受到种种压迫与迫害，再加上现实的不平等，天主教徒难以对新教徒和英国政府产生太多信任。这种状况使北爱尔兰和平陷入进退维谷的困境。这些也就是民族认同感会激化北爱尔兰问题的原因。

2.3.2 民族认同感改善北爱尔兰问题的原因

从北爱尔兰民族冲突的发展可以看出，暴力并不能使冲突得到缓解和彻底地解决。冲突双方民众对多年的暴力冲突已经感到了厌倦，希望能停止暴力冲突，通过和平的非暴力的方式来实现北爱尔兰地区的最终和平。于是，南北爱尔兰之间不断进行和平谈判。而北爱尔兰和平进程充分体现了冲突双方在妥协的基础上通过谈判来化解分歧和冲突，特别是《贝尔法斯特协议》本身可以被看成北爱尔兰冲突双方妥协的方案，民族认同感对北爱尔兰问题也起到了改善的作用。《贝尔法斯特协议》则是北爱尔兰冲突相关方通过谈判在北爱尔兰宪政地位等关键问题上做出了重大的妥协而实现的。该协议依据"英、爱共管的原则"对北爱尔兰的宪政选择做了规定，确立了北爱尔兰与英国的宪政联合关系，同时，该协议也照顾到了民族主义者对南、北爱尔兰联合的要求，如规定北爱尔兰与南爱尔兰通过建立"南北部长理事会"。这实现了在民族认同感下，民族冲突在各方妥协和合作下才能更和谐发展。而在妥协和合作下，这些也是民族认同感能改善北爱尔兰问题的原因。

第三章　民族认同的意义体现在国际环境下的分析

3.1　北爱尔兰和平进程的曲折发展

天主教和新教徒有着截然不同的民族认同感，面对天主教徒不断兴起的民族主义浪潮，新教徒害怕他们在爱尔兰的优势地位被摧毁，于是他们开始组织起他们的反爱尔兰独立运动。但是爱尔兰民族独立运动的迅速发展超乎他们的预期，于是，退而求其次，要求独立不得包括阿尔斯特地区，即北爱尔兰。1921 年爱尔兰独立战争为爱尔兰赢得《英爱条约》，条约承认爱尔兰西南 26 个郡为自由邦，脱离英国管辖，成立爱尔兰自由邦，并最终在 1949 年获得完全独立，成立了自己的民族国家。北爱尔兰选择继续留在英国，从此南北分治。但是北爱尔兰不仅仅全是新教徒，也有相当大一部分的天主教徒。在北爱尔兰地区，新教徒占据统治地位，天主教处于弱势和被动地位，所以北爱尔兰的民族冲突并没有因为南北分治而消失，反而因为两大教派的矛盾不断的激化。北爱尔兰的政治结构、教育文化结构和社会经济结构都严重不平等，政府人员主要由新教徒组成，对天主教实行歧视与打压。大多数北爱尔兰人（联合派）希望留在英国，但一个举足轻重的少数派（民族派）希望加入爱尔兰共和国。从 20 世纪 90 年代两派之间的斗争武装化。1972 年北爱尔兰的自治权为此被取消。从 20 世纪 90 年代中期开始，两派的主要半军事组织达成一个不十分可靠的停火协议。2002 年 10 月 14 日，英国政府宣布，中止北爱尔兰地方自治政府的运作，把北爱尔兰地区的控制权重新收归中央政府。2007 年 5 月 8 日，民主统一党和新芬党组成的联合政府宣誓就职，这意味着北爱尔兰正式恢复分权自治政府。近年来，国际社会一直在为北爱尔兰问题的和平努力着，这也被作为是世界局部冲突地区的一个蓝图。

3.2　统一民族认同在民族运动中的积极影响

第一次世界大战爆发后，英国忙于战争，给爱尔兰民族独立运动造成机会。

面对英国的殖民统治，"爱尔兰人民是一个民族，它应该被当成民族来对待"的思想传播得越来越广泛，民族认同感进一步加强。在这个时期，世界各地的民族解放运动又出现高涨。1916 年复活节后的星期一，约 1000 名爱尔兰人夺取都柏林约 14 个地区并声明成立爱尔兰共和国。起义的领导人皮尔斯在过去曾说要用流血牺牲来净化爱尔兰，还多次使用基督作为人类牺牲的类比。皮尔斯在邮政总局门口宣读成立爱尔兰共和国的声明："以上帝的名义，从逝去的先辈那里，爱尔兰继承了古老的国家传统。这些都通过我们号召爱尔兰的子民们站到爱尔兰的旗帜下，为自由而奋斗。"但是成功之前注定经历许多失败，2 万名英军被派往都柏林，包围了市中心并炮轰起义军所占地区，4 月 29 日皮尔斯和康诺利投降，15 个起义领导人经军事法庭审判被处死。一位起义领导人汤姆·克拉克在他被处决的前一天夜里对前来探视他的妻子说，领导人都相信他们为爱尔兰自由做了第一次奋斗。自由正在到来，爱尔兰永远不会再倒下。但他又加了一句："在此刻和自由之间，爱尔兰还要冲破地狱的桎梏。"是民族认同感让爱尔兰不再甘心受控于英帝国的统治，他们要自由要独立，要自己掌握民族的未来，爱尔兰人的爱国主义和民族认同感在不断加强。这种认同有着强烈的内聚力，有力地维系着民族的团结和统一，也正是由于爱尔兰人的团结，使得 1921 年爱尔兰自由邦的成立变为现实。起义者被认为是爱尔兰独立运动的英雄。尽管这次复活节起义在军事上是失败的，但起义可以被认为是通往爱尔兰共和国的最终成立道路上的一块重要的里程碑。

本论文一开始提到民族是被想象的共同体，但是人们为什么随时愿意为这个创造物献身呢？每当我们提起自己的民族，总是能激发起爱，而且通常激发起深刻的自我牺牲之爱。这种政治爱的某些性质可以从语言描述其对象的方式当中去解读，从关于亲族关系的词汇：祖国，motherland（母国），Vaterland（父国）。或是关于故乡的词汇：heimat（故乡）或 tanah air（印尼语的家乡群岛之意）当中去解读。这两类惯用的词汇都意指某种人们与之有自然联系的事物，在所有"自然地"事物中总是都存在着某些不容选择的东西。因此，民族的属性就被融入肤色、性别、出身和出生的时代等——所有那些我们无法选择——不得不这样的事物中。在这些"自然地连带关系"中我们感受到了也许可以称之为"有机的共同体之美（the beauty of gemeinschaft）"的东西。正因为这种连带关系是不容选择的，它们因此就戴上了一种公正无私的光圈。也正是因为这个理由，民族可以要求成员的牺牲。为革命而死之所以被视为崇高的行为，也是因为人们感觉那是某种本质上非常纯粹的事物。所以，爱尔兰人民愿意为了民族的独立去牺牲，去从容赴死。

南北分离后，一方面，北爱尔兰的民族冲突愈演愈烈，走过漫长的曲折道路，经过长期谈判与冲突相间的过程，谈判各方终于在 1998 年签订了《贝尔法斯特和平协议》，为北爱尔兰实现最终的和平即北爱尔兰将保留在联合王国境内直到大多数人投票脱离；另一方面，英国政府第一次承认该原则：即从所谓的"爱尔兰因素"视角来看，爱尔兰岛的人民作为一个整体有权利，不受任何外界干扰，在双方自愿的情况下解决南北问题。协议也确定在北爱尔兰建立一个权力共享的政府，该政府必须由联合派和民族派双方党派组成。北爱尔兰长期以来的冲突，导致数以千计的无辜群众死于恐怖暴力活动之中，严重影响当地经济的发展，人民痛恨暴力，渴望和平，强烈要求各派别和各党派停止冲突，和平谈判。人民渴望在北爱尔兰实现民族的和解，这是促使《贝尔法斯特和平协议》得以达成和实施的基石。

3.3 民族认同危机论

民族国家认同是现代政治认同的核心，对于其他认同具有根本性的塑造作用。在民族国家体系下，认同的单位或主体是以民族国家这个核心单位参照区分的。随着全球化的发展，它在不同领域，从不同角度和不同程度上对民族国家认同提出了挑战。在纵向上，认同单位可以分为超国家和次国家两大类。超国家包括地区性和全球性的单位，欧盟是超国家认同的典型。全球性认同虽然目前还没有一个有效的实体，但在一些领域存在着发展的趋势。次国家认同是国家范围内的，包括社区、地方、族群、种族等。在横向上，认同单位分散在私人部门，公民社会组织以及政治组织中。比如，企业、各种非政府组织、政党等。横向的认同单位在成员和范围上有可能跨越国家边界，成为跨国性认同。

在现有的国际体系和规则下，纵向和横向认同对民族国家认同产生的影响存在根本的不同。在"民族自决""地方自治"的原则下，以次国家认同为典型的纵向认同很容易替代国家认同，成为个人和群体的首要认同，并有可能寻求实体化。比如围绕这些认同形成的各种分离主义运动。横向认同通常是以承认民族国家为前提的，是在民族国家框架内实现的，并不会代替民族国家认同，但会制约或削弱民族国家认同，比如各种"少数民族认同"在不断因各种原因被人为强化后，会逐渐导致"本民族认同"高于"国族认同"，并可能形成部分公民更忠诚于小团体、建立"国中之国"的离心倾向。另外，"少数民族认同"也可能在全球化时代出现"跨国联动"，在少数极端主义分子的鼓励下，形成极端民族分离主义运动。总之，在后冷战的信息一体化、经济全球化时代，"超国家认同"和"少数民族认同"及各种"次国家认同"已经开始对传统的"民族-国家"认同提出了挑战。

结语

民族认同作为社会成员对自己民族归属的一种自觉认知，对北爱尔兰问题产生了深远影响。民族认同因其强大的聚合力而成为人们普遍重视的一种"政治资源"，但它是一柄双刃剑。当进步的力量对它进行有效的利用时，可以加强民族融合，深化人民友谊，可以促进民族繁荣、社会稳定、国家发展和世界和平；但与此同时，邪恶势力也可以利用它制造分裂、破坏民族团结从而危及国家安全与稳定，造成国际局势的动荡不安。在当代世界，因民族问题而引发的各种争端、因霸权主义对民族纷争的介入而导致的局势动荡屡见不鲜。因此，我们应正确理解民族认同，正视民族认同的影响，因势利导，学会正确利用这一重要的"政治资源"。

References

[1] Ann Hughes. *The Cause of the English Civil War* [M]. London: Macmillan，1991.

[2] Benedict Anderson. *Imagined Communities，reflections on the Origin and Spread of Nationalism* [M]. NewYork: Verso. 2016.

[3] Boyce C.D. *The Irish Question and British Politics* [M]. London: Macmillan Education，1988.

[4] Edmund C，McDowell R.B. *Irish Historical Documents，1172—1922*. London: Routledge，2013: 235.

[5] Ernst Barker. *Principles of Social and Political Theory* [M]. London: Oxford University Press，1976.

[6] Micheal Hechter: *The Celtic Fringe in British National Development，1536-1966* [M]. Berkeley: University of California press，1998.

[7] Mike Cronin. Irish History for Dummies. New Jersey: John Wiley&Sons，2012.

[8] Thomas Hennessey. Dividing Ireland: World War I and Partition [M]. New York: Routledge，1998.

[9] 埃德蒙·柯蒂斯. 爱尔兰[M]. 江苏师范学院翻译组译. 南京: 江苏人民出版社，1974.

[10] 埃里·凯杜里. 民族主义[M]. 张明明，等译. 北京: 中央编译出版社，2002.

[11] 安东尼·D. 史密斯. 全球化时代的民族与民族主义. 龚维斌，等译. 北京: 中央编译出版社，2002.

[12] 本尼迪克特·安德森. 想象的共同体——民族主义的起源与散布[M]. 吴叡人译. 上海: 上海世纪出版集团，2001.

[13] 成珞. 关于古凯尔特人在爱尔兰的播迁和发展——兼论凯尔特因素在爱尔兰近代民族形成过程中的影响[D]. 华东师范大学，2004：18.

[14] 费孝通. 费孝通民族研究文集[M]. 北京：民族出版社，1988.

[15] 菲利克斯·格罗斯. 公民与国家：民族、部族和族属身份[M]. 王建娥译. 北京：新华出版社，2003.

[16] 高岱. 近代爱尔兰民族独立运动评析[J]. 历史教学，1992（2）.

[17] 郭家宏. 民族、宗教与20世纪爱尔兰问题[J]. 史学月刊，2004（2）。

[18] 郝时远. 民族认同危机还是民族主义宣示[J]. 世界民族，2005（3）.

[19] 何树. 试析爱尔兰多元民族认同形成的原因[J]. 史学月刊，2002（2）.

[20] 何群. 论民族认同性与多民族国家民族政策的成功调整[J]. 内蒙古大学学报，2001（1）.

[21] 基齐·德拉诺瓦. 民族与民族主义[M]. 郑文彬，洪晖译. 北京：生活·读书·新知三联书店，2005.

[22] 邱显平. 当代世界民族冲突问题研究[M]. 南昌：江西人民出版社，2009.

[23] 君恩特·帕拉佛. 族群冲突管理——以南提洛尔、巴斯克及北爱尔兰为例[M]. 杜子信译. 中国台北：前卫出版社，2004.

[24] 刘玉华. 北爱尔兰民族问题的来龙去脉[J]. 今日民族，2001（4）.

[25] 罗伯特·基. 爱尔兰史[M]. 潘兴明译. 北京：中国出版集团，2010.

[26] 迈克尔·加拉赫. 爱尔兰岛上有几个民族[J]. 世界民族，2000（2）.

[27] 塞缪尔·亨廷顿. 第三波：20世纪后期的民主化浪潮[M]. 刘军宁译. 上海：上海三联书店，1998.

[28] 王晋新，薛桂芬. 爱尔兰与近代早期英国的殖民活动[J]. 北方论丛，2004（5）.

[29] 杨小明，邱显平. 谈判与妥协——北爱尔兰民族冲突的化解极致探析[J]. 浙江学刊，2007（4）.

[30] 袁小红. 对"文明冲突论"的批判与思考[J]. 理论探讨，2004（4）.

[31] 张锡镇. 十九世纪中期英国的殖民地自治政策[J]. 世界历史，1985（4）.

从摇篮到尽头：论20世纪70—80年代英国NHS 效率变化及成因

邓雪纯　张　娣　谭帮雁　刘雪妍

摘　要：英国在第二次世界大战后率先实行福利国家制度，其中国民医疗保健制度是最具特色的一部分。在伦敦奥运会中，英国向我们展示了令整个大不列颠民族自豪的社会医疗保障系统。然而，近年来英国的社会医疗保障系统却丑闻不断。通过围绕20世纪70—80年代英国国民医疗保健制度的效率变化展开阐述，国民医疗保健制度效率变化背后的原因将得到研究。

关键词：英国国民保健制度；20世纪70—80年代；效率变化；原因分析

Abstract: The United Kingdom took the lead in implementing the welfare state system after WWII, in which the national health care system is the most distinctive part. During the London Olympics, Britain showed the world its enviable system of social health insurance. However, in recent years, scandals have continued to plague the traditional reputation of such health insurance system. This essay focuses on the studies of the change of the efficiency of the National Health Care System the reasons behind. Based on that, the author continues to elaborate on the efficiency change of such British system in the 1970s and 1980s.

Key Words: NHS, efficiency change, the 1970s and 1980s, analysis of reasons

第一章　选题背景及研究意义

1.1　选题原因

本论文介绍20世纪70—80年代NHS效率的变化，着重分析其背后的原因。

英国国民卫生服务体系（National Health Service，简称NHS）是英国社会福利制度中最重要的部分之一，被英国国民称为最好的制度。全民免费就医，大规模的医疗覆盖让NHS广受赞扬，政府对此制度大量的财政投入和政策的支持，也不得不引起我们的关注，多年来，NHS不断在起伏中改善与发展。近日，俄罗斯卫生部部长在一个医疗媒体论坛上宣布，保证俄罗斯公民将永远在俄罗斯联邦内能够免费享受医疗服务，而且保证医疗服务项目每年都会增加。这意味着，俄罗斯公民在公费医疗上享受同等待遇，任何人都不会因没有钱而被医院拒之门外。笔者认为，这也是对英国NHS的借鉴。然而，近年却不断爆出的医疗事故和丑闻，让我们不禁怀疑，是制度本身的缺陷还是社会环境下产生的不利因素。

NHS体系起源于19世纪末的英国，经历了一个多世纪的风风雨雨，逐渐发展成熟，才有了我们今天看到的覆盖全民的免费医疗制度。工业革命时期，英国占尽工业技术优势，又广泛占领殖民地，成为世界强国。随着科技中心转移，一个世纪以后英国渐渐失去了领先世界的地位，但仍保持着资本主义大国的实力。而 NHS 体系见证了其全过程，我们可以看到 NHS 逐渐演变和成熟的过程中的每一阶段都渗透着浓厚的时代特色，有着各个时代独特的烙印。因此我们试图通过研究 20 世纪 70—80 年代 NHS 的效率变化的原因去了解英国社会概略，透视英国时代的变迁与转折。

谈到 NHS，我们首先想到的一定是它最大的优势，即全民覆盖和免费，然而这种突出的优势却孕育出 NHS 最大的弊端——效率低下。进入 20 世纪 70 年代，随着 NHS 已经成型并开始走向成熟，效率低下的弊端首次凸显，并成为今后许多年英国政府政策的核心关注点。效率这块短板常常被人们看成评判 NHS 体系的标准，效率的高低很大程度上取决于财政政策，并与 NHS 自身体制的完善有关。近年来，NHS 的效率问题常常引发丑闻，民众满意度降低，效率更成为 NHS 的关键词。我们认为研究效率变化的原因最能反映 NHS 的发展状况并解释 NHS 体系的先进性。

20 世纪 70—80 年代是 NHS 体系发展过程中的一个关键时期。从 1948 年建立之初到 20 世纪 60 年代，NHS 始终处于成长时期。直至 20 世纪 70 年代，NHS 的体制和运作都已经成型，开始进入成熟和稳定阶段，开始暴露问题并解决问题。可以说，20 世纪 70—80 年代是 NHS 发展中遇到的第一个困难时期，并且为英国政府带来了效率低下这一长久不能解决的难题。我们选取 NHS 的这个转折点的目的是通过这一个点去分析 NHS 发展的过程，包括 20 世纪 70 年代以前发展的盛况和 20 世纪 80 年代以后的低潮，以及这期间究竟有哪些原因导致 NHS 发展势头由盛转衰。

1.2 NHS 效率变化概况

NHS 在 20 世纪 70 年代末以前，经历了最辉煌的时代。在本论文中，我们试图从建立之初的非歧视原则、第二次世界大战对人民心理以及政府的潜在影响、政府在财政和政策上的支持等进行分析，从而得出 NHS 在这个时期效率高的原因。

但是，在 20 世纪 80 年代初期，NHS 却走向低潮，出现了"质"与"量"的下降。因此，我们对此进行探究得出，屡屡爆发的经济危机是导致低潮的重要原因，而 NHS 制度中自带的缺陷和私有医院对 NHS 的冲击也是不容忽视的原因。

1.3 关键词解释

1.3.1 什么是 NHS

英国国民卫生服务（National Health Service，简称 NHS）体系是英国社会福利制度中最重要的部分之一，它是由英国各级公立医院、各类诊所、社区医疗中心和养老院等医疗机构组成。英国所有的纳税人和在英国有居住权的人都享有免费使用该体系服务的权利。NHS 一词作为文章题眼之一，贯穿全文。因此下面笔者将简单介绍其结构，帮助读者了解 NHS。

NHS 的行政管理部门是卫生部。卫生大臣是卫生部的负责人，卫生部对整个 NHS 体系向议会负总责，并负责制定有关 NHS 的各项政策。在卫生部之下，整个英格兰分区设立了十个策略医疗机构（Strategic Health Authorities, SHAs），主要负责监督辖区内的 NHS 执行情况，确保体制正常运转。在其之下的是 152 家基础保健信托（Primary Care Trusts, PCTs），具体负责评估社区医疗需求并向有关 NHS 或私人医疗服务提供者采购医疗服务（一般采用招标方式，但实践中会更倾向公立的医疗服务提供者）。全科医生、牙医、医院信托、急救信托等则受委托直接向患者提供医疗服务。此外，另设有独立的医疗质量委员会（Care Quality Commission，CQC）监管所有公立和非公立的医疗服务提供者的服务质量（如图1所示）。

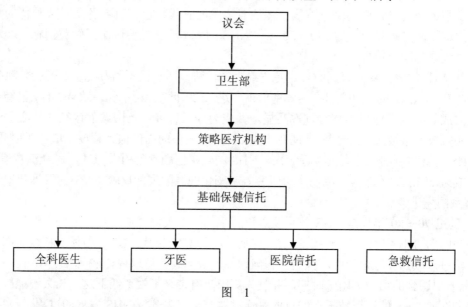

图 1

1.3.2 NHS 的分级制运作

NHS 通过两个层级的医疗体系向民众提供服务，分为基层护理信托 PCT（Primary Care Trust）和中层护理信托（Secondary Care Trust），或者叫以社区为主的基础医疗网（Community-based primary health care）和医院服务（Hospital-based specialist services）。

基层护理信托 PCT 是以地区为单位的医疗组织，它负责一个固定区域的居民的医疗服务。基层护理信托不仅仅满足居民基础医疗的需要，同时它还为该地区提供全方位的社会福利和保健护理。在英国，人们可以就近在社区的诊所注册并有一位自己的家庭医生。通常社区驻诊提供医疗保健的全科医生（General Practitioner，GP）及护士是自我雇佣者（self-employed），由 NHS 设在各地区的基础保健信托向其采购医疗服务免费向民众提供。这个"诊所"就是基层护理信托中的一部分，同时也是整个国家医疗服务的中心。当人们的健康出现问题时，首先会联系自己的家庭医生接受基层护理信托提供的服务。同时，它还有 NHS 非预约医疗中心和 NHS 直线为居民提供快速诊治的建议和保健常识以及一些当地的医疗监管机构。全科医师在 NHS 的体系中充当"看门人"的作用，90%的人在基层医疗服务体系接受诊断和治疗，不需转诊到二级机构。大多数患者都需持有全科医生的转诊单才能转到二级医疗服务处就诊。基层护理信托是国民医疗服务中最重要的基础，约占其总资金预算的 80%。由于基层护理信托是以地区为基础的组织，他们可以更清楚地了解到该地区居民的医疗需要，因此他们可以有效地提供社会福利和保健护理。

中层护理信托 SCT，不仅仅为地区内人口提供更高阶的或专项健康医疗服务，同时它也起到对全英医疗资源进行统筹调配的功能等。它包括国民保健信托（常规或专科医院）、精神健康医院和紧急救护系统等。GP 确认患者病情严重时，将患者转向中层护理。当然，所有的预约和治疗也都是免费的。在中层护理信托体系中，国民保健信托（Acute Trusts）负责运营公立医院，确保医院提供有效和高质量的服务并监管医疗资金的流转情况。这些信托规模庞大，一些是地方或者全国性的专科医院，另一些是与大学医学学院合作运营。

1.3.3　贝弗利奇报告

贝弗里奇报告（即《社会保险和相关服务》）是于 1942 年由贝弗里奇提出的。笔者在第二章盛况的原因之政治原因里将详细阐述贝弗里奇报告对 NHS 体系的作用。为了方便读者更好地理解论文的内容，笔者先对其做简要介绍。贝弗里奇报告是在对当时英国社会保险方案及相关服务（包括工伤赔偿）进行调查的基础上就第二次世界大战后重建社会保障计划进行的构思设计形成的具体方案和建议。

除导言和概论外，报告正文共分五个部分，分别阐述了英国当时保障制度所存在的众多问题以及报告所建议的二十三项改革的理由及具体方案。分重点讨论待遇标准和房租问题、老年问题以及关于伤残赔偿的途径问题和社会保障预算问题。这些建议与方案引领了医疗服务体系即 NHS 的建设方向。

贝弗里奇报告最值得注意的普遍价值在于其所主张的"3U"思想：普享性原则（Universality），即所有公民不论其职业为何，都应被覆盖以预防社会风险；统一性原则（Unity），即建立大一统的福利行政管理机构；均一性原则（Uniformity），即每一个受益人根据其需要，而不是收入状况，获得资助。

1.3.4　福利国家

福利国家一词对大多数人来讲并不陌生，之所以将它作为关键词讲解，是笔者认为我们对福利国家的概念较为模糊，对其的理解也有失偏颇。另外，NHS 作为福利国家的重要部分，对其特性的理解需要建立在对福利国家概念及性质的理解上。

福利国家是资本主义国家通过创办并资助社会公共事业，实行和完善一套社会福利政策和制度，对社会经济生活进行干预，以调节和缓和阶级矛盾，保证社会秩序和经济生活正常运行，维护垄断资本的利益和统治的一种方法。它不单是社会保险、公费医疗、家庭福利或社会救济计划，而是一种以福利为特性的国家形态。这种国家形态突出地强化了现代国家的社会功能，所以它是一个政治学的概念。

福利国家实质上是由国家进行国民收入再分配的一种形式，反映了分配领域社会化的趋势。它的前提是生产力的提高，其资金来源于个人缴纳、企业缴纳的税款和国家补贴。它将福利从单纯的救济发展成为公民的社会权利，得到立法和制度上的保证，以覆盖面广（包括医疗保险，失业保险，工伤保险和养老保险）和低收入阶层受惠多为特点。

第二章　20 世纪 70—80 年代 NHS 的盛与衰

在短短 30 年左右，英国的 NHS 体系经历了最辉煌的一段时期，又从黄金的发展时期慢慢走向衰落，在发展达到顶峰时，弊端也就慢慢暴露了出来。

2.1　20 世纪 70 年代末以前 NHS 发展的盛况

2.1.1　"你们从来没有享受过这样的好日子"

英国社会福利一度让英国人引以为傲，麦克米伦就曾对英国国民说："你们从来没有享受过这样的好日子。"的确，20 世纪 70 年代末以前 NHS 发展的盛况是让人艳羡的。

第一，民众受欢迎程度高。

在 1996 年举行的一次公民测验中显示，86%的人认为国民医疗保健体系是英国最重要的公共服务项目。更令英国民众自豪的是，在北京时间 2012 年 7 月 28 日举世瞩目的第 30 届奥林匹克运动会开幕式上，1000 多名医生和护士走上运动场，摆出 NHS 和 GOSH（意为赞叹，同时也是伦敦著名大奥蒙德街儿童医院缩写）。众所周知，奥运会展示的总是一个国家最好的东西。由此可见，国民健康服务在英国深入人心并备受殊荣。NHS 能取得民众的欢迎，最主要的原因是医疗服务中效率高。在此，效率高体现在质与量两方面。

一方面，就质而言，1948 年 NHS 建立之初，英国新生儿的死亡率为 34%，平均期望寿命是男的 66 岁，女的 71 岁。到 NHS 施行 51 年后，新生儿死亡率降到 7.6%，平均期望寿命为男的 74.7 岁，女的 79.7 岁。在这一时间段中，英国人的平均寿命一直是呈增长趋势。直观的数据显示了 NHS 所做，的确在对国民健康的改善中起了巨大作用。

另一方面，就量来说，在开展公共保健事业的头 20 年中，英国主要的问题是医院的严重匮乏。由于政府之前的错误估计，到了 20 世纪 50 年代末又出现了医生的短缺问题。在 60 年代中期，缺乏具有开业资格的全科医生达到了极点。当时，许多医生的病人实际上超过所允许的限度，最多时超过限额达到 3500 人之多。但是，随着一系列政策的出台，医生人数逐年增加。到了 1971 年，每个医生的人的平均人数下降到 2421 人。医生人数的增加，很大程度上减少了病人的候诊时间。同时，单位时间内，整个英国接诊人数大大提高。

第二，英国国民健康服务的范围广。这种广阔的覆盖不仅是指其在地域上覆盖整个英国，也体现在其涉及的服务项目，医护人员种类多和专业性强。其具体体现在以下三方面。

（1）地域，人口覆盖范围广。根据《国民保健法》规定，所有的英国人都可以享受免费的医疗。在英国，每 10 万～15 万人口必须拥有一所 600～800 个病床的医院。

（2）医护人员，健康服务项目的种类全面多样。当保守党在 1974 年组阁后，一开始就把重点摆在初级照顾、社区照顾以及预防医学上。国民保健系统规定有医师、护士、理疗师、职业病医生、语言障碍治疗师和心理学医师对老人、伤残病和精神病患者进行治疗，并会免费向他们提供假肢、假眼、助听器、轮椅等医疗手段。重伤残疾病人可以免费使用响铃、无线电、电视、电话和取暖器等设备。除了就医过程中的健康服务多，NHS 同时也致力于健康教育及预防工作。在每一个地方，健康部门都有一个社区医师（community physician），负责所有的生育、儿童福利、康复服务和健康教育等工作，推动更健康的饮食、鼓励运动、建议不要过量烟酒消费等项目。

（3）医院专业性强。国民保健由政府国民保健署负责管理在全国各地分设一个总医院，并设有普通医院、诊疗所、卫生中心、精神病院、传染病院、妇产科院、结核病院等专科医院。此种国民健康服务系统不仅增加了医疗界的权威和影响，也使其作用在各个层次都有良好的体现。

这种网状覆盖地区及服务项目的国民健康服务不仅可以满足民众在家里就医，出门有诊所、医院的要求，还大大减少了就诊和转诊的时间花费。此外，专业性的医院为病人提供了更为有效的诊治和对病情更准确的诊断，从而大大提高了医疗效率。

第三，低廉的价格。

20 世纪 70 年代以前 NHS 运行状况好体现在能够基本实现全民免费就医，而且对资金要求不高，自身运行良好。

（1）公民就医基本免费。众所周知，NHS 最大的特点之一就是免费，除了在一些特定时期有需要另外收费的项目，如 20 世纪 60 年代工党提出收取处方费和牙科费，公民就医基本是完全免费的。甚至一些在英国短时居住的居民也能获得这样的待遇。例如，一位在英国短期交流的教授，右踝关节不慎意外骨折，彻底感受了公费医疗的优越性，住院期间的饮食、救护车费用均为 NHS 提供。

（2）NHS 的运行模式反映这个体系能够节约成本。政府直接买进医疗机构的服务，再由医疗机构负责购买药品和器械，由政府代表公民利益从中控制费用，并规定了医院的服务范围及标准，这种明确的买方与卖方的关系会有效防止医生从中获利，既控制了成本，又保证了质量。1975 年英国用于国民健康服务的支出占国民生产总值的 5.5%，美国为 8.4%。

第四，良好的竞争环境。

众多医院的建立要求政府注意避免恶性竞争，合理分布金钱资源。三层级就医模式使就医有序化。全科医生，地区医院与专业医院之间是一种类似于"上下级"的关系。一般来说，地区医院只接受全科医生转诊而来的病人（急诊除外），因此地区医院一般不设普通门诊部，专业医院也是如此。这样一来，病人在三个层级之间的顺序已经固定，就医的层级由病情的轻重决定而非病人私自决定，防止了病人治病心切而集中就医和盲目就医的现象。

2.1.2 NHS 发展盛况之原因

对于 NHS 在20世纪70年代初以前发展的盛况，笔者通过分析，总结为以下三点：思想文化积淀、第二次世界大战后两党的共同努力和财政投入以及管理体系。

2.1.2.1 思想文化积淀

关于第一点，思想文化积淀。众所周知，NHS 的全民免费医疗制度得益于在 NHS 建立之初提出的非歧视原则，一视同仁。同时基督教与绅士文化也对 NHS 的产生和保障其在建立之初的发展提供了有利的社会意识条件。

英国是一个受基督教影响较深的国家。公元601年，奥古斯丁被教皇任命为第一任坎特伯雷大主教，并把基督教传播到整个英格兰。公元7世纪中叶，不列颠岛上的所有过往都成为基督教徒，英国成为一个典型的基督教国家。基督教也深深影响英国民众。基督教会督促所有的人要关心和照顾病人。Surely no one lays hand on a broken man when he cries for help in his distress. 人扑倒岂不伸手？与灾难岂不求救呢？正因为在基督博爱，仁慈理念的感染下，基督教义的博爱，在很多英国人心中形成了潜移默化的民族认知。

其次，绅士文化作为一种确定的观念系统和行为方式，其经历了一个长期的培养和形成过程，吸纳了欧洲多个国家的文化精髓，最终在英国通过继承和发展形成完整的绅士理念。英国的绅士风度大致包括以下几点行为准则：慷慨好客、乐于助人、富有社会责任心、举止大方、谈吐高雅等。较之于贵族精神，它少了份傲慢自负、居高临下的凌人气势，多了份不卑不亢、落落大方的从容和优雅。绅士文化也随着公学的发展，在英国不断发展和完善。在绅士文化下，英国上层人士很少出现对下层人民看不起，反而更多的是投身社会公益的建设中。这样便形成了帮扶的良好社会风气。在20世纪50—60年代，社会福利的资金有一部分是来自社会各基层人士的捐款（这其中很大一部分的英国社会上层人士的捐助），这是维持和保障当时福利制度良好运作的重要条件。

正是在良好的社会思想环境下，在19世纪20年代"友谊社"以及"共济会"等民间组织，它们逐渐发展成为地区自愿性包括健康在内的民间自愿保险机构。民间组织慢慢地如雨后春笋出现在英国社会，它们的影响也逐渐扩大。部分学者认为，这些民间组织便是社会福利制度的雏形。

此外，关于思想方面，就不得不提当时在英国盛行的凯恩斯主义。在1929—1933年经济危机中，资本主义固有的缺陷暴露。此后，在凯恩斯主义影响下，英国政府将自由放任主义逐渐转化为国家干预经济，强调平衡发展与社会公平。

2.1.2.2 第二次世界大战后两党的共同努力

国情与国民的心态在政策的选择上起着决定性作用。第二次世界大战中英国国民频繁遭受德军飞机的狂轰滥炸，人民的生命财产安全蒙受了重大的损失，这在人民的心中留下了阴影。战争所带来的死亡、失业、医药及教育问题十分严重，但在令悲恸的人们同时，对第二次世界大战后民众心理也产生了积极影响，民众前所未有的团结一致，对于第二次世界大战后重建和社会变革抱有极大期望，心里对于平均主义更加认同。媒体振奋人心的宣传调动起了人们的情绪，客观上为医疗服务制度的建立做了铺垫，给予政府充分的决心采取行动促成社会公平。政府该如何顺应民心，有序地第二次世界大战后重建，才能不辜负人们的期望呢？

贝弗里奇的《社会保险及相关服务》是政府的一个积极的探索。

就在民众期待政府提出一个不负众望的重建政策时，威廉·贝弗里奇写了一份轰动的 *Social Insurance and Allied Services*：

Medical treatment covering all requirements will be provided for all citizens by a national health service organized under the health departments and post-medical rehabilitation treatment will be provided for all persons capable of profiting by it.

他对于第二次世界大战后福利政策的原则及计划不仅可行性高，而且迎合了人们的预期。我们可以看出，早在这时贝弗里奇就提出了医疗机构由国家控制以及医疗服务覆盖全民的原则，大体确定了 NHS 今后发展的原则。从此社会政策连同其他项目，诸如全民免费保健服务等优先列入第二次世界大战后的公共议事日程。

第二次世界大战后，保守党与工党面对当时人民基本医疗问题得不到保障，特别是工业区及贫民区居民死亡率高的情况，一致认为应该改善医疗情况，全民享受免费医疗，以实现第二次世界大战后重建。早在 1937 年，道森报告就已经认识到私人医疗体系和公共医疗体系的重复性和浪费资源的问题；继贝弗利奇之后，1946 年工党卫生大臣安奈林·贝文提倡国民保健服务，提出了较好的设想。1944 年，保守党卫生大臣亨利·威林克发布了医疗保健白皮书，同样认为全民免费医疗是重要的。此时，除私人医院的存废问题外，医疗改革的计划已经自上而下达成一致，建立一个全民免费的医疗制度已经是大势所趋。保守党和工党在期间进行积极辩论，共同探讨出一个最适合当时国情的医疗保健体制。

贝弗里奇的方案基本被政府采纳。1945 年工党党魁克莱门特·艾德里出任英国首相时，各项工作百废待兴，第二次世界大战后重建工作处于停滞状态。首当其冲的问题是，实行全民免费医疗，而实行全民免费医疗的前提是取缔所有私人医生营业，我们不难想象这一步会受到很多医生的反对，为此许多政府曾努力争取，同时也做出了适当的让步。例如，为了假牙与眼镜的收费问题，卫生大臣安奈林·贝文就曾被迫辞职。当然，卫生大臣在实施中也做出了一些典型的英国式妥协。例如，奥根在他的《牛津英国通史》中介绍道，贝文本人迫于来自医生方面的压力，也不得不允许执业医生保留私人诊所和国有化医院里保留私人病房。通过政府的一系列努力，NHS 的建成取得了实质性的进展，其中所规定的一些原则和调理在今后几十年内被严格执行，NHS 体系的全面高效持续到 20 世纪 70 年代，经得起时间的考验正得益于这些条例。

2.1.2.3 财政投入以及管理体系

政府充足的财政投入。1962 年，国家制定了医院发展规划，加大以医院建设与改造的资金投入。规划确定建立大批区级普通医院。在 1952—1995 年，作为保守党政府中的卫生大臣伊恩·麦克劳德（Iain Macleod）和伊诺克·鲍威尔（Enoch Powell），见证了亿元建设的显著扩张，政府在健康服务方面的投资在财政支出中占较大的份额。直至 1960 年，政府用在人民保健事业方面（即不包括现役军人和退伍军人）的开支仍然不到 50 亿美元，只占国民收入的1%强。自 1965 年实施医疗照顾方案和医疗补助方案后，政府在保健事业方面的开支迅速增加，1977 年达到 680 亿美元，约占国民收入的 4.5%。政府在全国医疗总开支中所占的份额几乎翻了一番。NHS 的财政来源在 1949—1975 年平均有 85%是来自政府拨款，正是因为政府在前期的充足财政，保证了后来 NHS 的正常运行。如表 1 所示，第二次世界大战后近三十年间，英国国民健康服务的大部分资金都来自于政府拨款，可见政府对 NHS 体系的重视程度。表 2 记录了第二次世界大战后 50 年左右医疗卫生服务在 GDP 所占份额，其比重呈上升趋势，正是政府的长期投入，才使 NHS 得到了稳步发展。

表 1   1949—1975 年英国国民健康服务财政来源分析

（单位：%）

财政年度	政府拨款	国民保险供款	医疗收费	其他
1949—1950	87.8	9.8	0.7	1.7
1954—1955	86.9	7.9	5.0	0.2
1959—1950	80.4	14.5	4.9	0.3
1964—1965	79.6	15.0	5.1	0.4
1969—1970	85.9	10.3	3.5	0.3
1974—1975	91.3	5.7	2.6	0.4

注释：政府拨款是来自税收；国民保险供款是指，凡有职业工作的国民，每人每月交纳工资的0.75%，雇主交纳工资总额的0.6%，独立劳动者交纳收入的1.35%作为医疗保健费，即可包括其家庭在内的享受国家统一规定的免费医疗待遇。医疗收费是指，为遏制浪费，规定每张处方单需要个人交费以及享受较高档次的医疗服务支付的费用。

表 2   1949—1994 英国国家卫生费用

（单位：百万英镑）

年份	总值（百万英镑）	占 GDP 的比例（%）
1949	437	3.9
1955	608	3.5
1960	902	3.9
1970	2046	4.6
1975	5248	5.5
1980	11 875	6.1
1981	13 524	5.9
1994	37 800	5.9

政府在运行 NHS 系统中所面临的问题在于，如何做到效率和公平的最大化，协调发展效率和公平。因此，如果想要真正提高 NHS 的运行效率，首先要理顺两者的关系。在这一点上，英国政府将重点放在了提升硬件措施上：培养与管理全科医生，引进先进设备。

政府为了使全科医生取得国民的信任，规范就诊顺序，对全科医生的培训十分重视。每一个全科医生都要经过 9 年的专业学习与实践并通过考试，期间除了要接受医学基本教育外，还要学习医疗与社区管理，如何处理病人情境和与自身业务发展的知识。皇家全科医生学院作为英国权威的全科医生教育学校负责对全科医生进行考核，颁发或撤销行医资格。政府对全科医生如此重视，是因为全科医生与基层医疗服务在 NHS 的高效运行中起到了至关重要的作用。有人说全科医生是社区健康的守门人，这种说法也不为过。此外，政府也将财政支出的一部分用于引进与发展先进的医疗技术，更新治疗方法。

2.2　20 世纪 80 年代 NHS 的低潮

1973—1975年的石油问题带来的经济危机席卷整个西方世界，英国更是深受其害，经济萎靡不振，财政赤字严重，加上福利支出的不断增长，对医疗领域发起了巨大挑战。NHS 首当其冲，加上制度本身存在缺陷，运行效率一落千丈，失去了往日的辉煌，开始走向衰落，民众对此愈发担忧。

2.2.1　效率降低之表现

就"量"而言，医院数量减少。

英国医生马克思·甘蒙（Marx Khammouan）博士在 1976 年 12 月的一份报告中提出："在经过 200 年发展起来的民间医疗事业几乎已经完全毁灭，现行的强制性医疗制度经过改组实际上已经成为普遍的医疗制度。"（Over the past two hundred years, the folk medical career is almost completely destroyed）"国家卫生局建立的 13 年之中，实际上没有新建一家医院，而现在，1976 年，英国拥有的医院床位比 1948 年 7 月刚建立卫生局时还要少。"（It has been 13 years since National Health Bureau established. In fact, no hospitals have been set up. But now, in 1976, the number of sickbeds in hospitals is less than that in July, 1948）医院服务材料证明了这一理论，在这 8 年期间，医院工作人员总数增加了 28%，行政和协助办事人员增加了 51%，但按每日床位的平均使用率来计算的产量下降了 11%。从 1959—1980 年，医院数量不断减少，医生纷纷逃离英国，每年从英国移居国外的医生相当于英国医学院在校毕业生人数的三分之一，如 Table 3 所示。

Table 3　Hospital in England, 1959-1980: numbers and rates per 100 000

	1959	1969	1979	1980	Percentage change (1959—1980)
Population of England (million)	43	46	46.4	46.4	—
Number of hospitals	2441	2293	2023	1984	-19
Hospitals per 100 000	5.7	5.0	4.4	4.3	-25

私人行医、私人健康保险、私人医院和私人疗养所迅速增加也是对国家保健事业不满的结果。

就"质"而言，医疗服务质量下降。

与日俱增的服务费用与政府财政困难同时增长，大多数医院财政赤字严重，医院为了节省成本，降低服务水平，忽视病人最基本的需求，设备陈旧，医院卫生不合格，医疗费用大幅上涨，医疗服务质量急剧下降。医院就诊供求矛盾大，门诊要排长队等候，住院治疗更慢，一般要等几个月，有的地区甚至 1 年以上。据英国皇家医院统计，需要住院的慢性病人中有65%的病人至少要等一年，30%的病人需要等半年，5%的病人要等数月才能住院。有些人难以忍受超长时间的等待，转而去国外就医，但是出国就医不是所有人都能支付得起，大多数人还是忍受着漫长的排队过程。

2.2.2 效率降低之原因

2.2.2.1 政府的医疗垄断

NHS 在运行机制、管理模式以及经费来源等方面实行计划管理模式，医院属于国家和政府承担绝大部分医疗费用，医护人员领取国家固定工资。这种政府的医疗垄断造成了诸多问题。最突出的是，相比市场管理体制，计划管理使得医疗机构缺乏活力，效率不高。从医院的角度来说，采用新技术、购买新设备、雇佣高水平医生的积极性不高。从医生的角度来说，其报酬与付出没有直接联系，没有动力去做更多的努力，"干多干少一个样，干好干坏一个样"的不良风气逐渐散开，从而造成全科医生以预约为满为由拒绝给予患者治疗，并且对病人的服务质量也逐渐变差。例如，由纽卡斯尔大学（Newcastle University）领衔的团队对英国国民医疗保健体制中约 18 万年轻病人的医学档案进行研究后发现，对儿童进行多次 CT 扫描可增加患脑癌或白血病风险 3 倍。大多数医生对于这种潜在的危害是有意识的，但还是选择去给儿童做此检查。在英国国民保健制度（NHS）的指定医院中，很多病人被活活饿死，且数量让人震惊，被慈善人士称为 21 世纪的最大丑闻。一些老年人告诉后护士也不能及时帮助他们进食。据统计，英国 14 家国民医疗保健医院出于医护人员工作疏忽间接导致 1.3 万人死亡。政府的"手"对 NHS 管的多会兼顾到公平，但没有另一只市场的"手"参与，就会忽视掉效率。

2.2.2.2 经济危机的冲击

20 世纪以来屡屡爆发的经济危机导致英国财政危机的出现，NHS 缺乏资金支持。英国在1971—1972 年、1973—1975 年分别爆发了三次影响面广、损失严重的经济危机。可以说，英国经济在整个 20 世纪 70 年代是与经济危机并行发展的。石油危机后，经济滞涨使英国经济陷入了困境，经济形势日益严峻。英国经济增长速度和人均国内生产总值都已经降到西方国家的最低水平，国内财政状况恶化，1971—1979 年，政府财政赤字总额达到支出总额的 10.3%，达到同期国民生产总值的 5%；通货膨胀最高时曾经达到 25%，国债规模也急剧扩大。面对危机，政府意识到如果继续保持福利事业的高开支，政府就会成为一个毫无作为的政府，得不到公民的支持和世界的肯定。由此，政府不得不减少福利支出。1960 年，政府用在人民保健事业方面（即不包括现役军人和退伍军人）的开支不到 50 亿美元，只占国民收入的 1%。NHS80%的经费来源是政府的财政收入，首当其冲地遭受巨大冲击。医院无力承担经济压力，不得不节约成本，结果就是医疗费用大幅上涨，而医疗服务质量却大幅降低。设备老化，医生数量大大减少，医患矛盾激化，排队看病的现象层出不穷，从而使病人得不到较好的治疗。

2.2.2.3 新自由主义的影响

20 世纪 70 年代，随着经济滞涨对于英国社会的冲击，思想领域的凯恩斯主义渐渐失去了往日的主导地位。新自由主义，一种经济自由主义的复苏形式，自从 20 世纪 70 年代以来在国际经济政策上扮演着越来越重要的角色。它主张在新的历史时期维护资产阶级个人自由，反对国家对于国内经济的干预，调解社会矛盾，维护资本主义制度。NHS，一贯秉承着追求

"从摇篮到坟墓"般的公平原则，而新自由主义思想强调市场竞争和个人财富。毋庸置疑，二者存在着对立与冲突。为了使 NHS 与时俱进，政府试图引进"内部市场"机制，鼓励私人医院发展，通过植入竞争的方式推动其适应社会的发展。然而，改革并未收到预期的效果。比如鼓励私人医院的发展这一改革产生了较大弊端，对国家免费医疗制度造成了巨大冲击。这些冲击包括：①国家医疗卫生费用通过各种渠道直接或间接地流入私人医院机构，为私人所有，从而导致国家医疗保险财政收入减少，不利于国家医疗保险的可持续发展。②私人医疗机构不受政府财政控制，自由增添设备和招聘高水平医生，导致医疗费用上升。③国家医院的高水平医生流向高报酬的私立医院，削弱了国立医院的技术力量。④私立医院机构拥有先进的设备与高水平的医生，而受政府各种限制的国立医院医疗水平相对较差。中产阶层以上的有钱人愿意自费去私立医院就医，国立医院主要是那些慢性病人、老年人和低收入者就医，这就形成了医疗消费的不公平现象。另外，新自由主义强调个人财富与利益，为很多医生医德的沦丧找到了借口，很多医生把病人的需求置于个人利益之外，责任心不强，对病人不能做到悉心照料，致使丑闻频出。

第三章　NHS 在此后的发展及历史评价

3.1　透过 NHS 看时代

一叶落知天下秋，NHS 效率的降低实质上折射的是昔日的日不落帝国走向衰落的过程。同时也要看到，这位世界大国中的绅士面对颓势从容补救，始终不失大国风范。

第二次世界大战结束以后，英国出现过 8 次政权更迭，保守党执政 4 次共 35 年，工党执政 4 次近 24 年。随着工党和保守党两党轮流执政，英国包括 NHS 在内的福利制度也随之出现较大变化。英国在第二次世界大战后的 1945 年和 1979 年，既是政党政治发展过程的重要标志，也是社会保障制度演变过程的里程碑。1945 年大选使工党第一次取得决定性胜利，艾德礼首相领导的工党采纳了贝弗里奇的社会福利报告，建立起了福利国家，同时也改变了保守党的信仰，开始了两党福利共识的历程；1979 年大选使撒切尔夫人领导的保守党政府掌握了政权，两党间旧的福利共识被打破，新的共识开始形成，开创了新自由主义对福利制度的深刻影响时期。由于英国在政策制定过程中政党政治色彩较浓，福利政策的发展演变过程都表现出政党政治的痕迹，因而，与这两次共识政治相适应，在英国的社会保障领域中，也相应地出现过两次"福利共识"。从福利共识中，我们可以看出，英国福利国家能够走到今天，说明政党间并不总是对立分歧的。同时，福利共识是建立在两党政治共识的基础之上。例如，在 20 世纪初，自由党与工党在大选中，为了争取当时工人阶级的支持，自由党采取了一系列的改革措施，其主要包括改善儿童健康和工人的工作环境及劳动条件；在随后工党的政治期间，工党在福利保障领域，一直为工人阶级争取更多福利制度，同时也要求各种福利制度要在社会服务项目中保持"国民最低标准"。笔者认为，政党的执政理念、责任以及其福利主张是以追求满足人民的需求，从而稳固其政治基础为出发点。

自由放任政策的推行使英国在第二次工业革命已经处于弱势，一些传统工业逐渐老化并落后于时代，没有新技术的引进，英国经济正处于逐渐下滑的态势。美国、德国的新技术发展蒸蒸日上，对比之下，一味地故步自封使英国开始落后于时代，因此，英国彻底丧失了工业革命时期的领先地位，沦落成一个经济实力普通的资本主义国家。与此同时，英国经济工

人工资与所获得社会保障减少，甚至不能维持他们的基本生活，大量工人家庭的医疗问题亟待解决，这将是英国政府今后巨大的负担。在此基础上建立的 NHS 从建立之初就承担着巨大的压力，而从长远来看，NHS 运行所需的资金有 80% 来自于财政拨款，国家卫生医疗机构所需的资金日渐累积成为政府沉重的财政负担，更是增加了 NHS 发展的不稳定因素。可以说，NHS 的建立与发展是一个充满波折与困扰的过程。此外，资本主义世界的经济危机在英国影响尤为严重，自 1972—1974 年石油危机引发的经济危机到今天，平均不到十年就发生一次经济危机，每一次经济危机都导致英国经济出现一定的倒退，对于财政的额外需求就会加大，政府经常会面临财政重负问题，注定将 NHS 引向一个效率逐渐降低的方向。

20 世纪 30 年代的经济危机以时间长，范围广，破坏性强为基本特点，极大地冲击了资本主义世界，英国作为老牌资本主义国家，更是首当其冲。工农业生产下降，失业增加，股票市场崩溃，信贷危机严重。这些萧条的迹象造成了人们恐慌、疑惧乃至绝望的心理。与此同时，苏联社会主义运动搞得轰轰烈烈，两个"五年计划"均提前完成，苏联由落后的农业国发展为先进的工业国，社会生产力大幅提高，国民生产总值跃居世界前列，人民物质文化生活得到极大改善。一边是自称最先进的资本主义制度，面临着重重危机，一边是备受歧视的社会主义制度却如巨星般在世界冉冉升起。人们开始怀疑资本主义制度，羡慕社会主义人人平等、丰衣足食的生活。经济领域的凯恩斯主义思潮兴起，与亚当·斯密的自由资本主义思想不同的是，凯恩斯主义主张"市场是一只看得见的手"，要求加强国家的宏观调控，国家要干预经济。

面对危机，英国没有像日本、德国那样走上法西斯道路，而是加强了国家的宏观调控，发展福利事业，缓和社会矛盾。NHS 服务方面的免费和普遍性，医院的国有化等特点均体现了一些社会主义的特色。NHS 的建立体现了资本主义意识形态中对于社会主义制度的借鉴。NHS 虽然提高了医疗服务的质量和公民的身体健康，但由于在运行机制、管理模式以及经费来源等方面实行计划管理模式，到了 20 世纪 60—70 年代，NHS 运行效率一落千丈，尤其是住院手术需要长时间排队，引起了民众的强烈不满。在这个时候，为了鼓励竞争，政府的改革引入了"内部市场机制"，出发点是结合计划调节与市场调节两者的优点，把国民健康服务制度建成一个完美的制度，既具有政府调节公平性和成本可控性，又具有市场的高效性和灵敏性。可见，计划调节与市场调节，或者更确切地说，资本主义制度与社会主义制度并不是完全对立的两种制度，它们可以相互借鉴，取长补短，从而实现共同繁荣的良好局面。

3.2 NHS 在此后的发展

1979年大选把保守党的撒切尔政府推上了英国的政治舞台，从此英国的 NHS 体系进入了新的时代。但是，总的来说，在前两个任期中，撒切尔政府对免费医疗制度的态度非常谨慎。1979年，保守党《竞选宣言》在这一领域未作任何激进的承诺。1983年大选前撒切尔夫人请选民"放心"，声称免费医疗制度在她的政府任期内是"绝对安全的"。

在前两个任期中，撒切尔政府对 NHS 进行了一些改革，但都没有从根本上改变这一体系，到了第三任期内，由于财政困难，撒切尔政府围绕医疗供求关系，对 NHS 体系进行反思，对其进行改革和完善。

首先，打破以前大一统的医疗管理机构，建立小而灵活的管理机制。200 个左右的"地方卫生局"，他们拥有从管理，提供医疗服务，帮助病人挑选医院的权利。设立地区卫生局的目的是在尽可能小的地理范围内最大限度地发展医疗服务事业，因地制宜发挥小地区优势与特点。同时，在 NHS 体系之外，培育私营医院。在保守党政府鼓励政策下，私营医院有了很快的发展。从 1979—1984 年，私立医院病床增加了大约 50%。

其次，在 NHS 体系内还实行商业医疗保险。20 世纪 70 年代商业保险围绕付费病床业务展开（付费病床主要是满足支付能力强的病人的需要），但是规模不大。到了 1981 年，全国有 350 万人参加商业医疗保险，占全国总人口的 6.4%。人们参加商业医疗保险主要是为了减少排队时间，另外，也可以通过此种方式获得一些 NHS 体系不提供的服务，如一些保健性的服务（特殊的老年护理、整容等）。政府发展商务医疗保险的目的是为了减轻国家财政负担，增加国民医疗保健服务经费来源。

再次，在管理机制方面引进竞争机制。改变传统专业人员操作下的国家垄断现状来提高 NHS 体系的运作效率。私营部门可降低国有垄断的程度。为提高医疗资源的使用率，卫生局将不得不引入为某项服务竞争的投标制度，把医院的工作承包出去，确保了私人合同者可以就某项服务进行平等竞争。医院如门卫、食物供应、洗衣服务、病理服务、建筑工程等可以承包给私人。

1990 年年底，梅杰首相上台后，延续了撒切尔政府的医疗保障制度改革，力图既减少政府财政支出，又能提高医疗服务效率，实现医疗资源的有效利用。为此英国颁布新的国民健康服务与社会关怀法。1991 年的机构改革大量录用了管理人员、会计和办事员等，导致管理费骤升。1993 年以后，梅杰政府又对国民医疗保健体系进行了重组。总之，这些改革提高了医疗服务效率，降低了成本，但是医疗管理费用始终没有降下来。

商业保险和私人医院的发展导致医疗费用变相流入私人机构，国家财政减少，对医疗的投入减少，NHS 机构内的医疗服务质量下降。同时私人医院的发展使高收入群体能够享受到更高质量的服务，低收入群体只能在 NHS 制度内就医，这就造成了医疗的不公平。

1997 年，工党领袖布莱尔上台后，肯定了市场机制的作用，鼓励自由竞争；针对撒切尔改革重视效率忽视公平从而造成的不良后果，主张在追求经济效益的同时，兼顾社会公平公正，照顾中下层居民的利益。布莱尔提出"新英国，新经济"的口号，寻求 NHS 的新方向，把重点放在公共健康上，政府承诺结束所有香烟广告的正式形式，至于 NHS 的组织，政府说将会结束"内部市场"，购买方与提供方相分离被保留下来，但是全科医生资金持有者将会被淘汰，简单的管理方式将会取代内部市场的合同制度。公共服务之间将会是合作而不是竞争。新政府的工作重点是提高 NHS 和地方当局社会服务的效率。针对 20 世纪 80 年代以来两届政府在国民医疗保健领域里的改革过分强调压缩医疗保障费用，削减民众医疗保障待遇而忽视中下层利益情况，布莱尔政府发布了新的国民医疗保障制度白皮书，增加医疗经费来源；批判由"准市场"带来的盈利主义等不良风气，实行代理和计划机制；降低医疗成本。

2000 年 7 月，布莱尔公布了一份《NHS：投资改革计划》的白皮书。NHS 制度不断受到批评，权威人士认为根本原因是投资不足。所以政府在白皮书中把目前每年 500 亿英镑的预算增加到 690 亿英镑，增长幅度史无前例，由于民众对全科医生制度持普遍的认同态度，认为它提高了 NHS 体系的运行效率，因此这次改革主要针对公立医院，目标是提高公立医院的工作效率和医疗质量，缩短病人排队等候的时间。

通过历届政府改革，我们看到英国对 NHS 的重视以及这一体系对国民和社会的重要性，在几次改革中执政党的不同理念，对于公平与效率，市场调节与国家干预的偏重，国民医疗体系的效率出现了一系列变化，由盛转衰。然而在每一次问题突出时所采取的措施却未能真正改变 NHS 的命运。时至今日 NHS 依然以其较低的财政支出比例，较全面的医疗覆盖而引人注目，同时也以病患等待时间长，医护缺乏责任心而备受争议。

NHS 是英国社会福利制度中辉煌的一笔，其突出特点为全民免费，服务覆盖面广，长期以来为人民提供了较好的服务水平。全面分析 NHS 效率的变化需要联系政党斗争，经济稳定程度和计划、市场的运行机制的结合，不能孤立地看待 NHS 体系。透过效率的变化我们可以窥视英国社会乃至整个世界的发展变化。NHS 体系从成立至今经历了不少波折与非议，但近几年英国政府推出了被宣称为不同以前的改革措施，究竟 NHS 体系能否获得进一步的完善呢？且拭目以待。

References

[1] Chris Ham. Why the Plans to Reform the NHS May Never Be Implemented[J], British Medical Journal , 2010, 341 (7773): 586-586 .

[2] John Kindom, Government and Politics in Britain[M], Bristol: Policy Press, 2000.

[3] Lawrence Buell. New England Literary Culture[M]. London: Cambridge University Press, 1986.

[4] Perry Miller and Thomas H. Johnson, eds. The Puritans, A Sourcebook of Their Writings [M]. New York: Henry Holt and Company, 1963, Vol. I

[5] 陈晓律，陈祖洲. 当代英国——需要新支点的夕阳帝国[M]. 贵阳：贵州人民出版社，2001.

[6] 蒂姆哈弗得. 卧底经济学[M]. 赵恒译. 北京：中信出版社，2006.

[7] 肯尼斯·奥根. 牛津英国通史[M]. 王绝非，等译. 北京：商务印书馆，1993.

[8] 李英. 从第二次工业革命看历史的变化[J]. 历史学习，2007（3）.

[9] 毛锐. 撒切尔政府私有化政策研究[M]. 北京：中国社会科学出版社，2005.

[10] 米尔顿·弗里德曼，罗斯·弗里德曼. 自由选择：个人声明[M]. 北京：商务印书馆，1982.

[11] 钱承旦，陈晓律. 在传统与变革之间——英国文化模式溯源[M]. 杭州：浙江人民出版社，1991.

[12] 全继凤. 论英国撒切尔梅杰政府的医疗保健制度[D]. 湖南科技大学，2007.

[13] 孙炳耀. 当代英国瑞典社会保障制度[M]. 北京：法律出版社，2000：108.

[14] 孙洁. 英国的政党政治与福利制度[M]. 北京：商务印书馆，2008.

[15] 孙晓莉. 英国国家卫生服务制度的起源及几次重大改革[J]. Chinese Health Resource，2001：280.

[16] 谢洪彬. 英国卫生改革进展及启示[J]. 中国医院管理，2005（4）.

[17] 阎照祥. 英国思想政治史[M]. 北京：人民出版社，2010.

[18] 禹亚男. 谈绅士文化[J]. 时代文学，2010（8）：23.

[19] 于宗河. 英国医疗制度及其改革[J]. 中华医院管理杂志，1994，8（10）.

[20] 赵秀荣. 近代英国医疗行业中利益追求与人道追求的并存[J]. 学海，2009（4）.

[21] 张为佳. 英国的全科医生与全科医生教育[J]. 中医教育报，2001，20（5）.

[22] 郑晓曼，王小丽. 英国国民医疗保健体制探析[J]. 中国卫生事业管理，2011（12）.

[23] 钟国发. 英国社会保障制度源流浅探[J]. 新疆师范大学学报（哲学社会科学版），1997（2）.

[24] 周子君. 英国的医疗服务体系简介[J]. 英国医学中文版，2006（6）.

[25] 乌日图. 医疗保障制度国际比较[M]. 北京：化学工业出版社，2003：130.

[26] Copper, S. The Health Benefits, London Policy Studies Institute , table 2.7, p.27.

[27] John Fry. Health and personal social statistics. Table 4.2. NHS DATABOOK, MTP Press, 1984: 91.

论西进运动对美国民族精神的影响

周 霜 王 蓉 张秋思 芦吉强

摘 要： 通过简析西进运动的兴起、发展模式及特点来对西进运动有一个宏观概述，进而展现其对美国民族精神的积极影响，即对美利坚民族的塑造、对美国个人思想的影响以及对美国民主主义意识的促进，以及负面影响，即种族主义，同时还有反平等精神和自然观的缺失。发生在19世纪的西进运动是美国历史上一场规模浩大的群众性的对西部开发的运动，经过殖民者将近100年的开拓，西进运动取得了巨大的成功。西进运动是一场"使美国成为真正的美国"的运动，是美国从自由农业向商品农业、由农业国向工业国转换并最终实现美国崛起的运动，对美国经济、政治、社会、文化等方面都产生了巨大的影响。通过从西进运动的角度来分析美国民族精神的孕育、锻造及影响，可以总结出对于当代中国的西部大开发的经验与教训。

关键词： 西进运动；美国民族精神；经验与教训

Abstract： This paper first attempts to analyze the origin, development patterns and features of the *Westward Movement*; then through the analysis of a series of federal government's policies of the westward movement, the situation of immigrant populations and their objective and subjective demands and the rich and fertile natural conditions of western region, to analyze the driven reasons of the westward movement. Finally, we draw a conclusion about the influence of the American ethos, which is shaping the American nation, the impact on the United States and promotion of the personal ideas of the American democratic consciousness. Mainly occurred in the 19th century, westward movement is a vast scale mass movement of western development in American history, after nearly 100 years of colonists' pioneering westward movement has achieved a great success. Westward Movement is a "make America a truly America" campaign, which ultimately convert the United States from Freedom Of Agriculture to Commercial Agriculture , from an agricultural country to an industrial country and achieve the rise of the United States. This campaign has had a huge impact on the U.S. economic, political, social, and cultural aspects. We analyze this paper from the perspective of the nurture, forging and effect of the American national in the westward movement, and summarize the experiences and lessons for contemporary China's Western Development.

Key Words: Westward Movement, American ethos, Experiences and lessons

西进运动（Westward Movement）又称西部开发，是美国历史上最具里程碑意义的事件之一。在此过程中，大量移民涌入西部，开垦西部，修建道路，把先进的资本主义推广到荒凉的西部地区。这不仅促使美国西部地区经济高速发展，更促进美国国家的整合与巩固，使美国形成了独属于自己的美国民族精神，为统一美利坚民族奠定了良好的基础，给美国人民留下了丰富的精神财富。本文拟在其他学者研究的基础之上，从原因到影响来分析西进运动，在中国大力开发西部的今天，借鉴美国西部开发的成功经验，吸取其教训，对当今中国的发展有着重大的现实意义。

第一章　西进运动的概述

1.1　选题意义

美国西部与中国西部在地理位置、地形地貌、自然资源和重要性等方面有许多相似之处，且中美两国都经历了从东部向西部逐步开发的过程。

中美两国幅员辽阔，发展皆以先东后西的过程进行，出现区域经济差异问题，是我国应解决的问题之一。在区域开发中，交通运输的优先发展对美国西部开发和国民经济增长具有深远的影响。交通运输业的发展促进了西部经济的地区专业化，促进了全国统一市场的形成，促进了西部经济发展。交通运输业的发展使得吸引东、中部大量私人资本建设通往西部，直接推动西部的发展。在西进运动过程中，因寻求更快发展，直接促进了工业革命和粮食改革，良好的教育为美国西部的发展提供了良好的基础。中国西部幅员辽阔，自然资源丰富，蕴藏着巨大的投资机会、巨大的市场潜力和发展潜力，但因地形及历史原因，经济及交通相对东部落后，应大力发展交通运输业，不仅仅发展西部地区的交通，应在全国形成一个较大的交通网。还应改变西部教育现状，投入足够的人才、技术及物质支持，使得西部经济发展，缩小区域间经济的差异。

在西部开发和发展中，我国还可学习西进运动中美国根据西部的自身优势发展与开发和发展优势等特点。美国根据西部资源丰富的特色开发当地资源，从资源开发到资源在当地加工利用，从资源导向型到市场导向型，并发展一批西部城市，如芝加哥等。我国可以利用西部自然资源丰富、历史文化遗产丰富等优势，西部特色农牧业等特点来发展。农牧业发展结合商业等综合发展，使得所产生的经济价值更高。自然资源的输出可转换成直接在西部加工和相关产业的发展，国家可加大人才、科技及资金的支持，以一些城市为重点，利用当地资源，带动整体发展，如云南个旧利用当地的锡矿资源发展，四川攀枝花也利用铁矿资源发展城市，使得当地钢铁业在全国占有举足轻重的地位。西部地区曾在历史上也繁华过，历史文化遗产丰富，再结合西部独特的自然景观，可大力发展旅游业，带动西部经济发展。

在西部开发进程中，我国还应考虑西部少数民族众多和文化差异大的特点，可从中得到经验。西进运动在某种意义上可以说是一部印第安人的血泪史。在西进运动的过程中，印第安人不得不离开自己的家园，打破自己长久以来的生活习惯，被迫迁往更加荒凉和贫瘠的土地。这是西进运动存在的民族问题之一。我国西部，民族众多，地区文化与中、东部差异大，与中国主体文化差异大，且因地理、自然、历史的制约，西部发展起步晚、发展慢，再加上文化差异，一些适合东部发展的产业不一定适合西部发展。我国应在尊重西部各民族的前提下，因地制宜，根据当地特色和特点发展该地经济。重视发展过程中随时出现的各种社会问题，保持整个社会的和谐和安定。

"他山之石，可以攻玉"。西进运动的经验对正在进行的我国西部开发具有重大的借鉴意义，而它所暴露的缺陷曲折则是不容小觑的反面教材。

1.2　什么是西进运动

西进运动是一场以大规模移民为特征的大型国内殖民运动。其历史背景可以追溯至殖民时代，而作为一场大规模的移民运动它却是在独立战争后才兴起的。西进运动的遗产既有骄人的辉煌成就，也有辛酸的人间悲剧；既产生了史诗般的深远影响，也犯下了不可忽视的严重错误。The Westward Movement in the United States is a great movement of domestic colonization featured by the massive migration of people. Its historical background can be traced back to the colonial era, though as a massive immigrant movement it did not spring up until the Independence War. The legacy of westward expansion is a mix of great accomplishments and grim tragedies, heroic persistence and terrible errors. 西进运动对美国的经济、政治和社会都产生了重大而深刻的影响。从某种意义上说，不研究美国西进运动就不可能了解美国迅速发展的重要原因。

西进运动的"西"是指，在美国独立以后，废除了英国政府颁布的禁止移民向西进的敕令，许多来自东部沿海地区和欧洲的移民纷纷越过阿巴拉契亚山脉涌向西部。西进运动历时约一个多世纪，涉及的疆域东至阿巴拉契亚山，西至太平洋的广大地区，相当于美国国土的四分之三。独立战争打开了通向西部的第一道大门，美国人不仅在独立以后得到一大片土地，而且在观念上形成了一种新看法：新获得的西部土地是十三个殖民地共同用生命和财富换来的，因此这些土地应该是属于人民的公共财产，人民有权去开垦、种植。当时流传的"西部神话"，激发了人们的想象：穿过阿巴拉契亚山屏障，深入内地，一直向西部延伸到密西西比河沿岸，是一片富裕的"黄金宝地"。

西进运动的"进"是指，从土地政策、交通运输、工业发展、教育科技等方面进行西部大开发。他们开采矿藏，但是，随着西进运动的进行，大批印第安人遭到屠杀。据统计，阿巴拉契亚以西的人口在 1810 年只占美国总人口的 1/7，10 年以后增长为 1/4。这些移民中，既有南部的奴隶主，也有北部的土地投机商；但人数最多的还是一般贫苦的拓荒者——猎人、矿工、牧民和农民，后者是为谋生来到西部的，他们成为西部早期移民的主体。

总体来讲，西进运动经历了三个阶段。第一阶段：始于独立战争后的 18 世纪末。在这次西进高潮中，开拓者们涌入宾夕法尼亚、纽约、乔治亚州的西部地区定居下来，最终形成了肯塔基、田纳西和俄亥俄州这三个美国的新成员。第二阶段：发生在 1812 年第二次独立战争之后，规模更加庞大。其结果是印第安纳、伊利诺斯、路易斯安娜、密西西比、阿拉巴马和密苏里州 5 个美国新州的诞生。第三阶段：兴起于 19 世纪 30 年代，在阿肯萨斯、密歇根、得克萨斯、依阿华和威斯康星州的创历史上写下了光辉的篇章。经过几十年的西进运动，美国的疆土也得到了数倍的扩张，几乎相当于整个欧洲大陆的面积，人口也从 1790 年的 300 万激增到 1860 年的 3100 万。经过西进运动，美国所拥有的州数也由原来的 13 个州增加到 33 个。在西进运动中，美国经历了政治、农业、工业和交通的四大革命，与此同时具有美国特色的民主制度和美国文学也已基本成型。

1.3 西进运动的发展模式及特点

1.3.1 以联邦公共土地政策为核心

美国西进运动及西部开发的前提首先是西部有广大"自由土地"的存在。独立后，国家宣布西部土地为"公共土地"，然后进一步宣布向移民开放这些土地（以不同方式向移民出售这些土地），即通过市场陆续将公共土地转化为私有土地，从而形成了一种资本主义的土地所有制度。这一土地制度为成千上万自由移民以相对低廉的价格获取土地创造了条件，使几百万独立的农场主得以形成，并在不受任何封建残余束缚的情况下自由发展。一般来说，这一土地政策是优惠的，在此基础上西部的拓荒农场主绝大多数都经历了一个由自给农民到商业

农民，再到资本主义农场主的演变发展阶段。与此同时，这一政策也鼓励对土地的投机，因而吸引了东部和欧洲资本源源不断地进入。由于公共土地政策实行之初很重要的一个目的是"充实国库"，因而出售土地采取的是"整卖兼零售"的方式，国家鼓励大量购买土地，大多数移民只能从土地投机者手中（后来是从铁路公司手中）购买土地，致使财富集中到土地投资者的手中，加重了移民的负担。但是也要看到，这种土地投机在开发西部的资本原始积累过程中发挥了重要作用，正是通过投机和投资交织在一起的土地开发活动，从而完成了西部资本的原始积累，使西部开发最终得以实现。公共土地政策是美国全部西部开发政策的基础和核心，是美国西部开发模式的一个重要的特点。

1.3.2　以交通运输业为龙头

美国独立时，交通运输业的基础并不好，由于美国的河流一般是从北部流向南部的，而西进运动中，人口、物资的流动主要又是由东部移向西部，因此，运输方面真正需要解决的问题是东西交通问题。从 19 世纪 50 年代起，美国交通运输业的发展便进入了它的铁路时代。铁路的大发展为成千上万移民的西迁提供了交通上的便利，从而加快了西部的开发。铁路为正在走向工业化的东部与尚处于拓荒阶段的西部之间架起了交往的桥梁，从而促进了西部拓荒业由自给经济向商品经济的转化，推动了政治、经济、文化和技术以及社会生活的全面交流，使社会成为一个有机的息息相通的综合体。

1.3.3　以私人企业、个人创业活动为动力

毫无疑问，政府在美国西部开发过程中发挥了十分重要的作用。但是我们也必须看到，私人企业（民间资本）对西部开发的完成也是至关重要的，甚至可以说他们才是西进运动和西部开发真正的动力。事实上，在联邦公共土地政策形成的过程中，私人企业始终都是一种促进力量。

1.3.4　以法律为保障

纵观美国全部西部开发的历史，我们随处可见政府立法对整个经济开发活动提供保障、引导和规范的事例。西进运动之初，国会通过制定 1787 年《西北法令》对移民在蛮荒的土地上从事生产和生活提供了必要的政治、经济、社会方面的保证，从法律上消除了东部各州打算前往西部的人们害怕失去原有政治地位的顾虑，从而消除了西进运动的巨大障碍。

在农业方面，国会于 1887 年制定了资助农业实验站的"海琪法案"，扶持和鼓励农业科技的研究和开发，以形成完善的农业教育、科研与技术推广体系。与农业有关的还有 1873 年通过的《鼓励西部草原植树法案》，它规定任何个人只要在自己的地产上种植 40 英亩的树木并保持 10 年以上，就可以另外获得 160 英亩的联邦土地。1877 年颁布的《沙漠土地法》规定，如果移民在产权申请登记后三年内灌溉了土地，既可以按每英亩 25 美分的价格购得 64 英亩土地。这两项法案对土地开发中滥砍滥伐及对土地过渡使用有所制止，对水土保持和土壤改造起到了很好的作用。

在工业方面，1866 年通过的关于矿产地的法令规定，公共领地上的矿产地包括已测量和未测量的都将被勘测和占领，并对所有美国公民开放。这一法令将公共土地出售的政策扩大到矿产领域，对推动美国矿产业按资本主义方式开发起了决定性的作用。

在教育科技方面，1785 年土地法已为市镇学校的建立专门保留了土地。1862 年《摩利尔法》成为西部发展高等职业教育的重要基础。自 1825 年伊利诺伊首次制订教育法，规定国家

有义务办理公共教育以增进公民的知识和发展他们的智力，到 1919 年亚拉巴马州最后通过义务教育法，美国用 60 多年的时间基本普及了义务教育。教育的普及以及以教育为基础的科技的发展是 19 世纪美国迅速赶上和超过欧洲先进国家的重要原因。

正是通过各方面的立法，美国政府为整个西进运动和西部开发创造了良好的投资创业、生产生活的环境，从法律上保证了西部开发活动的顺利进行。

以上所述以联邦公共土地政策为核心，以交通运输业为龙头，以私人企业、个人创业活动为动力以及以法律为保障这四个方面，共同构成了美国西部开发模式的主要特点。

第二章 西进运动对美国民族精神的积极影响

民族精神是一个民族的思想观念、心理意识、价值选择和精神追求，它是一个民族在长期共同生活和实践中逐步形成的一种优秀传统，反映了民族的价值观念、心理素质、性格意志和精神风貌，是一个民族赖以生存的精神支柱和发展的内在动力。西进运动过程中，拓荒者在恶劣的自然环境和艰苦的辛勤劳作中所造就和孕育的民主独立、自由平等、勇于冒险、乐观自信、创新进取和注重实效的独特的民族性格、民族价值观以及生活方式，形成了美国特有的西部拓荒精神，成为美国民族精神的象征。National spirit is an ideology, the psychological consciousness, the ethical values and the pursuit. It is a fine tradition for a people living long time together and practicing together, which is the backbone for the people's survival and the motivation of people's inner heart, mirroring a people's value standard, psychological quality, perseverance, cultural pattern and the features.

2.1 西进运动对美利坚民族的塑造

2.1.1 西进运动对美国民族冒险精神的催生

西进运动对于培养美国民族冒险与拓荒精神有着不可估量的作用，甚至在一定程度上可以说，是西进运动催生了美利坚民族的冒险精神。

西进运动从某种意义上来说是一种冒险运动，不仅仅是个人的冒险，更是群众性的集体冒险。在西进运动的初期，移民对西部边疆的认识是相当匮乏的。人们没有任何相关的可靠资料，甚至连目的地的可靠位置都不清楚，就是凭借一腔的热情和对西部的美好憧憬，他们踏上了西进的漫漫征程。丹尼尔·布尔斯廷在《美国人》一书中写道："美国人生活在一个鲜为人知的大陆上，但是他们并不知道他们的知识贫乏到何种程度。然而，如果他们了解得多些，他们反而不会像初生牛犊那样全然无畏了。"正是由于专业知识的缺乏，移民西进征程中的艰难困苦与各种各样的危险才更加致命。特纳曾经这样描述过西进的路途："封锁去路的莽莽森林，峭然耸立的重峦叠峰，杳无人烟、荒草丛生的草原，寸草不生、一望无垠的荒原，还有干燥的沙漠，剽悍的蛮族，所有这些都是必须加以征服的。"移民行进在陌生的土地上，必须忍受饥饿、寒冷、疾病、印第安人的袭击这一系列的不可预料的艰难险阻，正是这样的危险让无数人在路途中丧命。然而美好而未知的将来与机遇使得他们都选择孤注一掷，排除万难，坚定地向着西部迈进。据记载，在 1846—1847 年的冬季，一支前往加利福尼亚的 87 人的旅行队被大雪所阻挡，在救援来临之前已有 39 人因饥寒交迫而死，剩余的人仅靠吃死人的肉才得以活命。但是即使这样，一个幸存的成年女子在写给她东部朋友的信中，还是大谈西部的美好，并敦促她的朋友一定要做此行，不管路上有什么艰险和苦难。勇敢与冒险是美利坚民族精神的重要组成部分，而这种精神恰恰在西进的艰苦磨炼中确立并巩固。冒险是西部开发过程中的一个重要品质，也是西部移民开拓精神的一种体现，西进运动则进一步催生了美国人的冒险与拓荒精神。

喜欢迁徙是美利坚民族冒险精神的另一个体现，也正是西进运动培养了美国人喜欢迁移的性格。

"美国民族无疑是世界上最流动转移的民族"，一位芬兰移民在 19 世纪 40 年代这样写道。在最初的时候，移民点往往只有几户人，通过后来的不断加入，居民区不断扩大。于是有些已在本地定居的移民便会放弃现有的生活继续西行，向更开阔偏远的西部开发。到 19 世纪的时候，"西行"似乎已成为一种国民习惯甚至成为一种精神状态。许多移民是个人单独行动，或步行或骑马，一路向西进发。但在这向西跋涉的人流中更为常见的是以一家一户为单位，带着谷场用具，甚至还带着黑奴。间或也有团体组织，如摩门教移民向他们自己的、在沙漠中的锡安山进发。可以在西部改变经济状况甚至是社会地位的思想让移民热衷于不断的迁移，这种一次又一次的迁移又进一步削弱了那种比较固定的社会所具有的对乡土的依恋情结。迁移的观念逐渐融入民族的性格中。直到今天，美国仍是一个好迁移的民族，很少有人终其一生都居住在一个地方。因此美国又被称为"轮子上的国家"，就是因为美国人永远不安于现状，不断地迁移搬家，不停地追寻梦想的独具特色的生活方式才塑造了最独特的美国民族。

2.1.2　西进运动对美国民族乐观向上精神的培植

西进运动过程中艰苦的环境锤炼了美利坚民族乐观进取的性格。乐观进取、昂扬向上的精神是美国人不断向西部开拓的力量源泉之一。而西进运动的特殊经历又反过来进一步锻炼了美国人的乐观进取精神。美国历史学家康马杰就曾经说过这样的话："地球上没有任何地方自然条件如此优越，资源如此丰富，每一个有进取心和运气好的美国人都可以致富。由于大自然和经验都告诉他们应该保持乐观，美国人的乐观精神是异乎寻常的。"

美国西部是一片肥沃富饶、尚未开垦的辽阔土地，这是美国得天独厚的有利条件，也是西进运动的基本前提。这里的陆地、山川、河流、森林构成了一个至高无上、牢不可破的自然秩序体系，同时也奠定了人民的物质文明基础，所以，这里是人民渴望已久的圣所和乐园。因此，西部被看成是机会、力量和财富的象征，在时刻召唤着他们去开发和探索。在这样的情况下，面对即将开始的行程，移民理所当然地充满了极大的乐观和保持锐意进取的精神风貌。美国历史学家布罗姆这样认为："美国人乐观主义的根源之一就在于西部那似乎无边无际的空间和取之不尽的资源，足以保证美国人民的日子能够过得比欧洲老百姓所曾梦寐以求的生活更加尊严、更加富足。"美国著名学者利德基也曾经有这样的言论："美国民族的个性与价值观点，美国社会与政治的构成，最终是与其自然资源和得天独厚的气候条件密不可分的。这一观点从未受到过怀疑。"李其荣先生也在其关于美利坚民族个性与价值观的著作中这样写道："得天独厚的自然条件，对培育乐观进取精神起了特殊作用。"

美国人的乐观还表现为不断进取，总会"把眼睛总是盯着前方"。究其原因，首先，是他们热心追求物质生活享乐；其次，西部地区的所有人都可以自由改变自己的地位而不受法律和习惯的限制；再次，人们普遍相信各种职业都是平等开放的，谁都可以依靠自己的能力登上行业的顶峰。对移民而言："仅仅活下去并不能使他们感到满足；他们追求的目标是发财致富。移民的流动性同他们保持自己的希望之火不灭的决心是成比例的。"不断努力、不断锐意进取成为西部开拓过程中的一种品质，因此在西部充满艰难困扰的条件下，生活就是一场持续不断的斗争，在此过程中美利坚民族乐观向上锐意进取的民族品格也被逐渐培植起来。

2.1.3 西进运动对美国民族艰苦勤奋精神的塑造

西进运动塑造了美利坚民族艰苦勤奋的精神，即艰苦创业勤奋工作的精神。

移民可归为三类，即投机家、普通人（大多为东部落魄者）和奴隶领袖。Varied as they were, the frontier settlers generally fell into three groups: hunters or trappers; a mix of hunters and farmers, the first true settlers; and people from all walks of life, including doctors, lawyers, storekeepers, editors, preachers, mechanics, politicians, miners, and land speculators. All were heralds of civilization, and as they marched westward civilization followed in the wake. Among them the main driving forces of the Westward Movement were three groups of people: land speculators, common people and slave owners, rather than just one or two groups of them. 第一类的东部落魄者以小农为主，包括大量其他劳动者，如工人和自由职业者，以及少部分失去地位的奴隶主。导致这些移民"西进"的主要原因是他们在东部的处境普遍是属于难以果腹的境况。投机者中最主要的是土地投机者。这些投机者抢占了西进运动的先机，出于利益最大化的原则，加剧了对西部的拓殖，直接或间接地成为这个运动的组织者和推动者。此外，由于美国领土不断扩大，加上欧亚大陆战乱不断，使得大量的移民潮来到了美国。国外涌来的移民对于西部开发、对美国整个经济的迅速发展都起了巨大的作用。尽管各阶层的人去西部的动机有所不同，但他们都有一种共同的品质，即艰苦创业的精神。他们在向西部开拓过程中呈现出一派锐意进取的气氛和改善自我和成功的决心和意志。在一个没有任何基础的遥远陌生的西部，实现成功是一件十分艰难的事情，只有依靠艰苦创业，开拓者才能得到生存发展以及他们渴望的成功。虽然政府也曾鼓励移民向西部疆域拓殖，但在拓荒初期却不愿给移民个人提供资助。正如一位美国历史学家所指出的，在美国，"没有一个政府曾向拓荒者提供交通工具，或者在到达目的以后给予帮助。"早期的拓荒者所经历的苦难可想而知，当来自北方的第一批移民冒险踏向西部的征途时，在一个没有城市，没有道路，没有任何通信系统和资金的情况下，能提供给他们的只有自然通道，移民在面对崎岖道路的过程中只能走一站看一站，不断地开拓前进。在路途中，他们不仅要与自然搏斗，与险恶的生存环境搏斗，还要与不愿轻易让出土地的印第安人搏斗。但是在这种极其艰苦充满险恶的条件下，人除了需要勇敢之外，更需要有坚强的意志和坚忍不拔的精神。美国早期的开拓者用他们超凡的果敢和艰辛的劳动，使本是一片荒芜的地方开发成为以后的"小麦王国""棉花王国"及"畜牧王国"，他们靠的就是拓荒者艰苦创业孜孜以求的精神。这种艰苦奋斗锐意进取的创业精神在美国人的民族性格中铸造培育出一种吃苦耐劳、艰苦创业的拓荒精神和强烈的进取心，这种精神因素使得移民在西进运动中以及日后都显示了强大的力量，进而成为美利坚民族宝贵的精神遗产。

"美国民族的勤奋价值观，同时也表现为推崇、钦佩白手起家的英雄。"早期开荒者们刚到西部，首先需要寻找中意的土地，定居后就在各自的土地上建造家园。在辽阔的西部，每家每户都居住得非常分散，无法相互协作就使得新生活的创立需要自身的勤劳辛苦，因此当时美国人成功的本钱就是勤奋和不断劳作。随着时光推移，那些勤劳勇敢的农户就可以把自己开垦出来的土地以更高的价格卖给新到的开荒者，然后再携家向西，寻找属于自己的下一块更加便宜的土地。西部的丰饶土地对于一个强壮的男人而言绝对是一片任他发挥驰骋的战场。对于他们，白手起家绝非奇迹。因而当时个人的成功与失败，大部分是取决于自身的努力。因此在这种背景下，人们自然更看重一个人通过自身努力获得的成果，而非他的家庭背景或所继承的财富。这种艰苦创业、努力工作的精神演变成当今美利坚民族典型的性格特征——艰苦独立。这种在艰苦环境里铸造的思想和精神在美国的家庭教育中显得异常重要，使美国人从小就养成独立生活、独立思考、独立工作和独立学习的习惯，更使他们从小懂得劳动的价值和含义。

在当今的美国社会中，勤奋具有更为广泛的含义，那就是为了获得经济的好转和赢得尊重而努力工作。霍夫施塔特评价说："有很多农场雇工、职员、教师、技工、船工以及劈围栏横木者——以后终于成为农场主、富裕的食品商、律师、批发商、内科医生和政治家。他们的理想就是：做人只要勤劳节俭，克己自制，锲而不舍地发挥能力，有朝一日终能跻身有产阶层或职业阶层，即便不能致富成名，也可赢得独立和尊敬。"美国人相信只要依靠自己的艰苦劳动和勤奋工作就能获得生活的改观和社会的尊重，因此视工作为乐趣便成为他们的信条，甚至还在许多领域涌现出不少的工作狂。

2.2 西进运动对美国人个人思想的影响

2.2.1 西进运动促进了美国人自治精神的发展

西进运动中，美国人崇尚民主、渴求自由平等的性格得到了充分发展，也就是说，美国人的自治精神在这一时期产生并且得到很大程度的发展。

西进运动发展了美国民主政治与公平社会的自由意识，培植了美国式的自由、平等和竞争。西进运动是荒野之上的运动，移民所到之处根本不存在政府和管理机构。为了维持居民点最起码的安全和秩序，大家需要一起选举一个管理公共事务的人员或者机构来维持秩序、保护移民安全。在这种情况下，凡是重大事件都要经全体居民讨论才能决定，因此西部新建各州的宪法借用了东部诸州宪法中最自由化的内容，从而显示了他们比东部更为民主。在艾伦·比林顿的书中有这样的描述："几乎所有新州的宪法都赋予立法机构以非同一般的权力。据信，立法机构更关心的是社会舆论，而不是州长的意见，并且大都规定较短的官职任期以便迅速轮换立法人员……尤为明显的倾向是边疆社区把掌权职位交给了出身于各阶层的普通公民。"由此我们可以得出一个结论，即西部没有开创政治民主，但是向西部的扩张扩大了对人民政治的信念，同时，美国人民渴求自由与平等的观念在西部更是得到了充分的发挥与进一步的巩固，西部体现了19世纪使美国社会充满活力的对自由的向往。梭罗更是在他的书中写下这样的句子："朝东我不自由，西行则感到自由。"西进运动中，移民们摆脱了东部思想堕落和精神束缚，甚至不少的美国人觉得它是"纯洁心灵的精神寄托"，觉得可以利用这一机会改变自己的社会经济地位。边疆社会给人们提供了一个追求平等地位的大舞台，移民们自己建立政府，自己立法，自己用更加民主的方式进行管理，自治精神就这样一点点地渗透到社会的各个层面，更重要的是，渗透到了每个西部美国人的心中。

总而言之，西进运动充分体现了美国人民对民主和自治的不懈追求，并在美国文化的形成中将其发展为一种靠全体公民的自觉遵守才能得以实施的契约关系。

2.2.2 西进运动推动了美国个人主义的进步

西进运动时期，美利坚民族的个人主义精神得到了进一步的强化。这一时期的个人主义可以高度概括为"开拓进取、自我改善、蔑视惯例和传统"。美国人的个人主义思想是美国文化的核心，其渊源可以追溯到美国历史的最初阶段，但西进运动和边疆生活使美国的个人主义价值观得到前所未有的发展，因为作为贯穿整个美国自由资本主义时期，并且持续了百余年的西进运动，其中艰苦的环境实际上使美利坚民族的精神和品格接受了一次洗礼，并培育出美国特有的个人主义精神。

首先，西部特殊的自然地理环境锻造了美国的个人主义精神。美国的个人主义精神与在西进运动中特殊的环境是密切相关的，在特纳著名的论文《边疆在美国历史上的意义》中有这样的描述："欧洲文明和美国文明的区别在于，美国文明在一定意义上是新世界特殊环境的产物。"其中最不同寻常的环境特征是自由土地的存在，自由土地的消失和美国人向西部推进。正是这样的自由土地吸引了企图获得经济收益的广大移民作为欧洲人或东部人来到西部，但是他们很快认识到："原有的习惯、制度和社会文化观念在荒野环境中是不适用的。复杂的政治制度在小小的边疆前哨是不必要的；传统的经济是实践在一个孤立的、自给自足的经济社区是无用的；严格的社会习惯在依赖斧子和来复枪的技术，而不是依赖世袭的天国的土地上成为过去。"因而，他们自力更生，开发西部，进而维持了美国人的生存及发展，其中的勇气就是个人主义的一种体现。

其次，在西进运动中，个人主义的本质就是开拓进取。布尔斯廷曾指出："迁往新地方和探索新事物的勇气就是单干的勇气，是完全、彻底、雄心勃勃地专注于自身利益的勇气。"为了独立和财富，广大的移民来到西部之后便展开了一场与大自然的殊死搏斗。拓荒者一踏上旅途便要经受艰苦的磨炼，他们只能携带种子、农具、枪支、口粮和牲畜等最重要的生活必需品，一路风餐露宿，有时候，移民们带的粮食甚至不能让他们坚持到目的地。因此，路途中的野菜和浆果也是拓荒者的救命粮食。除危险的旅行之外，移民们还要承受疾病和死亡的打击。一位叫迈纳尔德的大夫 1850 年西行的日记中有这样的记载："途中看到了昨天刚死去的新坟，我看到三个霍乱病人；我也得了霍乱；上帝啊，蚊子真凶残，人和牛都无法停下小憩；只能把同队的布朗迪和波丽留下等死；在路旁有一个淹死的孩子，我们埋了他。"正是由于这样无尽的艰辛，西进运动被称为资本主义、个人主义的长征。

最后，"西进运动对个人主义的影响另一个重要方面，在美国人反对社会和社会上各种势力对个人的各种控制上。"特纳在《边疆在美国历史上的意义》中写道："边疆是产生个人主义的场所。它对控制，特别是对任何直接的控制有反感。"在美国的边疆地区，社会相对原始的状态为移民在这片自由的土地发展自己提供了机会。他们在艰苦劳作，也享受着自由，摆脱了历史与传统的重负。他们只根据良心、常识和一些约定俗成的规矩办事，对于权威和特权有一种反感和不信任。他们要求经济和政治权利的平等，认为利用机会和抓住机会是这里最重要的事情。他们尊崇那些白手起家的英雄——也许这些英雄没有绅士风度和学识，却有着倔强的意志和尊重他人平等的态度。广袤的边疆为个人主义的培育、发展和确立提供了一个巨大的试验场，美国人追求自由、民主，摆脱各种束缚，不受传统惯例的影响，极力追求个人主义的精神。

总之，在西进运动时期，个人主义精神强调的就是移民们按照自己的意愿充分自由和独立的生活创业。因此，西进运动塑造的典型的美利坚民族精神，最重要的就是个人主义精神。但个人主义带来的天命观和以强凌弱的边疆精神则对美利坚民族精神产生了一些消极影响。比如"老子天下第一"的傲慢神态仍然存留在今天的一些美国人身上。

2.2.3　西进运动培育了美国人实用主义哲学观

在西进运动特定的环境里，在美利坚独特的民族精神中，美国人的实用主义哲学观就这样孕育产生了。

实用主义是美利坚民族精神特别是西部精神在哲学上的高度凝念和升华，它促进了美利坚民族精神内涵的完善和发展，成为美利坚民族精神的本质。繁多的民族，多元的文化，丰富的资源，古朴的民风，使移民们到达西部后就树立起一种为生存、为创业服务的全新价值观念。特殊的西部环境要求人们正视现实，追求实效，发扬开拓进取的精神，坚持功利主义原则，解决开发所面临的一切实际问题。因此，开拓进取、注重实效的西部精神在理论上升华成为实用主义，成为创业时期美利坚民族精神的重要内容。实用主义的基本内涵是：立足现实，积极行动；注重目的，讲求实效；崇尚进取，重在开拓。实用主义的形成与西进运动有着不可分割的联系，在西部开拓的过程中，移民们必须着眼于自然与社会的现实基础，服从现实，努力摆脱原有的各种道德、理念的束缚，以生存为首要目的。勤奋进取，注重实效，形成以经验为根据的思想，重视现实的可塑性，把经验作为适应和控制现实的工具，讲求实效，身体力行逐渐成为这一时期的主要思想观念。西部拓荒者的奋斗史证明，观念、信仰或主张的意义在于它在实际使用中所带来的实际效用。美国一个著名的历史学家曾在他的著作中这样记录美国西进运动中产生的实用主义过程："西部政治、经济制度的建立，西部社会文化观念的产生，西部法律的制定，无不体现出实用主义的本质特征。在把西部这片神奇而恐怖的土地变成人类美好家园的过程中，美国人培养了务实、奋斗和注重效用的精神，当代美国人厌恶思辨、崇尚具体；不屑空谈、追求行动；轻视传统、注重现实的人生态度是实用主义基本精神在价值观方面的最为恰当的说明。"现在的美国社会中，实用主义被称为美国的"本土哲学"，其实用主义哲学观、相对主义真理观、个人主义价值观、行动主义实践观、民主主义政治观长期流行于美国，是美国人最突出的生活信条。实用主义的哲学观已深深植入美国人的思想、文化和行为中，是美国人求实进取精神的继承和总结，协调了美国民族性格与美国社会发展的关系，最终发展成为美国民族精神，它是西部精神在哲学上的升华和提炼。

实用主义在西进运动中起步，到了 20 世纪初盛行。它是美国独一无二的贡献。无论在美国人的思想上，还是在美国表现出的各种文化上，都存在着实用主义哲学观的影子。以行动求生存，以效果定优劣，以进取求发展，这是美国实用主义中的积极内容，也是当代美国社会的主要价值取向和人生信念，它深刻影响了美国人的价值观，就像美国的血液，流在美国的每一道大小血脉之中。

2.3　西进运动对美国民主主义意识的促进

2.3.1　西进运动对民主观念的建立和发展

"美国人民渴求自由与平等的观念在西部更是得到了充分的发挥与进一步的巩固。西部的开发体现了使美国社会充满了活力和自由的向往。"西进运动则进一步加速了美国民主主义精神的建立和发展。

富饶、开放的西部是演示民主制度的巨大场所，而西进运动则是发展民主观念的征程。"边疆是美国民主得以扩大和加深的广阔而深厚的土壤。"正如比林顿所指出的："几乎所有新州的宪法都赋予立法机构以非同一般的权力。前文已提到，立法机构更关心的是社会舆论，并且大都规定较短的官职任期以便迅速轮换立法人员。后来在 19 世纪，新成立的西部各州开创利用创制民主，这种形式在西部边疆不仅是一种政治制度，还是一种社会生活方式。西部从来没有传统意义上的仆人，仆人不但要求别人称他们为'助手'，而且坚持与雇用他的那一家人同桌吃饭，并作为地位相等的人与客人交际。"西部民主观念的形成和发展与边疆的生活环境和生活习惯是分不开的，"美国人对政治与社会民主的态度是以人人都可以通过开发自然而获得平等这一信念为基础的"。西进运动中的移民对"先到先占"自然法则的认可使得民主平等精神渗入每一位美国人的思想。长期生活在以"优先原则"为主体的社会环境中，人们的等级观念逐渐地消失，平等意识渐渐萌生。追求民主、平等成为生活在当时的人们的一种自觉行为和普遍的社会价值观。在西进运动中，西部独特的社会价值取向为美利坚民族精神的形成提供了更加丰富的思想养料，升华了美利坚民族精神的内涵。移民们抛弃了传统的习惯和思想的束缚，进而培育锻造出一种比东部更为激进的平等观和民主观，他们抛弃身份和阶层的限制，蔑视传统和惯例来最大限度地利用西部蕴藏的丰富资源。"边疆人拒绝一切不具有直接满足自己需求价值的东西，希望用新的未经实验的民主政体来取代训练有素的贵族政体"正是这一时期民主观念的体现。

美国人在此基础上所形成的民主价值观是推动美国前进的动力。也正是西进运动加速了美国政治民主化的进程，使民主观念在西部得以确立和发展。

2.3.2 西进运动对民主制度的建立和完善

特纳在他的"边疆学说"中，特别强调西进运动"创建了美国式民主，建立了美国人对美国体制和思想的认可。"西部是美国民化运动的重要基地，西部移民的民主化观念发展并完善了美国的民主政治制度。

西进运动后的西部疆域中，由于当时的边境居民来源地不同，民族不同，信仰差异较大，因此人民要求政府不干预宗教信仰，要求教会与政府分离；他们信奉民主参与制，推行候选人任命权体系。随着边疆的推进，西部范围的扩大，西部新州的不断建立，西部在国家的政治生活中也发挥着越来越重要的影响，乃至在许多方面，西部的民主政治以及其政治制度甚至走在了全国的前列。The newly-admitted Western states constituted a region somewhat different from the South and the North in terms of interests and tipped the regional balance of power in the US legislature, exerting significant influence upon its legislative activities. In fact, legislation concerning the protection of common people's interests was largely first proposed by delegates from the West. 在 19 世纪中期以后，西部拓荒者日益成长为农业资本家，西部农场主也逐渐成为美国政治舞台上的一支重要力量，随着一些边疆州先后加入联邦，美国的国力也得到了增强。1828 年田纳西州的安德鲁·杰克逊成为第一个来自西部的总统，这表明西部在全国性政治大事中的影响与日俱增。到南北战争之际，著名的美国总统亚伯拉罕·林肯同样来自西部。就西进运动对民主制度的作用而言，一方面，公民的选举权尤其是在给予妇女选举权的问题上表现得最为明显。例如，从印第安纳州和伊利诺伊州开始，西部州宪法都规定成年男子的选举权；密西西比和亚拉巴马两州的宪法都不要求有财产才能有投票权，都给予凡在该州居住满一年的男性以选举权。西部普选权的实行，同时带动了东部各州普选权的扩大。在妇女选举权方面，1787 年联邦宪法颁布后最先给予妇女选举权的也是西部。早在 1860 年，堪萨斯州就允许妇女在学校享有选举权，1869 年，怀俄明州第一个在法律上确认妇女的选举权，随后，科罗拉多、爱达荷、华盛顿、加利福尼亚、俄勒冈等 12 个州也相继承认了妇女的选举权。而直到 1920 年 7 月，美国才以宪法第十九条修正案的形式在全国范围内确认妇女选举权。Westward Movement stimulated and accelerated the trend toward democracy, for example, the lifting of property qualifications for voting and office-holding, the gaining of women suffrage, and the adoption of direct democratic institutions（Initiative, Referendum and Recall 主动，全民公决和召回）。另一方面，西进运动在美国两党制的形成与确立上也发挥了重要的作用。美国民主政治的重要表现形式就是两党制，而两党制的产生与发展及其相互斗争的内容都与西进运动有着密切的关联。共和党与民主党的对抗及南北战争后的轮流执政就标志着美国两党制度的最终确立，西部力量在两党制的形成与确立过程中发挥着不可忽视的重要作用。

综上所述，西进运动对美国整个民主制度的完善有着不可忽视的重要作用，可以说，西进运动建立和奠定了美国式民主的基础。

第三章　西进运动对美国民族精神的负面影响

在从回顾美国历史角度的方面来看西进运动，我们不难看出西进运动的确对美国民族精神的形成和发展产生了不可磨灭的影响。但是，任何事物都有两面性，我们在歌颂其丰功伟绩的同时，也不得不承认西进运动过程中出现的一些罪恶和人性丑陋的一面。正如前文提到，西进运动的遗产既有骄人的辉煌成就，也有辛酸的人间悲剧；既产生了史诗般的深远影响，也犯下了不可忽视的严重错误。正视历史，才能避免悲剧的再次上演。但是由于这方面的相关资料和文献较少，不少学者也是更多地将目光放在西进运动的建设者角色上，因此我们的负面影响也不成体系。

3.1　西进运动中透析出的种族主义

前文提到，西进运动在传统意义上是指从阿巴拉契亚山脉以西，到太平洋沿岸都是广阔富饶的土地。而这些土地被定义为"未开垦"，但是未开垦不代表荒无人烟。相反，这里是印第安人世世代代居住的故乡，差不多在各个地方都生活着印第安人，甚至在生活条件十分艰苦的沙漠地带也有他们的足迹。

西部地区的开发，其实就意味着一个驱赶和屠杀印第安人的过程。在这个过程中，不仅仅是一些美国人用他们手中的猎枪去屠杀手无寸铁的印第安原住民来获取土地，甚至联邦政府都动用武力来灭杀印第安人。美国政府对印第安人的政策就是不断地夺去印第安人的土地，"以满足政府的一切需求，在一定时期内不仅能容纳来自联邦其他州的移民，而且能容纳来自外国的移民"。通过诱骗、胁迫、军事等手段巧取豪夺获得了大量的土地。更有甚者，在对印第安人进行掠夺战争时疯狂叫嚣"野蛮人必须消灭！""一个好的印第安人就是一个死了的印第安人"这样的口号。就是在这种对印第安人残酷的屠杀中，美国扫除了西进途中的障碍，才使得西进运动通畅无阻。

从这整个过程中，美国无论是从个人角度还是政府角度，为了发展西部促进经济，对印第安人都是采取了屠戮灭绝甚至碾压的方式来获取土地和所有权，其体现出来的无非是出于对自己民族的优越感和对印第安种族的蔑视。归根结底，种族主义、白人中心主义在这里面起了至关重要的作用。虽说白人中心主义及其衍生的种族主义在美国尚未建国之时就深深扎根于公民当中，但是西进运动中他们对待印第安人的方式却进一步催化了他们内心深处的劣行根，进而导致以后美国人对待其他民族的傲慢、歧视以及黑人问题的一再激化等等问题的出现。

3.2　西进运动中呈现出的反平等精神

美国的建国是基于一篇大名鼎鼎的文献《独立宣言》（*United States Declaration of Independence*），并且在这篇文献之中有这样的话："We hold these truths to be self-evident, that all men are created equal, that they are endowed by their Creator with certain unalienable rights, that they are among these are life, liberty and the pursuit of happiness."人人平等的思想，作为全人类最基本的权利，被写进了这份堪称是美利坚民族最引以为傲的文献之中。

但是可惜的是，在整个西进运动，尤其是在对待印第安人的方式和问题上，人人平等的思想消失得无影无踪。他们叫嚣着"野蛮人必须被消灭"，然后把印第安人烙上野蛮的印记去消灭、碾压，然后堂而皇之地占用别人的栖息地肆意妄为。在整个平等精神荡然无存的西进运动中，平等精神的缺少带来的不仅仅是印第安人的毁灭，还有美国人内心深处平等精神的缺少，更进一步来讲，还可能有对民族信仰的一种迷惘和不安。作为被写进《独立宣言》的精神，作为所谓的全人类共同遵守的信仰和准则，当被放在西进运动中的时候，就不再适用了，这是作为一个美利坚民族的伟大，还是悲哀？

或许从另一个角度来讲，其实美国所宣扬的平等不过是他们所认为的"民族"的平等。在他们内心深处，印第安人作为一个卑劣、野蛮的民族，不配跟他们讲平等。这也恰恰照应了我们的题目，这才是真正的"平等精神的缺失"。诚然，《独立宣言》所宣扬的平等思想伟大且高尚，但是这种高尚也只是限定在"白人"身上的华而不实的石头而已。真正的平等在美国，至少在西进运动中，还没有被运用。

3.3 西进运动中自然观的缺失

西进运动是一个美国资本主义向西发展的过程。在这个过程中，为发展资本主义，获取更大的利润，为东部和中西部本身的发展提供所需的原材料，难免就会出现不顾一切地开发和挖掘自然资源的行为。因此，在这个过程中，遭受灭顶之灾的不仅仅只有印第安人，更有与印第安人为伴的动植物，还有大自然。原本富饶美丽的土地被资本主义蚕食得千疮百孔，原本茂密繁盛的原始森林也因为家园的建设和采矿、制作业的侵蚀而消失在土地表面，这直接带来的是整个生态系统的紊乱，无数动植物的栖息地被破坏，被蚕食。

人与自然应该是和谐相处的，一味地索取都是带来人类自身的灾难。西进运动对于自然的破坏可以呈现出其正确自然观的缺失。对土地森林的压榨只是为了发展经济，这无异于饮鸩止渴。诚然，通过这种方式，西进运动在经济上获得了巨大的发展，但是，这更需要几十年的时间去恢复生态，更何况，有些破坏是无法挽回的。西进运动中正确自然观生态观的缺失，不仅仅对以后的美国，对整个人类的经济发展也是一个警钟。

第四章 总结与反思

西进运动的进行，对美国社会的经济、政治、文化等方面都形成了重要的影响。在这些影响中，西进运动对美国民族精神的影响尤为耀眼。西进运动为美国的发展提供了必需的条件，声势浩大的西进拓荒场景使普通人通过自己的艰苦努力和敬业精神在一贫如洗的情况下能创造奇迹，并通过白手起家，积累丰厚财富之梦得以实现。美国人用依靠自己作为发展的精神核心，以实用主义为原则，以开拓进取为动力，再加上宽松的民主政治环境，在西进的百年锤炼中形成了独特的民族精神。在西进运动过程中，拓荒者在恶劣的自然环境和艰苦的辛勤劳作中所造就和孕育的民主独立、自由平等、勇于冒险、乐观自信、创新进取和注重实效的独特的民族性格、民族价值观以及生活方式，形成了美国特有的西部拓荒精神，成为美国民族精神的象征。

然而西进运动中的糟粕却不可忽视。美利坚合众国在独立后的宣言中称人人平等的精神——美国民族精神中不可或缺的一部分，这种精神在西进运动中却被毫不留情地抹杀掉。西进运动和美国的大陆扩张是同时进行的，由于运动发生在资本主义制度下，不可避免地同侵略、掠夺和屠杀印第安人等血腥暴行结合在一起，"几乎每一批向西挺进的人流都踩着印第安人的白骨和血迹行进"。随着西进运动的发展，印第安人在自己世代居住的土地遭受野蛮的屠杀，在这片"平等"的土地中遭受剥夺。在西进运动中，印第安人遭受的不仅仅是不平等，而是遭受到种族灭绝和资源被无情掠夺。在很长的一段时间里，美国白人和西进者等都对印第安人歧视和不公平待遇，是美国历史上不光彩的一页。同时，西进运动的过程也是美国资本主义向西发展的过程，在这个过程中，为发展资本主义，获取更大的利润，为东部和中西部本身的发展提供所需的原材料，不顾一切地开发和挖掘自然资源。可想而知，当富饶宽广的自然被毫无顾忌地掠夺开发后给这片印第安人赖以生存的土地以及生存在这片土地上的生物带来的灭顶之灾。人类对自然的适度利用是正当的。但当人类把自己当成世界的中心、自然的主宰，对大自然毫无顾忌地破坏和攫取时，人类也将走向自我的灭亡。现今，人与自然和谐相处的重要性愈加明显，许多天灾也源于人祸，人类更需清楚认识到尊重大自然、和自然和谐相处的重要性。

美国历史上轰轰烈烈的西进运动虽然有功也有过，并且功过不可相抵。但是它都有一个不变的特征，"真实性"：真实地表现独立后腾飞的美国。

参 考 资 料

[1] 陈丽屏. 试论西进运动对美国民族精神的影响[D]. 山东大学，2008.

[2] 陈朝晖. 美国[M]. 北京：京华出版社，2001.

[3] 丹尼尔·布尔斯廷 .美国人[M]. 时殷弘译. 上海：上海译文出版社，2006.

[4] 端木万义. 美国社会文化透视[M]. 南京：南京大学出版社，1999.

[5] 段西宁. 美国西进运动的社会影响探析[J]. 淮北煤炭师范学院学报，2000，21（5）.

[6] 弗里德尼克·特纳. 论边疆在美国历史上的作用[M]. 北京：商务印书馆，1984.

[7] 何顺果. 美国边疆史[M]. 北京：北京大学出版社，1992.

[8] 黄绍湘. 美国通史简编[M]. 北京：人民出版社，1979.

[9] 布罗姆. 美国的历程[M]. 北京：商务印书馆，1988.

[10] 姜德琪. 西进运动对美国民族精神的影响[J]. 山东社会科学，2003（3）.

[11] 江泽民. 江泽民文选（第二卷）[M]. 南京：江苏人民出版，2006.

[12] 江泽民. 十六大报告辅导读本[M]. 南京：江苏人民出版，2002.

[13] 科曼. 远西部经济的兴起[M]. 北京：北京出版社，1912.

[14] 康马杰. 美国精神[M]. 北京：光明日报出版社，1988.

[15] 卡尔金斯. 美国扩张与发展史话[M]. 王岱译. 北京：人民出版社，1984.

[16] 柯恩. 美国划时代作品评论集[M]. 北京：生活·读书·新知三联书店，1988.

[17] 兰建英. 美国西进运动中的土地政策研究[D]. 四川大学，2004.

[18] 雷·艾伦·比林顿. 向西扩张——美国边疆史[M]. 韩维纯译. 北京：商务印书馆，1991.

[19] 李其荣. 美国精神[M]. 北京：长征文艺出版社，1998.

[20] 刘祚昌，光仁洪，韩承文. 世界通史（近代卷上册）[M]. 北京：人民出版社，1997.

[21] 南开大学历史研究所美国研究室. 美国历史问题新探[M]. 北京：中国社会科学出版社，1996.

[22] 容新芳. 论美国西进运动的原动力[J]. 河北大学学报（哲学社会科学版），2003，28（2）.

[23] 唐晋，大国崛起[M]. 北京：人民出版社，2006.

[24] 滕滕. 大熔炉的强音：美国百年强国历程[M]. 哈尔滨：黑龙江人民出版社，1988.

[25] 托克维尔. 论美国的民主[M]. 北京：商务印书馆，1997.

[26] 王恩铭. 当代美国社会和文化[M]. 上海：上海外语教育出版社，1997.

[27] 王荣堂. 世界近代史（上册）[M]. 长春：吉林人民出版，1986.

[28] 王蕊. 略论西进运动对美国民族精神的影响[J]. 赤峰学院学报，2011，32（3）.

[29] 王苏敏. 西进运动对美国社会发展的影响[J]. 黑龙江教育学院学报，2005，24（6）.

[30] 姚艳梅. 美国西进运动与中国西部大开发的对比及启示[J]. 河北学刊，2011，31（1）.

[31] 余志森. 美国史纲——从殖民到超级大国[M]. 上海：华东师范大学出版社，1992.

[32] 张琼. 西进运动对于美国文化的影响[J]. 杭州师范大学学报，2001（1）.

[33] 张旭辉. 美国西进运动的几个直接趋动因素[J]. 吉林华侨外国语学院学报，2006（1）.

[34] 张友伦. 美国的独立和初步繁荣[M]. 北京：人民出版社，1993.

[35] 张友伦. 美国西进运动探要[M]. 北京：人民出版社，2005.

[36] 张友伦. 美国通史[M]. 北京：人民出版社，2002.

[37] 张小路. 美国的西进运动及其西部开发模式[J]. 社会科学战线，2002（2）.

[38] 郑巧珊. 西进运动对美国民主的促进作用[D]. 上海外国语大学，2004.

美国宪法第十九条修正案历史研究

易　薇　张新璐　蒋天庆

摘　要：笔者试图从美国宪法第十九条修正案入手，分析和论证了 1920 年美国妇女争取到政治选举权的斗争过程，从女性角度出发，以期对美国女性选举权运动有一个客观的评价。论文共分为三个部分。第一章初步概述了美国宪法第十九条修正案，然后探讨了美国妇女争取选举权的历史背景；第二章是美国宪法第十九条修正案通过的艰难历程；第三章章则分析了美国妇女力争选举权运动的深远影响，和对中国的现实启示，以便中国在解放妇女运动和法律制定中得到一些参考，以及让女性自身得到一些启发。

关键词：美国宪法；第十九条修正案；妇女选举权；女性

Abstract: The Nineteenth Amendment is known as "Women's Suffrage Amendment". This paper analyzes and demonstrates the American woman's struggle for suffrage before 1920, aimed at having a complete and objective understanding of the American Feminism Movement. It consists of three parts. The first chapter gives a brief introduction of the Nineteenth Amendment to the United Constitution and indicates the historical background of the American women's struggle for suffrage; the second chapter introduces the development of the Nineteenth Amendment; in the last chapter, the paper concludes how the American Feminism Movement influences upon America and even other parts of the world. The author is expected to learn something that can be applied in China's Law, China's Feminism Career and modern women themselves.

Key Words:　the Constitution of United States, the Nineteenth Amendment, American women's struggle for suffrage, Woman

《1787 年美国宪法》是世界历史上第一部成文宪法，它确立了资产阶级的民主原则和共和政体，但是没有赋予美国妇女以公民选举权。美国制宪者们（全部是男性）在起草和修订宪法过程中没有对妇女权利问题做任何说明。美国宪法规定，选举权属于州权范畴。在 19 世纪，仅有个别州出于自身的政治和经济利益需要，授予妇女以选举权。美国历史学家艾伦·卡洛尔·杜波依斯在《女权主义与选举权》一书中指出：在西方经典的民主政治理论中，公民选举权与其独立的经济地位联系在一起，妇女在家庭中的从属、依赖地位决定了她们不能享有独立的个人应有的权利。从 19 世纪中期开始，美国妇女开始了争取选举权的漫长斗争，终于在 1920 年取得了选举权。

美国妇女争取选举权运动以 1848 年塞纳卡·福尔斯大会的召开为起点，以 1920 年妇女获得选举权暂时告一段落，大约有半个多世纪的时光。在这半个多世纪里，美国妇女为获得选举权进行了长期不懈的斗争。美国妇女争取选举权的斗争是美国女权运动的重要组成部分，其内容涉及政治、经济和文化等诸多方面，在美国社会生活中留下了不可磨灭的印迹。因而，探讨和研究美国妇女选举权运动，对于我们认识美国历史有很大帮助。虽然我国一些史学工作者发表了一些期刊论文和翻译了一些专著，从多方面多角度研究了美国妇女的选举权运动，并取得了一定的成果。然而，目前这方面的研究仍存在不足，如这些文章和专著没有对美国妇女选举权运动进行系统的总结，以至于我们还不能看到其整体面貌。

因此，为了展现美国妇女选举权运动的整体面貌，对美国妇女选举权运动有一个全面客观的认识，特著此文。

第一章　第十九条修正案的背景和概观

为了对美国宪法第十九条修正案有一个全面的了解，开篇有必要谈一下它的背景和通过过程。它的通过是美国民主进程的进步，更是美国女权运动的里程碑。在此之前，"资产阶级的民主在口头上答应给平等自由，事实上，任何一个资产阶级共和国，即使是最先进的资产阶级共和国，对于占人类半数的妇女，也没有给予在法律上同男子平等的地位"。

1.1　妇女权利的理解和实施

若干年来，富有意义地实施妇女权利的问题一直是国际公共关注的事项。在国家制度下有效地实施妇女权利是致力于实施妇女权利的关键部分。此外，国家对公私领域两分法所要求的传统价值的尊奉构成了实施妇女权利的巨大障碍，因为传统价值尤其鼓励妇女的屈从地位。妇女被普遍排斥在公共生活之外，被归于家庭中的从属角色，不能参与政治生活，更不用说拥有选举权了。

在美国和其他西方国家，妇女权利倡导者的回应，特别是对政府制度没有能够大力实施妇女权利的回应是要求扩大个人的诉权，强化并大力起诉侵犯权利者的角色。评估特定国家的妇女权利保护现状可以依照以下两个标准：首先，该国是否规定了妇女平等的成文法，其次，是否有权利收到侵犯的妇女可利用的实施行动。

按照国际法的要求认可对妇女权利阐释的国家面临无数重大的抉择，这些抉择都涉及如何实施权利。第一，国家可以优先安排那些有义务予以实施的权利，识别出"基本"的权利清单，而这些"基本"权利是实施一切其他权利或更为紧迫的权利所必不可少的。第二，国家可以侧重保证妇女可利用的法律机构，从而使她们的权利在平等基础上得到实施。第三，妇女权利可以通过承认不同的妇女特点或在国家社会结构中的地位而得到实施，由此必须从实体和程序上修改国内立法，以确保妇女权利得到保护。

1.2　第十九条修正案的哲学基础

现代的公民权利和政治立法建立在支持 1688 年英国革命及一个世纪后其法国和美国的继任者们的哲学基础上，它继承了男子的兄弟会公民资格居首位而排斥妇女的观念。根据卢梭的观点，男子是理性的且是人，而妇女是自然的，不是完全的人，这就意味着妇女被驯服和控制。这种哲学被很多其他国家所追随和重申。

19 世纪，民族国家的激增造成了推进哲学和法律两种倾向的最高统治权的扩展；20 世纪，反抗国家和集团压迫，为权利和自由而战的解放运动—解放了男人，却没有解放妇女。她们和国家只有间接关系。女性在越来越私有化的家庭中的工作价值和地位均未得到承认，由于她们享有行使自己的政治权利，因而她们普遍没有能力捍卫或促进自己的经济权利。

在 20 世纪之交，美国北方和男方的妇女组织开始为选举权的斗争进行合作。妇女委员会是第一个政府间机构，其成立的目的明确在于使妇女的公民权利和政治权利在全美洲得到保证。委员会以辩论、起草和游说的方式致力于在美洲通过起草的有关妇女公约草案，也因此使妇女问题在美洲取得了政治地位。

1.3 第十九条修正案的艰难通过

1.3.1 塞内卡·福尔斯会议

1848 年的塞内卡·福尔斯会议是美国早期一次的关于妇女权利的会。The Seneca Falls Convention, which advertised itself as a "Women's Right Convention". —A Convention to discuss the social, civil, and religious condition and rights of woman, was the first women's rights convention[1]. 此次大会套用了《独立宣言》（Declaration of Independence）的格式，起草了《感伤宣言》（Declaration of Sentiments）。宣言称"男人和女人是生而平等"，并历数了妇女在政治、经济、法律、教育等各个领域所遭受的不公正待遇及其应有的权利[2]。这次大会被公认为标志着美国妇女选举权运动的开端。

1.3.2 西部四州的胜利

怀俄明州。1869 年，在怀俄明领地的立法机构会议上，通过了赋予妇女选举权的法案。1890 年 3 月 28 日，众议院以 139 票赞同，127 票反对通过了批准在宪法中赋予妇女完整选举权的怀俄明加入联邦。三个月后，在参议院以 29 票赞成，19 票反对获得通过。

犹他州。犹他领地在邻区怀俄明领地通过给予妇女选举权法案的三个月后也赋予了妇女选举权。不过犹他领地妇女选举权的获得在很大程度上是源于宗教势力。1895 年犹他州摩门教宣布放弃一夫多妻制，犹他领地召开第七次制宪大会，妇女们积极斗争，终于将妇女选举权列入了讨论事项，并以 28 618 票赞成，2687 票反对获得通过。犹他州的妇女选举权终于失而复得。

科罗拉多州。在 1876 年召开的申请加入联邦的制宪会议上，科罗拉多的妇女们首次提出了妇女选举权的请愿，虽未获成功，但却获得了在学校事务上的选举权。1876 年 8 月 1 日，科罗拉多加入联邦。新成立的州立法机构制定了一个新的有关选举权的规定，即可以制定一个扩展选举权资格的法律而不需要通过宪法修正案，而这项法律在公民复决中以绝大多数形式通过。

爱达荷州。爱达荷在批准加入联邦之前，来自俄勒冈的妇女选举权领袖阿尔盖比·斯科特·达尼韦（Abigail Scott Duniway）一直在此大力宣传妇女选举权。她口才十分出众，得到了许多人的支持。1895 年，州议会通过了赋予妇女选举权的宪法修正案，并定于 11 月由公民复决通过。1896 年 11 月爱达荷州最高法院裁决此次复决有效。于是，爱达荷州成为第四个赋予妇女选举权的州。

妇女争取选举权的斗争率先在西部取得胜利主要取决于西部特殊的社会历史条件。首先，在开发西部的过程中，和殖民地时期一样，妇女在社会中起着十分重要的作用。当时为了鼓励妇女在西部定居，西部的各个领地都采取了一定的鼓励措施。比如俄勒冈的土地捐赠法案就规定，来俄勒冈定居的夫妇可以得到 640 英亩的土地，妻子有权支配自己的部分。其次，

---

① From Wikipedia, the free encyclopedia.

② 当时怀俄明州只有 8014 人，而需要 60 000 人才能申请加入联邦.

获得妇女选举权的这四个州都不是政治敏感度很高的区域。从反对妇女选举权的势力来看，大都集中在工业发达和人口众多的州，而南方更是反对妇女选举权的堡垒。

1.3.3 东部少量选举权的获得

与西部的胜利相反，"美国妇女选举权协会"试图通过制定州宪法修正案的运动却在东部历经了一次次的失败。

所有这些在各州开展的运动几乎进入同样的境地：它们可供运作的资金很少，妇女们在筹集经费上困难重重，承诺提供赞助的政党和报业常常在临近选举时就人间蒸发。困境使得"美国妇女选举权协会"的成员开始了另一种策略的尝试，他们把之前的目标——获得可以参与各个领域选举的完整的选举权（Full Suffrage），调整为争取在特定领域的选举权，即有限选举权（Limited Suffrage）的获得。这样的调整可以让州选举权的获得不再通过修改州宪法，而只需要修改相关的选举法。

而有限选举权对妇女选举权获得的另一个障碍则是并没能吸引足够多的妇女参与投票，这使得认为妇女对选举根本不感兴趣的反对主张显得更加证据确凿。

1880年，"美国妇女选举权协会"在新英格兰、纽约州、爱荷华州、伊利诺伊州、印第安纳州、密歇根州、堪萨斯州展开了市政选举权的斗争。1887年，堪萨斯州的妇女在"全国妇女选举权协会"和"美国妇女选举权协会"的共同努力下获得了市政选举权。1887年，蒙大拿州的妇女纳税人可以就纳税事务进行投票。1901年，纽约州立法机构赋予了纳税妇女在征税上的表决权，并且于1910年又通过法案将此权利扩展到了债券发行上。

"美国妇女选举权协会"虽在各州做出了努力，从总体上看仍是收效甚微，距离以各州通过宪法修正案的途径赋予妇女选举权的目标仍是非常遥远。

1.3.4 第十九条修正案的最终通过

1920年8月26日凌晨4点，由田纳西州州长签字的第36份"修正案"批准书送到了华盛顿的国务院，经验证及一系列程序之后，早上8点钟美利坚合众国国务卿班布里奇·科尔比（Bainbridge Colby）发表声明，美国宪法第十九条修正案获得通过。这一修正案的原文是：

第一项：合众国公民的选举权不得因性别缘故而被合众国或任何一州加以否定和剥夺。The right of citizens of the United States to vote shall not be denied or abridged by the United States or by any State on account of sex.

第二项：国会有权以适当立法实施本条。Congress shall have power to enforce this article by appropriate legislation.

笔者认为，它的通过主要得益于以下两点。

一是理念从公正性到有益性的转变。运动前期的领导人强调的都是妇女选举权的公正性。而"全美妇女选举权协会"成立后的选举权运动中，更多强调的是妇女拥有选举权的有益性。正是有益性理念在政党中的成功运作，直接促成了第十九条修正案的通过。二是州和联邦两种策略的统一。在美国，一项宪法修正案的通过究竟取决于联邦国会的通过，还是州立法机构的批准，实在很难对其进行权衡和比较，因为这两个条件本身就是互相统一的。美国妇女选举权运动的这两种策略，看似矛盾分裂和各行其是，其实质却是在修正案通过的两个必备条件上分别而共同的发挥作用。

第二章 第十九条修正案提出的历史背景

2.1 美国宪法第十九条修正案概观

美国妇女争取选举权的斗争是美国女权运动的重要组成部分，其内容涉及政治、经济和文化等诸多方面，在美国社会生活中留下了不可磨灭的印迹。美国宪法规定，选举权属于州范畴。在 19 世纪，仅有个别州出于自身的政治、经济利益需要，授予妇女以选举权。美国历史学家艾伦·卡洛尔·杜波依斯在《女权主义与选举权》一书中指出：在西方经典的民主政治理论中，公民选举权与其独立的经济地位联系在一起，妇女在家庭中的从属、依赖地位决定了她们不能享有独立的个人应有的权利。从 19 世纪中期开始，美国妇女开始了争取选举权的漫长斗争，终于在 1920 年取得了选举权。

美国第十九条修正案（the Nineteenth Amendment to the United States Constitution），一般简称为第十九条修正案（Amendment XIX），又称"妇女选举权修正案"（Women's Suffrage Amendment），于 1920 年 8 月 26 日获得通过，其内容有两项：第一项，合众国公民的选举权，不得因性别缘故而被合众国或任何一州加以否定和剥夺(The right of citizens of the United States to vote shall not be denied or abridged by the United States or by any State on account of sex)；第二项，国会有权以适当立法实施本条（Congress shall have power to enforce this article by appropriate legislation）。虽然此前已经有 30 多个州的妇女获得了不同程度的选举权，但是该修正案的意义和作用在于全美适龄妇女的选举权有了联邦宪法上的依据和保护，在美国女权运动（American Feminist Movement）发展中具有里程碑的意义。

第十九条修正案从 1918 年年初在众议院的首次表决到 1920 年 8 月 18 日田纳西州众议院的批准，前后仅用了两年多的时间。而妇女选举权运动者（Suffragist）为之所付出努力的时间则要长得多。早在 1878 年妇女选举运动者就已经在国会提出了"妇女选举权修正案"。该修正案与 42 年之后与最终确立的第十九条修正案几乎一字不差。而妇女选举权运动者第一次意识到应该争取妇女选举权联邦宪法修正案则可追溯到美国南北战争期间。实际上，早在建国初期就已经有妇女开始关注于自身的选举权问题。可以说第十九条修正案的通过是妇女选举权运动者一百多年来不断努力的结果。但是妇女选举权运动与第十九条修正案的关系绝不能简单地理解为过程和结果。第十九条修正案还是一种目标、理念和策略，它贯穿于选举权运动的全过程，并在很大程度上决定了运动的走向。它是美国宪政实现其平等历程的重要组成部分。

2.2 美国女性争取选举权的原因

2.2.1 思想上：西方启蒙思想的传播

约翰·洛克在《政府论》一书中明确阐明：自然法则统摄着自然界，它要求每个人都要遵守这一法则，这种法则即理性。它教导所有思索的人：他们全都平等、独立，没有谁可以损害他人的生命、健康、自由，或是侵犯他人的财产。但洛克所说的人是特指人类中的男性。"天赋人权学说"深深地影响了美国的开国元勋们，他们以此为依据制定了《独立宣言》，并且也认为，"公民"的含义应该有限度。"妇女、奴隶、无产男子以及儿童等没有独立能力和理性判断能力为大众谋取福利，因此不应该享有选举权。"这样，美国革命后，一方面，自由、民主、平等这些自由主义思想广为传播，有一定财产的白人男性在政治、经济、社会各个方面享有更多的个人权利；另一方面，这个新生的合众国仍然拒绝给予妇女和黑人选举权和其他平等权利。然而"天赋人权"思想却不可避免地影响美国中上层妇女。

当代美国妇女运动的思想先驱、著名妇女运动领袖贝蒂·弗里登（Betty Friedan）在她的《女性的神秘》（The Feminine Mystique）一书中指出，自美国进入工业化和都市化的社会后，尤其是第二次世界大战后，美国妇女一直在受着一套可概括为"女性的神秘"的思想观念和伦理道德观的熏陶和毒害。这种观念弥漫于整个社会，渗透于很多家庭。它的主要思想是宣扬妇女的最大幸福在于全身心地承担起母亲和妻子的角色，即做个贤妻良母。弗里登尖锐地抨击道，在鼓吹、宣扬"女性神秘"观念时，美国（男性）统治权贵可谓不遗余力、不择手段。如，商业广告大肆宣传，说妇女可通过使用最新式的家用电器来取得自我满足感；又如男子控制的《妇女杂志》把家务琐事浪漫化，竭力把妇女的欢乐、愉悦和惬意地定位与"寝室、厨房、孩子和家庭"等范围。与此同时，一些心理学家也跟着遥相呼应，煞有介事的大作论证，说任何不满意全日制家务工作的妇女大多有心理失调毛病，从而把妇女的失落感归咎于个人心理因素，而不是社会性矛盾。弗里登在此基础上得出结论，生活在这种文化氛围下的妇女，从出生之日起就深受这种观念的浸染和熏陶，以为妇女一生中最大的职能就是照顾好自己的丈夫，抚育好自己的孩子。弗里登指责说，美国社会文化对妇女做这种职能定位严重地限制了妇女的智力发展，迫使她们放弃自己的理想追求，因而，家庭实际上已成了美国妇女"舒适的集中营"。该书在 19 世纪上半叶被称为女权主义的圣经。她在书中说，上帝在颁布天赋人权时，既不想让男性做暴君的奴隶，也不想让女性做男性的奴隶，所以男女两性平等才是真正符合天意。她还指出，既然男性可以举起天赋人权的旗帜去反对英国君主不公正的君主制，那么美国女性也可以用天赋人权的思想武器去反对男性暴君式的统治。同年 7 月，一位美国妇女给《妇女杂志》写信道："我们反对婚姻中的'遵从'一词……婚姻不应该被视作一个尊者和一个卑者的契约，而应是一个双向的权力联盟、一个不言而喻的伙伴关系。"朱迪·默里和独立运动领袖约翰·亚当斯的妻子阿比盖尔·亚当斯更是对性别的不平等进行了系统的反思。

默里于 1790 年发表一篇《伦性别的平等》的文章。她认为既然男性在没有考虑女性利益的前提下制定了社会准则，就不应该苛求妇女去遵守；阿比盖尔则主张在法律上保证妇女的权利。1776 年 3 月，她在给丈夫的信中写道：在为独立的美国制定新法律时，务必"记住广大的妇女，……如果不给妇女以特别的关心和注意，我们决定煽动一场暴动，我们将不遵守我们在其中没有任何发言权和代表权的法律。"当约翰·亚当斯说她的要求不可能达到且违背自然规律时，阿比盖尔愤恨无比，她写信驳斥丈夫，还给女友写信，建议成立一个请愿团。此后，她这种以法律为基点争取妇女权利的思想便慢慢传开。

2.2.2 文化上：反抗社会传统的束缚

西方女性的从属形象是由基督教确立的。《圣经》在谈到女性时，说她来自于亚当的"肋骨"，而且是为了使亚当不受寂寞而创造出来的。这样，上帝创造的第一个女性——夏娃，也就自然而然地降至从属位置了。《创世纪》第三篇十六节里明确地记载上帝对夏娃的讲话："你的欲望将从属你丈夫的欲望，他将全权统治你。"（and thy desire shall be to thy husband, and he shall rule over thee）由此，《圣经》以它的绝对权威，为"男尊女卑"提供了神圣的依据。

17 世纪，英国的习惯法规定：女性完全处于男性的依附状态，婚前从父，婚后从夫，她的一切法律权利都归丈夫所有。更有甚者，在中产阶级和上层社会里，妻子甚至不允许有自己的收入。殖民地时期的法律明确规定，已婚妇女的一切都处于丈夫的"限制、保护和庇荫下，包括动产和不动产，全归丈夫所有；妻子婚前拥有的一切财产：土地、房屋、奴隶、牲畜、家具、钱财，连同她的衣服和首饰，婚后都自动成为丈夫的财产；假如她有机会外出工作，所得收入也归丈夫，雇主常常把工钱直接付给她的丈夫。"殖民地时期，北美社会的权力中心主要集中在乡镇会议、殖民地会议和各地的教会组织。然而，无论是乡镇会议，还是殖民地会议，妇女都被排斥在这些政治权利之外。在教会方面，妇女既不能参与教会事务的讨论，也不能担任神职人员。所以，尽管教会组织里的女教徒占相当高的比例，但由于其在教会组织里卑微的地位，她们不得不受制于教会的男性神职人员。正如国内一位研究北美殖民地妇女地位的学者所说："殖民地议会期的妇女在社会生活的各个方面都处于对男性的从属地位。她们没有经济地位，在家庭中没有财产权，在社会上独立从事经济活动的机会很少；她们没有政治地位，一切政权机构都无例外地将她们排斥在外，选举权和担任官职的机会为男人所独占；她们没有法律地位，只能事事处于丈夫的'限制、保护和庇荫下'；她们没有宗教地位，在教会中没有发言权，不能担任神职。因此，殖民地时代不可能是美国妇女的'黄金时代'。"

1776 年，美国独立战争爆发，广大妇女在爱国主义的感召下积极参战，从事各种形式的反英活动。当殖民地人民发动抵制英货时，大量殖民地妇女自己纺纱织布，而不去购买英国的布料。当殖民地与英国在茶叶税问题上发生矛盾时，殖民地妇女组织起"反茶叶协会"自己采集干草和叶子调制"自由茶"，代替英国进口茶叶。甚至还有一些妇女跟随大陆军南征北战。但是，随着独立战争的结束，不论是《1787 年宪法》，还是后来的《人权法案》（十条修正案），都把妇女、黑人、印第安人及不符合财产规定的人排除在外，这激起了广大资产阶级妇女和有色人种的强烈不满。在这些压迫下，一部分妇女对自身地位觉醒，并自行组织起来进行斗争，有利社会环境的促动。

影响美国女性争取选举权的原因不仅仅是因为西方启蒙思想传播后，女性的思想得到了解放，出现反抗社会传统的现象以及工业化和城市化的发展，推动了女性思想进一步的解放，加之对女性劳动力的需要，更使得女性为自己的利益做出了不懈努力的斗争。这也是女性争取选举权的另一因素。对女性劳动力的需要，促进了女性的就业。

就业及教育使其智力得到进一步的开发，更加地关心社会进步，并且在工作中切身体会到妇女社会地位低下的现状，这些都促使妇女为自己的权利展开斗争。

1795—1835 年，美国经历了史称"第二次大觉醒"的宗教复兴浪潮，再次推动美国新教派脱离英国教会枯燥无味的理性主义，朝向虔诚的福音派教义。该运动中声势最大、影响最深远的是它的第三个阶段，即查尔斯·芬尼从 20 世纪 20 年代起在纽约州中西部进行的福音布道。与宗教复兴其他支派不同，芬尼派允许并鼓励妇女积极参加复兴机会，捍卫"妇女姐妹"在集会中祈祷及表达意见的权利。芬尼派著名活动家西奥多·韦尔德尤其支持妇女在公共集会中畅所欲言，他号召："让有才智的妇女祈祷并演讲……当（男人）对此习以为常了，他们就会喜欢，不再有所顾虑。"受芬尼福音教义的感召，中产阶级妇女不仅参加了男性领导的团体，还成立各种妇女团体从事慈善行业的改革，其中最有影响的是妇女道德改革运动（Female Moral Reform）、禁酒运动（The Temperance Movement）和废奴运动（The Antislavery Movement）。

第二次大觉醒运动换起了一批先进中产阶级妇女的宗教热情,同时新教教义的改革也为女权运动主义者争取女权的斗争扫清了一定的障碍，为提出妇女选举权的问题做了成功的铺垫。

2.2.3 经济上：工业化和城市化的发展

现代美国社会的出现是两次工业革命的结果。在两次科技革命的推动下，美国经济发展突飞猛进。19 世纪最后 50 年，美国总产值增长 12 倍；1894 年跃居世界第 1 位；19 世纪末，美国工业生产总值超过英、法、德三国，取代了英国"世界工厂"的地位。城市化也伴随着两次工业革命而来。1800—1890 年，全国人口增加 11 倍，而同期城市人口增加 86 倍。19 世纪末最后 20 年，大城市的发展更是达到了前无古人的速度，芝加哥面积扩大 2 倍多，纽约人口从不满 200 万增加到近 350 万。工业化和城市化对社会的方方面面都产生了巨大的冲击，所有的美国人都被卷入工业化和城市化中，其中美国妇女的生活环境和社会地位发生了深刻的变化。首先，随着工业化的发展，家庭的生产功能被剥离开来，男性逐渐脱离家庭从事有酬劳动，而女性则承担家务，照顾家庭成员。男性是主要的工资劳动者，成为家庭的"养家糊口的人"。其次，工业化和城市化的发展带来了居住环境和日常生活的巨大变化，现代的家居环境在 20 世纪的美国初步成型。居住环境和日常生活的变化对美国妇女的婚姻家庭生活和观念有巨大的影响，19 世纪末 20 世纪初，美国妇女一改维多利亚时期的深居简出，以健康、摩登的形象出现于公共场所中，她们在家庭中的地位和角色也有新的变化。最后，工业化和城市化也动摇了维多利亚女性观。维多利亚时期社会性别分工明确，"妇女的位置在家庭"，只有在道德上高于男性。但到 19 世纪末 20 世纪初，随着工业化和城市化的加速，妇女更为广泛深入地参与社会各种活动，并一度成为一支重要的社会力量。

但工业化和城市化也滋生了混乱和贫穷。各种社会问题越来越严重，城乡之间的距离也逐渐拉大。城市中的美国妇女充分享受着工业化和城市化所带来的利益。与此相比，美国农村妇女的生活却与工业化之前没什么变化。但不可否认的是农村女性的生活也受到了现代化的冲击，城市的繁华和机会吸引着农村的女性，20 世纪 20—30 年代许多农村女孩常出于家庭经济需求和实现自身的梦想来到城市寻找职业，逐渐融入城市生活。

工业化和城市化使经济飞速发展，彻底改变了美国人的生活面貌，也为妇女创造了参与社会发展进步的条件，促进了她们自我意识的觉醒和群体力量的发展，其世界观和生活方式发生巨大的改变。

2.2.4 教育上：妇女受教育水平的提高

随着第二次工业革命的发展，经济结构、生产方式、管理模式发生了巨大的变化，对各种专业技能提出了更高的要求；同时，在"共和国革命"和"工业革命"两大历史巨轮的推动下，妇女得以坐进课堂接受启蒙教育，学习基本文化知识。此时妇女受教育的机会大为增加，初、高中的中学普遍招收女生。1880 年，1.3 万名妇女从高中毕业，而相比之下男性高中毕业生只有 1 万多名；1900 年的对比数字相差得更加悬殊，有 5.6 万名女高中毕业生和 3.8 万名男高中毕业生。在基础教育向女性开放的同时，高等教育也陆续向她们敞开了大门。到 1900 年，全美 80%的学院、大专和专业学校接纳了女性。据统计，到 1890 年，女性在获得学士学位的总人数中占 17%，在获得硕士学位的总人数中占 19%，在获得博士学位总人数中占 1%。从 1890—1930 年，美国受过高等教育的女性比例呈稳步上升趋势，完全把女性排除在外的仅仅是医学、牙科和法律专业。

另外，19 世纪 20—30 年代，美国还出现了一批全新而且更为严格的私立学校。它们的创建者都是女性，如妇女教育家埃玛·威拉德于 1807 年在佛蒙特州的米德尔伯里创办了一所女子专门学校，1821 年 6 月又在纽约州的哈特福德创办了一所女子学校，在迁到特洛伊后改为特洛伊女子学院，这是美国第一所女子高等院校。凯瑟琳·比彻于 1828 年在康涅狄格州开办一所女子专门学校。玛丽·莱昂斯于 1837 年在马萨诸塞州南哈德利开设芒特霍利奥克女子学院，声明该学院创办的目的是向女性提供相当于男生在当时专科学校所能得到的教育。美国西部和南部也相继开设了女子学院。1860 年，招收女生的高等院校已有 61 所，大多数大学开始实行男女同校。美国教育对妇女开放的宗旨是培养贤妻良母，但始料未及的后果是推动了妇女走出家门。

美国女子教育发展的重要意义不仅在于有越来越多的妇女受到了正规教育，而且在于促使全社会逐步正视妇女受教育的权利。同时，女子学校的学生们毕业后不仅仅在家庭中充当更合格的妻子与母亲，懂得营养学与卫生学，而且在她们身上体现出来的妇女智力的开发，对生活技能的掌握，特别是生活期望的提高促使其他的妇女学会用自己的头脑思考问题，关心社会进步，而且为自己的自由和权利展开斗争。在参与过社会实践后，她们体会到工作的价值，不愿再回归家庭，从事琐碎沉闷的家务劳动，而且她们在工作中切身感受到，由于妇女社会地位低下，致使自身利益受损。这些都使妇女体会到要通过不断的斗争来争取自己的权利保障。

2.2.5　就业上：就业机会的扩大与就业岗位的多样化

除了以上几个比较主要的因素外，妇女就业机会的增加和就业范围的扩大也对其争取选举权有一定的影响。

女工的形成比其他职业都早。1790 年塞缪尔·斯莱特引用水力于纺棉成功，使其后纺织工厂大兴。美国一直缺乏劳工，厂主开始雇佣廉价的女工。但到 19 世纪劳动力市场中女性仍占少数，只有一部分女性由于家庭经济需要进入劳动力市场。19 世纪末 20 世纪初工业化和城市化的发展以及妇女受教育水平的提高，使女性就业出现新的变化。此时随着第二次工业革命的发展，经济结构、生产方式、管理模式发生了巨大的变化，对各种专业技能提出了更高的要求，各个领域中的专业化趋势加强，劳动分工更加专门化；同时，随着女性受教育水平的提高，为她们进入办公室和教师、护士等白领职业提供了前提，此时教师、办公人员、护士、社会工作者以及图书馆工作者发展成为女性化职业，就业领域中的性别分割更加明确。1910 年，77%的教师都是女性，办公室中女性的比例从 1880 年的 4%跃升到 1890 年的 21%，到 1920 年，女性已占据办公室工作的半壁江山。19 世纪末，随着城市公共卫生运动的进一步发展，人们的卫生意识加强，医院大规模建立，对护士的需求不断增加，大量的女性加入这个职业中。与此同时，中产阶级妇女参加白领工作成为女性就业的一个新现象和发展趋势，已婚妇女就业也逐渐发展并成为 20 世纪的一个长期趋势。1900 年，已婚妇女在劳动大军中的比例为 5.6%，1910 年上升到 10.7%。

妇女的就业使其智力得到进一步的开发，更加的关心社会进步，并且在工作中切身体会到妇女社会地位低下的现状，这些都促使妇女为自己的权利展开斗争。

第三章　第十九条修正案的客观评析及成败原因

从 1848 年在塞内卡·福尔斯大会明确提出妇女选举权，到 1920 年终于用联邦宪法修正案的形式将这一权利确立下来，妇女选举权运动者们付出了艰辛的努力，过程也是相当漫长，历经72年。从第十四条法案和第十五条法案的确立，再到西部四州的胜利，东部少量妇女选举权的获得，美国第十九条修正案的形成其实是美国妇女的女权斗争史。第十九条修正案可以说正是在妇女选举权运动的推动下产生的。那么在围绕第十九条修正案对美国妇女选举权运动进行了一番历史考察之后，本章将对修正案进行一些简要的评析。

3.1 美国妇女选举权实现的意义

3.1.1 对白人妇女的影响

1920 年 8 月 26 日，美国妇女因宪法第十九条修正案的通过获得了选举权。因而该条修正案又被称为"妇女选举权修正案"。该条修正案不仅是美国第一次女权运动的里程碑，更是美国民主进程中的重要一步。

妇女选举权运动的胜利，不仅沉重打击了旧的社会伦理观，还使美国妇女获得了参与政治中的权利，男女政治权利的平等第一次得到宪法的承认。经过一个世纪的斗争，美国妇女在为自己争取权利的同时，也锻炼了妇女的能力，为以后女权运动新浪潮的来临奠定了深厚的基础。

经过长期的斗争，美国女性公民"开始把政治看作是走向公证社会的关键所在"。合众国宪法承认了妇女选举权，美国妇女选举权修正案也正式成为美国宪法的一个组成部分。美国2600 万适龄女性获得了与男性一样的选举权。美国宪法第十九条修正案正式生效后，美国各州针对本州的具体情况对法律进行了不同程度的修订，允许妇女拥有、继承和遗赠财产，对原来的离婚法也做了相应的修改，以便保障妇女的经济和监护子女的权利，同时妇女在接受高等教育的权利和妇女就业的机会等方面也得到了一定的改善。

首先，在 20 世纪 20 年代美国的政治舞台上，出现了两个女州长和一个女国会议员。她们是 1922 年进入美国参议院的丽贝卡·费尔顿夫人以及分别与 1924 年和 1925 年出任怀俄明和德克萨斯州州长的内莉·罗斯夫人和米里亚姆·费格森夫人。尽管这三人担任公职的时间并不长，但她们开创了女性选举的先河，从而为 20 世纪 20 年代美国女性解放运动增添了重要的一笔。政治获得平等的同时，20 世纪 20 年代的女性在经济上也获得了更多的机会，妇女所能从事的职业范围得到了很大的扩展。当时的妇女可以驾驶飞机、开出租车、架设电报线路、从事深水潜水员和高空作业建筑工的工作等。妇女们因此更加独立，单身女性搬进了她们自己的公寓。已婚女性大多仍在工作，由于离开了家庭，她们获得了更多的行动和选择的自由。妇女在家庭中的地位也因此发生了变化，男女逐渐趋向平等。

除了上述妇女在政治和经济上地位的提高之外，20 世纪 20 年代妇女更大的解放在于观念上的解放。这场所谓的性道德的革命则是弗洛伊德等人潜意识理论、性心理分析理论在美国传播的结果。在这种思想的影响下，男女之间有了更多的自由，他们在一起工作、游玩。更重要的是未婚妈妈们不再被逐出家门或成为社会排挤的对象。女性不再需要从一而终，也可不必在忍受痛苦的婚姻了，男性在婚姻家庭中的优势地位受到了严重的挑战。离婚率在当时不断上升。1914 年，美国的离婚率第一次突破了 10 万对；而到了 1929 年，仅当年一年的离婚率就超过了 20.5 万对。总之，获得选举权是妇女权利的重要标志，使妇女走向解放的第一步。同时，美国妇女选举权运动也是美国妇女运动史上的一道分水岭。美国妇女争取选举权的胜利，改变了她们的政治从属地位，促进了资产阶级民主制度的发展，推动了社会的进步，为美国向现代化迈进做出了重要贡献，是美利坚文明提升的重要标志。

美国妇女选举权运动是一场政治教育运动，极大地提高了妇女的素质。在漫长的斗争中，妇女选举权运动为广大妇女提供了政治锻炼的机会。由于妇女选举权活动的需要，他们不断地向公众发表演讲、对议员游说，撰写宣传材料，召开会议，组织团体……正是妇女选举权运动为妇女提供了进行公共活动、演讲、组织的机会，从而在实践上克服了维多利亚时代的性别领域分离，这实际上为妇女日后的政治参与打下了基础。在这种过程中，中产阶级妇女克服了思想文化上和个性上的局限，挨家挨户游说，征集签名，参与公共集会，参与游行，参加代表团，与政治家会面，从而培养自己的政治意识，锻炼了自己。运动中各个阶层的妇女团结一致，为妇女的共同事业而并肩战斗，使运动超越了阶级间的界限，成为妇女的共同事业。

3.1.2 对黑人妇女的影响

在美国不足 250 年的历史中，黑人历史是不可分割的一部分，同样，黑人妇女也是美国妇女中不可或缺的部分。美国黑人妇女首先是黑人，其次是女性，这两种属性决定了她们比黑人男性更悲惨，争取教育权的斗争更艰难。在大多数黑人生活的南方，白人殖民者不仅用军事镇压黑人的反抗，而且通过立法剥夺黑人的诸多权利，尤其是受教育的权利。

黑人妇女从一开始就是一个特殊的群体，遭受着民族的歧视，忍受着性别的屈辱，但她们始终坚忍不拔地立于社会之中。

奴隶制作为一个合法的体制存在，它对黑人的压迫和奴役是不言而喻的。在这种体制下，黑人连最起码的做人的权利都没有，更谈不上什么自由了。黑人作为一种财产，经常是被变卖。黑人女奴所受到的压迫更是惨重，她们不仅受到种族压迫，还受到性别压迫，甚至经常要遭受种植园主的性侵犯。

黑人女性主义者批判主流女性主义运动是"白人和中产阶级"的运动。以《女性的奥秘》的作者贝蒂·谢里丹（Betty Friedan）为例，她是美国主流女性主义的代表人物，并担任了 4 年"全国妇女组织"主席。她坚信妇女只有通过走出家门获得工作这一唯一一途径来获得与男性平等的地位。在她女性主义运动的生涯中，她将目光始终停留在"主流美国妇女"即白人中产阶级妇女身上。她呼吁妇女去争取的大多也是要求有高等教育背景的高薪工作，而这对于大多数黑人妇女来说简直是天方夜谭，因此从思想观念上，黑人妇女已经被排除在外。此外，除非是专门针对黑人或第三世界妇女的会议，黑人女性时常收不到参会邀请。

3.2 美国妇女选举权实现后存在的问题

"宪法第十九条修正法以法律形式正式明确了美国妇女在政治上男性公民有一样的权力，从此美国妇女可以通过参政部门反映自己的要求，这无疑是个巨大的进步，它为以后妇女争取其他的权利铺平了道路。"但是，美国妇女选举权的获得并没有给她们带来真正的平等，美国妇女的"黄金时代"并未到来。正如列宁所指出的："在任何一个资本主义国家里，甚至在自由的共和国里，妇女都没有完全的平等的权利。"她们在选举、就业、工资待遇等方面，尤其是职业方面仍受到严重的歧视。

3.2.1 政治上

第十九条修正通过后，男人们说："感谢上帝，这场旷日持久的女权运动终于结束了。"而妇女们则说："现在，我们终于可以开始了。"第十九条修正案究竟是为妇女选举权运动画上的完满的句号，还是妇女争取自身权利斗争的开始，有人认为修正案虽然把选民增加了一倍，但事实上妇女对政治并不是真的感兴趣，妇女拥有选举权后并没有体现出实质的意义。

在参政方面，据统计，从 1917—1945 年，美国 15 届国会中，只有 38 名妇女当选为两院议员。第 80 届国会众议员中只有 7 名妇女，第 81 届国会的参议员中只有 1 名妇女。1920 年是美国全国范围内行驶妇女选举权的第一年，这一年增加了 2600 万女选民。全国适龄选民大约有 6000 多万。可是这一年合格选民的投票率却下降，仅为 44.2%。这是自 1828 年以来 90 多年来里 24 次大选中投票率最低的一年。大多数妇女都与其丈夫、兄弟及父亲投一样的票，这不是因为她们被迫跟着男人走，而是因为具有同样的对阶级、民族群体和地区的忠诚。与许多新获得投票权的群体一样，妇女也比长期使用投票权的人参加投票的次数少。1920 年，当美国妇女首次在全国范围内走进投票站时，她们仅占投票人的三分之一。

3.2.2　经济上

在就业、工资待遇尤其是职业方面，美国政府和社会仍坚持传统的性别角色观念，妇女在战争时期，经济地位的变化并没有改变各行业中的性别歧视状况。妇女有就业机会，却没有和男子一样的提升机会，妇女在整个劳动力比例的增长没有改变妇女处在各行业等级的低层状况。男女同工不同酬的现象也很普遍。私营企业实行按性别区分的两套工资级别制，使妇女无法和男子有同样的收入。美国工会为了维护男工人的利益，也坚持男女分工和划分等级。男女同工不同酬的现象仍很普遍。从 1920—1945 年，政府从未颁布过一个哪怕是形式上的同工同酬法令。做同样工作的男子和女子在工资上存在巨大而明显的差异，女工的平均工资比男子低 15%～20%，女公务员比男公务员的工资少 18%～20%，而女书记员比男书记员的工资少 25%～30%。在制业，妇女的工资仅为男子的 65%。不仅如此，妇女总是被先解雇。据统计，从 1948—1966 年，美国就有 885 000 妇女被解雇。最突出的是"太特里塞姆钢铁公司"，第二次世界大战中，该公司雇用了 1200 名妇女，但到 1949 年，就剩下一名了。性别歧视在职业领域内也很严重，职业妇女甚至在战争年代仍然难以找到合适的位置。护士、图书管理员、社会福利工作者、售票员、低等秘书等成为 20 世纪美国女性的职业。1950 年，在各"女性职业"里，女护士占 98%，女接线员占 96%，女打字员、女秘书占 94%，女图书管理员占 89%，女小学教师占 91%，女社会福利工作者占 66%；而在所谓的"男性职业"里，妇女仍不能有所突破，1950 年女律师占 3.5%，女医生占 6.1%。

因此，从 1923—1948 年，妇女们每年都会向国会提出一项修正案，要求废除联邦、州以及各个城市的各种歧视妇女的法律条文，但每年都遭到拒绝。后来，经过女权主义者的不懈努力，加之在 20 世纪 60 年代民权运动中，联邦政府这才在 1963 年立法规定男女同工同酬，禁止就业和工作中的性别歧视。但其他形式的性别歧视还在，旨在从法律上消除性别分类的"平等权利修正案"虽然在 1972 年已经被国会通过，但直到 1982 年也没有被足够的州批准（当时，平等权利修正案必须得到美国 38 个州批准才能生效，但直到 1982 年也只有 32 个州批准该修正案），最后这项修正案被迫流产。

3.3　美国妇女获得选举权成败原因

第十九条修正案最后得以通过是多种因素共同作用的结果，如运动理念上从公正性到有益性的转变，策略上有关联邦和州策略的统一。实际上，美国联邦宪法在建国初期对于选举权的立场是授权州宪法加以规定，因而此时的联邦宪法并没有提及妇女选举权的问题，既没有授予，也没有剥夺。在一些州拥有财产权的妇女都可以进行投票选举总统。但是第十四条修正案和第十五条修正案明确的以"男性"的字眼剥夺了妇女的选举权。从这种角度来看，美国妇女的选举权是被宪法强制剥夺的，而第十九条修正案在某种程度上是对第十四条修正案以及第十五条修正案的抗争。

美国特殊的宪法修改模式决定了妇女选举权运动的走向，但是历时一百多年的运动过程则仍然取决于一个基本的社会问题：男女并不平等。相比于黑人问题的种族不平等，男女不平等不仅历史更长，情况也更为复杂。第十九条修正案的通过作为美国第一次女权运动的一个高峰，不但没有将女权运动者更加紧密地结合起来，反而使不同种类的女权运动者在其共同目标——选举权实现后迅速分化。加上这一时期物质文化的繁荣，许多妇女在当时享乐主义的影响下又重新回到了家庭。虽然性别歧视的问题仍然十分严重，但女权运动的领导者却很难提出一个和选举权一样富有号召力的目标来团结大家，因此，美国女权运动在选举权获得之后逐渐走向了低潮。

获得选举权的美国妇女在社会上仍然遭受歧视的现象，使得一些女权运动者意识到，选举权的斗争只是开始，争取真正平等的道路还十分漫长。第十九条修正案通过以后，女权运动者认为应该致力于消除一切"基于性别基础上"的法律区别。激进女权运动者保罗认为，无论是妇女不能作为陪审团成员、没有独立财产权还是离婚中不平等的所有问题都应通过一个宪法修正案进行解决。因此，在 1923 年，塞内卡·福尔斯第一次女权大会召开 75 周年之际，保罗所代表的"全国妇女党"向国会提交了平等权利修正案，并将之命名为"柳客丽霞·莫特修正案"。其内容非常简单，只有短短一句："在美国及其所辖每个地区，男女应拥有平等的权利，国会有权指定适当立法实施这一条款"。

这条几乎意味着"取消妇女一切特殊优惠"的平等权利修正案的结果可想而知，屡次提交屡次失败，虽在 20 世纪 70 年代复兴得以在国会通过，但在各州批准的过程中则是困难重重，历经十年终以三州之差而宣告失败。妇女选举权的获得尽管存在着形形色色的障碍，但民主制度的承诺和进程使得这样一种寻求公民身份接纳的运动最终必将走向成功。相对于选举权的斗争，号召妇女们追求平等权利的斗争虽然具有更大的感染力，也的确再次将她们团结到了一起，然而平等权利却比选举权涉及更加广泛和纵深的利益。如果说争取选举权的斗争是一个寻求接纳的历程，追求平等权利的过程则更深入地触及了男女平等的问题，试图用一条宪法修正案去改变男女不平等的社会现实自然更加艰难。

再者，造成男女同工不同酬的情况的原因是多方面的，除了复杂的社会条件外，归纳起来主要有以下几个原因。

第一，妇女获得选举权后，不同种类的女权积极分子失去了团结的纽带，所以先前有着共同目标而紧紧团结在一起的女权运动在妇女获得选举权后迅速分化，这些不同的团体都在为自己理解的自由而奋斗。例如，凯特女士领导的"全美妇女选举权协会"变成了"妇女选民同盟"，其会员只有原来的十分之一；选举权运动的先驱斯坦顿的女儿哈里奥特·布拉奇女士加入了迅速消失的社会主义党；思想激进的保罗小姐则认为，妇女选举权获得后，妇女应该努力反对一切"基于性别基础上的不平等"。她在 1921 年组建"妇女党"，企图以第三党的身份来改变美国的政治局面，消除尚存的不平等现象。

第二，美国宪法只在形式上给予妇女选举权，却没有订立一个保证这一权利实施的统一选举制度。美国各州分别规定的各种各样诸如教育、财产、定居、纳税等项关于选举权的限制不但对妇女有效，而且有的州还额外增加条款限制妇女选举权，使得经济、社会地位仍然较低的广大妇女比起同等地位的男子来，就不可能参加投票了。

第三，"进步运动"时期的美国女权运动的基本力量是工业化的主要受益者——中产阶级妇女。而工人阶级妇女同政治上受排斥相比，更直接受经济不平等的压迫。给予她们选举权并不能帮助她们摆脱贫困和压榨。因此，选举权运动没有能对中产阶级以外的广大劳动妇女产生强大的吸引力，她们明显对投票缺乏热情。

第四，在美国，再也没有哪一个词汇比"公民权"（Citizenship）这个概念在政治上更为核心，在历史上更加多变，在理论上更具有争议。而政治权利平等则正是美国公民权的首要标志。选票一直是社会正式成员的一纸证书，其主要价值在于它能将最低限度的社会尊严赋予人们。正是由于上述原因，公民权从来就不仅仅是代理和授权的问题，而是一个社会身份问题。美国哈佛大学政治学教授茱迪·史珂拉说："在美国民主社会，构成公民身份的两大核心要素是选举权和收入权。"

因此，在美国，如果没有选举权，他们就觉得自己不是公民，就觉得自己脸面无光，甚至他们也会遭到其他公民同胞的蔑视。身份是美国妇女争取选举权的重点问题。但是，一旦获得了选举权，选举权又不能赋予个人其他好处。具有深远意义的是权利，而不是对权利的行使。一个人没有选举权就不是完整的公民，一旦他获得了选举权，这个权利就实现了它的功能，拉开了这位公民与地位低于他的人尤其是奴隶的距离。美国妇女最后得到了这种权利，至于她们是否行使它，则是妇女们自己的事情。

第五，进入 20 世纪以后，美国社会风气发生了很大变化。女权主义者试图继续争取妇女平等权利的事业，但已经无法在年轻一代妇女中产生影响。20 世纪 20 年代的时髦女郎们生活在一个新的社会环境中，在道德观念和生活追求上同前一辈妇女有很大的差异。她们对投票选举、集体事业和社会妇女兴趣淡漠，而热衷于个人自由、自我实现，表现出很强的个体主义精神。具有讽刺意义的是：女权主义的初衷是让妇女加入个体主义化的过程，获得和男子一样的个人权利，而年轻一代的个体主义倾向却成了女权主义者推进妇女事业的一个障碍。

但在一定意义上，美国宪法第十九条宪法修正案应该说还是前进了一大步。这是在美国女权运动的推动下，统治集团在保留原有宪法形式下，通过补充宪法使其适应不同历史条件的需要。然而，这个修正案正如资本主义制度下其他的法律一样，仍然反映了资本主义制度的阶级本质，是维护资产阶级利益的法律。尽管美国资产阶级革命是以争取人权为口号的，但是所谓"天赋人权"只是它用来反对封建专制统治的思想武器，一旦资产阶级掌握了政权，它的法律就只是维护统治阶级的人权，而践踏广大劳动人民的人权。美国宪法第十九条修正案的产生和实施，说明了美国妇女想要得到真正的解放，获得真正的平等权利，只争取选举权是绝对办不到的。因为从历史发展的角度讲，私有制是造成男女不平等的根本原因。只有废除了资本对男女双方的剥夺，即"废除土地和工厂的私有制，才能为妇女真正彻底的解放开辟道路"，才能逐渐地真正地享有"人人平等"的"天赋人权"。我们相信，对于广大美国妇女来说，这一天终将到来。

美国妇女选举权运动是工业化和城市化发展到一定阶段的产物，是在走向民主社会历史进程中出现的。事实上，女权运动是伴随近现代化进程所产生的。政治的进步，思想的启蒙，使平等权利观念深入人心，这才催生了美国妇女争取选举权的运动。但美国妇女选举权运动基本上是在传统的性别观念主导下追求妇女政治选举权的改革运动。它并没有从根本上突破男性中心社会的性别观念，并没有去颠覆男性的话语霸权或思想霸权，或者说主流社会的性别观念已经深深地内化成为妇女自己的信念。所以，从这个意义上说，妇女得到了选举权，仅仅是获得了初步的解放，她们前面的路还很长，她们要面对的仍然是一个充满偏见的男性社会。当妇女在真正意义上取得平等的社会地位时，那将是人类从自然走向文明的巨大进步。

References

[1] Carol Hymowitz, Michaele Weissmam. A History of Women in American[M]. New York: Bantam Books, 1978.

[2] Carol Ruth Berkin , Mary Beth Norton. Women of American History[M]. Boston: Boston Press, 1979

[3] Eleanor Flexner. Century of Struggle, the Woman Rights Movement in the United States [M]. Cambridge: Harvard University Press, 1973.

[4] Frances M., Bjorkman. Woman Suffrage History Arguments and Results[M], Whitefish: Kessinger Publishing, 2010.

[5] Linda Kerber. Women of the Republic: Intellect and Ideology in Revolutionary America [M]. Chapel Hill; The University of North Carolina Press, 1997.

[6] Reva B. Siegel. She the People: the Nineteenth Amendment, Sex Equality, Federalism, and the Family[J]. Harvard Law Review, 2002, 115 (4): 947-1046.

[7] Sara M Evans. Born for Liberty: A History of Women in America[M]. New York: Collier Macmillan, 1989.

[8] William H. Chafe. The American Women: Her Changing Social, Economic, and Political Roles, 1920-1970. Oxford: Oxford University Press, 1972.

[9] 埃里克·方纳. 美国自由的故事[M]. 王希译. 北京：商务印书馆，2002.

[10] 布卢姆，摩根，等. 美国的历程（下册，第一分册）[M]. 戴瑞辉，等译. 北京：商务印书馆，1988.

[12] 加加林娜. 资本主义国家的妇女[M]. 华群译. 北京：中外出版社，1951.

[13] 林艳. 19 世纪后期 20 世纪初期美国西部妇女参政权运动及其作用[D]. 东北师范大学，1998.

[14] 陆丹妮. 论北美殖民地时期妇女的地位[J]. 世界历史，1991（2）.

[15] 洛伊斯·班纳. 美国现代妇女[M]. 侯文惠译. 北京：东方出版社，1987.

[16] 李昌道. 美国宪法纵横论[M]. 上海：复旦大学出版社，1994.

[17] 列宁. 列宁全集（第 28 卷）[M]. 北京：人民出版社，1993.

[18] 马克垚. 世界文明史[M]. 北京：北京出版社，2004.

[19] 玛丽·沃尔斯通克拉夫特，约翰·斯图亚特·密尔. 为女权辩护/妇女的屈从地位[M]. 王蓁，等译. 北京：商务印书馆，1995.

[20] 玛丽莲·亚隆. 老婆的历史[M]. 许德金，等译. 北京：华龄出版社，2002.

[21] 萨拉·M. 文斯. 为自由而生——美国妇女历史[M]. 杨俊峰译. 沈阳：辽宁人民出版社，1995.

[22] 王恩铭. 20 世纪美国妇女研究[M]. 上海：上海外语教育出版社，2002.

[23] 王政. 女性的崛起——当代美国的女权运动[M]. 北京：当代中国出版社，1995.

[24] 王希. 原则与妥协：美国宪法的精神与实践[M]. 北京：北京大学出版社，2000.

[25] 王加丰，周旭东. 美国历史与文化[M]. 杭州：浙江大学出版社，2005.

[26] 许卓. 美国第二次女权运动中平等权利修正案的失败及其原因[D]. 东北师范大学，2006.

[27] 余志森. 崛起和扩张的年代[M]. 北京：人民出版社，2001.

[28] 约瑟芬·多诺万. 女权主义的知识分子传统[M]. 赵育春译. 南京：江苏人民出版社，2003.

[29] 朱迪·史苟拉. 美国公民权寻求接纳[M]. 刘满贵译. 上海：上海世纪出版集团，2005.

[30] 中华人民共和国全国妇女联合会. 马克思恩格斯列宁斯大林论妇女[M]. 北京：中国妇女出版社，1990.

[31] 张明芸，韦澍一. 社会变革与妇女进步[M]. 长春：东北师范大学出版社，1998.

百家争鸣与西汉独尊儒术

董虹宇

摘　要：中华文明上下五千年的历史中，汇集了成千上万、不可数的优秀的独特的文化瑰宝，这篇文章抓住的是春秋战国时期著名的一个文化现象：百家争鸣。百家争鸣中最为重要的学说之一便是儒家学说，它不仅属于文化范围，其思想主张还涉及政治、经济等范畴。而文化与政治的关系向来密不可分，本文讲述的便是儒家学说与百家争鸣的概念以及西汉政治统治中儒学的参与：参与背景、原因、改革变化。

关键词：百家争鸣；儒学；西汉

Abstract: In the five thousand years of history of Chinese civilization, there are thousands of excellent and unique cultural treasures. This article focuses on one of the most famous cultural phenomena of the Spring and Autumn Period and the Warring States Periods: the contention of one hundred schools of thought, among which the most important one is Confucianism that is cultural, political and economic in its philosophical scope. As culture and politics have always been inseparable, this article thus seeks to study on the concept of Confucianism and the One Hundred School Contention, and the Confucian involvement in Western Han politics, especially the background, reasons and reforms of such kind of Confucian participation in politics.

Key Words: Contention of 100 Schools, Confucianism, political involvement, the Western Han

1　引言

大二的时候我选修了一门核心通识课程，叫中华文明史，课程上的内容就如同它的名字，从华夏商周时期开始讲述中华民族的文明史，讲到了明清时期，当然课程的学时有限，老师只是挑选了几个具有代表性的特别的，或是著名的文化现象、历史事件进行授课。在这之中，我发现百家争鸣这一个内容，并非我们从初高中学校学到的那样简单，其中还有很多细节、很多流派是我们从未听说的，而稍微深思一下，就发现其中的儒家学说的博大精深，其与秦王朝之后的汉朝更有着千丝万缕的联系，值得我们思考和探究。所以我仅根据自己浅薄的知识去对其进行了分析，许多地方定有缺漏或错处。虽然这个课题在国内外都已经被讨论研究过很多次了，但我还是以为它有很多细节值得现代人深究，思考过后，我们定能为自身的素质提高、文化界的繁荣和当今的社会发展得出体悟，出一份力。

2　百家争鸣与西汉独尊儒术

百家争鸣指的是春秋战国时期知识分子之间关于政治、学习、修身养性等主题进行的激烈丰富的争论。这一时期由于诸侯争霸、社会混乱、周代的礼乐制度崩坏，社会面临巨大变革，于是学术上涌现了各种各样的新观点和新见解。各知识分子对于政治经济等面临的问题提出了自己的独到见解，于是逐渐形成了一些学术流派。而这些具有影响力的学术流派之间不同观点的摩擦、争论，便被人们形象地称为"百家争鸣"。然而一些人认为："百家"泛指的是数量多，其实并不是真的是 100 家。据《汉书·艺文志》记载，能被说出名字的就有 189 家，著作多达 4000 多篇。而之后的《隋书·经籍志》等书说明这个"百家"其实有 1000 多家。可见当时争鸣之激烈。当然，我认为这些学派数目众多，但观点往往有不同，也有相同，有冲突，也会有融合，观点的内涵与价值也良莠不齐。所以后世提到诸子百家与百家争鸣，常谈的只有十家学派，分别是儒家、墨家、道家、法家、阴阳家、杂家、名家、纵横家、兵家、小说家。西汉刘歆将小说家去掉称"九流"，后来发展为我们口中的"十家九流"。

如果要说百家争鸣在中国历史的地位，我首先会想到同时期西方的古希腊哲学体系，因为读高中的时候老师就经常把两者放在一起比较。诚然，两者都对后世以及周边国家、世界产生了相应的影响，但我认为：百家争鸣的地位不应局限于纯理论的哲学史，它对中国历史的影响还远远涉及社会变革、文化艺术、政治军事和人性品德、中外交流等方面。春秋战国时代的百家争鸣是我国思想文化史上的第一座高峰。在这个"轴心时代"里，各种学说与学术都出现了基型。从此以后，两千多年后续的封建中国便一直行进在它的巨影之中。可以说，直至近代，我国"一直靠轴心时代所产生的思考和创造的一切而生存，……轴心期潜力的苏醒和对轴心期潜力的回归，或者说复兴，总是提供了精神动力。[1]"

首先，春秋战国时代是中华文明的一个成型时期，以前的教科书里也多次提到：百家争鸣是中国历史上第一次思想解放，促进了古代思想文化的发展进步。这里的思想解放是指知识分子阶层的意见交流和学术讨论十分激烈，各种观点的碰撞融合影响广泛，甚至开始涉及农民大众阶层。首当其冲就是儒家，当时主要是孔孟之说以及荀子的观点，以"仁"为核心，在人的品德修养、君主治国、家庭关系、教育等方面都提出了具体的看法；还有"虚无"的老庄之学，重点就是因循自然，以不变应万变，老庄的思想超越功利，看中精神上的追求，因此对中国历史上的文学艺术、诗歌、美术还产生了极大的深远的影响，因此后世很多文人的审美偏向于自然，喜欢聆听天籁，"清水出芙蓉，天然去雕饰"，作画力求达到虚无的静与自然，不像西方更强调人力的技巧、人工的创造；还有实用主义的墨家等等。各种各样的观点，针对各种各样的领域，不同的主张相互争讨，还有各位诸侯的支持和应用，使得百家思想极大地发展与流传下去，在当时社会的地位不可谓不大。甚至中华人民共和国建立以后，毛泽东也受其启发，提出双百方针"百花齐放，百家争鸣"，当时大家争相发言，为中华人民共和国建设建言献策，还有各类艺术文化创作层出不穷，比如文学上：阿城的《棋王》、宗璞的《红豆》、茹志鹃的《百合花》、刘心武的《班主任》、格非的《迷舟》、余华的《鲜血梅花》、白先勇的《游园惊梦》，电影有《上甘岭》《五朵金花》《英雄儿女》，戏剧有《蔡文姬》《文成公主》等等，文化事业大大繁荣起来，也为人民生活提供了丰富的娱乐消遣，其影响可见一斑。

更深入一点地说，百家争鸣其实还是第一次人性和理性的解放。那时候人们多迷信鬼神之说，认为人的生活处处与神仙鬼怪有着紧密联系，对很多当时无法解释的现象和无法靠自己解决的问题都喜欢推给未知的鬼神。而百家争鸣中则出现了这样的观点：不再过多关注鬼神，而是更多地关注"人"自身，主张依靠自身的努力；或是更多关注人与自然的联系。比如孔子对鬼神持敬畏态度，李路问孔子鬼神、死生之事时，孔子回答："未能事人，焉能事鬼？未知生，焉知死？"意思是人的事情都还没处理好，怎么去管鬼不鬼的事呢？还不知晓活着的那些事，怎能知道死了后的事呢？可见孔子注重"人"大于"鬼"，强调人的理性，先关心人活着的事情。当然还有很多人认为孔子提倡"远鬼神"就是一种迷信，因为他好像承认了鬼神的存在，其实孔子是避而不谈，他完全不讨论鬼神之说，甚至都不表示自己承认鬼神的存在，因为他完全强调的是"人"在社会的作为。又比如老庄，崇尚自然，认为人与自然是一天的，应该顺应自然，无为而治。就是说人处在自然中，受自然支配、影响，而自然的一些规律则通过人表现出来，所以人应该顺应自然，不要改变自然，面对未知的现象也顺应自然规律，不受鬼神迷信之说摆布。当然百家中还有承认鬼神的思想，比如墨家的"明鬼"还提到人死后为鬼，分善恶，入地狱或升天的问题。但同时墨家的"非命"又是对天命的否定，因为他强调人的主观能动性，要通过自己的努力去改变现状，我认为这也是对迷信依赖心理的一种反驳。总的来看，百家争鸣是中国历史上第一次对迷信鬼神思想的松动，开始了对理性的解放。

其次，百家争鸣在中国政治史上的地位也不能不说。因为几乎每个大大小小的学派都有自己的政治观点，而很多统治者往往喜欢从中寻找、挑选对自己有利的部分，加以应用。从这一点上来说，百家争鸣对中国政治产生了深远的影响，为以后各个朝代的统治思想和方式都奠定了一个基调，为中国古代政治画了一个较为明确具体的方向，提供了许多实用的学说。比如西汉统治者对儒家的推崇。

那么为什么西汉统治者不采用墨家、法家、道家等学说呢？为什么偏偏采用了秦朝禁用的儒家学说？首先我们会想到的理由就是顺应统治的需要。对封建王朝来说，一切都是为了君主的统治而服务的。秦王朝刚刚统一六国，社会还很混乱，生产力亟待发展，此时统治者需要的是集中统一的管理和治理，法家思想讲究功利，非常适合秦的发展。而到了西汉，社会相对稳定，战争已经结束，对统治者来说"治天下"成为主要的目的，法家那套针对地主阶级的理论主张过于激进。西汉需要一套更"柔"的理论思想来改善和发展已经比较稳定和富足的国家。其实汉初，统治者偏爱的是道家理论发展而来的黄老之术，实施的是休养生息、轻徭薄赋，这在一定程度上与儒家的民本思想十分相近，然而随着社会不断发展，"无为而治"使得西汉逐渐出现问题，而儒家思想讲究"仁政""以德治国"的同时，还强调对人的约束和对社会秩序的管理，适合彼时的西汉。统治者通过宣扬儒学的克己复礼、尊师重道、君臣秩序、仁义礼智来达到天下归心的目的，即：人民依照儒学说的那样生活，安分守己，恪守自己的本分，不做出格的事情，听从君主、听从老师与父母，社会越来越稳定，等级秩序也得到维护。这就是西汉君主想要的。当然，由董仲舒引起的著名的"罢黜百家，独尊儒术"其实是对孔孟之说进行了改变的一种"新儒学"，其特点是外儒内法，就是说吸收了一些法家的主张思想。

具体来说，西汉时期：（1）政治上出现王国问题，又一次面临春秋战国时的诸侯割据危机，同时北方匈奴虎视眈眈，西南夷也成问题。董仲舒提出的新儒学主张君权神授、天人感应，完美地适应了"大一统"的需要。而其他学说的主张并不能帮助君主巩固等级秩序，比如墨家，它调解君主与劳动人民矛盾的方法是"兼爱"，主张人与人之间平等对待，互相关爱。然而在封建等级社会，这个主张无疑与统治阶级的利益相悖。（2）西汉初土地兼并严重，地主阶级与农民阶级矛盾激化。在儒家的"仁政"与"民本"思想指导下，统治者实行轻徭薄赋，鼓励人民生产，有利于经济发展。然而如果是道家的无作为，就只能眼看着农业生产一步步滑落。（3）西汉作为封建王朝，自然希望建立森严的等级制度，统治阶级自然希望享受普通人民享受不到的待遇。此时儒家的主张又一次派上用场，"君君，臣臣，父父，子子"，它强调对上层阶级的绝对依顺，为统治者的至尊地位提供了理论支持。而其他学说，如墨家代表的是小生产阶级者的利益，"尚贤""尚同"都是要求凭实力选拔人才，这无疑触碰了官僚阶级贵族阶级的家族利益，使得他们的子孙的荣华富贵无从保证。"节用""节葬"是墨家的精华思想，强调节俭，反对铺张浪费，反对"厚葬"就是禁止把过多财物放到棺材里，并

且主张人人死后都只需要简单的葬礼，其他人参加完葬礼后马上去参加生产劳动，不提倡儒家的"久丧"，比如我们熟知的父母去世后守丧三年。这绝不是西汉统治者乃至任何一个朝代的统治者想要的，他们不仅活着的时候喜欢享受，死了以后也希望风光的厚葬，希望留名历史被后世永远关注。我们看历代皇帝为自己大肆修建的陵墓就可以知道这一点。再者，墨家提出"非乐"，反对统治者花大量金钱欣赏音乐、观看歌舞表演，认为这是一种铺张浪费，同时占用了君主治理国家的时间和人民生产的时间，甚至提出废除音乐，这又一次与上层阶级的享乐需求相悖。总的来说，汉武帝为了实现大一统，需要一套统一的思想体系来规范人民、百官，而这套思想体系需要站在统治阶级的利益上，为统治者服务，同时却不能过于激进、绝对，它还需要适当地为劳动人民着想，准确地说是为劳动人民的生产活动着想，推动他们安居乐业，从而保证社会稳定，统治者的利益也就得到了维护。

而除开儒家、道家、法家和墨家的学说外，名家主要是一套逻辑理论，没有太多的政治主张，并且它的逻辑思想主要都是围绕一些抽象的哲学问题，对西汉王朝可以说没有现实意义。也因此，后世多称名家为"诡辩"。阴阳家的观点也主要在自然观和历史观上，其关于政治的思想后来也被后人"取其精华，去其糟粕"了。纵横家、杂家等思想主要针对的是春秋战国那样的乱世，到了西汉便没有发展更新，自然也就不适用于西汉王朝。

再说回到百家争鸣的地位，它不仅在当时解放了思想、促进了思想的融合交流、推动了政治的发展与变革，为后世留下了许多有意义的精华，还为以后的朝代、社会提供了可贵的交流模式，即：各种思想相互碰撞，有冲突的同时，即使是完全对立的学说也有可以融合的地方。统治者应当学会广纳言论、吸收各家之所长，并且善于改进。这甚至影响近代的中国，在引进西方先进言论的同时，我们也保留了自己文明中有特色有意义的部分，并且根据本国特色对西方文明进行改变再加以应用。

百家争鸣还有利于当时中国与世界的和平交流与交往。在与日本、朝鲜等周边国家来往的过程中，对方都非常推崇百家争鸣中的各种学说，比如儒家的仁德思想、法家与兵家的政治理论、道家的自然观和其他一些哲学思想。再比如日本天皇举办过关于佛教等文化的辩论活动，都是借鉴了我国古代的百家争鸣。甚至远到另一个半球的西方也传入了百家争鸣的学说，以儒学为主。众所周知，法国伟大的思想家伏尔泰对孔子的学说就十分赞赏，并且表示自己的一些观点主张都受过中国儒家的影响。从这一点来说，百家争鸣在中国外交史上还占有重要位置。

除大家最关注的政治、经济、文化理论，百家争鸣著作数以万计，其中还有很多关于古代手工艺、农业生产、中医药、音乐等方面的知识。这些在当时促进了社会生产力的发展，各种生产技术开始流传，改善了人民生活，诗经等著作更是丰富了人民的生活，流传到后世也产生了深远的影响，从中还可以了解到我们祖先的博大智慧。

百家争鸣可以说开创了中华文明中的宗教文化。中国的宗教文化在世界上并不突出，但我们并不能忽视他的存在。道教是最具中国本土特色的民族宗教，与百家争鸣的道家一字之差，可见两者渊源。道教奉老子为太上老君，将其神化，同时继承了道家的思想理论，信仰"大道无形""生道合一，长生成仙"与"天道承负，因果报应"，其中贯穿道家思想中的因循自然、天人合一。道教关于宇宙生成、万物本性的观点也基本与道家、老子的看法一致。然后便是佛教，它由印度传入中国，并非本土自产的宗教，但传入后，对中国影响广泛，其著作在翻译过程中也受到百家争鸣中儒家和道家思想的潜移默化，本地佛教的不断钻研和辨析使得中国佛教出现了许多宗派，"百家争鸣"又一次出现在佛教的领域。而这些宗教文化又衍生出许多相关的艺术文化，产生了许多珍贵的历史文化瑰宝，比如龙门石窟、敦煌石窟、道教的各种道观遗址。北魏崔浩更是将百家争鸣中的阴阳学说融入道教，为统治者服务。还有一些统治者也信奉宗教，但他们在这里的信奉多表现为追求长生不老，从而大肆修建教观、召集人手研究这些宗教著作，还鼓励相关的绘画、书法等作品发展。

总的来说，百家争鸣在中国历史上不仅影响时间深远，从春秋战国到后来的历代王朝，再到近代中国与当代中国；影响的范围领域也很广大，思想、学术、文学、政治、艺术、品德教育甚至宗教和外交。

而西汉独尊儒学，使其成为千百年来中国历史的主流文化，我认为把上文中的原因简单概括来有以下几点：（1）儒学自身的合理性与科学性。（2）巩固统治的需要，西汉社会生产状况、历史背景更适用儒学的主张。（3）统治者的正确选择与适当改善。（4）儒家代表的阶级利益符合西汉君主利益。（5）其他学派代表的阶级利益与统治阶级利益不符，或是其主张不适用于西汉国情，或是许多学派自身的理论体系不够完善、没有改进。

对于第一个理由，我认为是最重要的，正因为儒家思想自身的科学与合理，才使得它不仅在西汉被统治者采用，还能被后人沿用至今。从儒学本身来看，到了西汉中期，它已成为一种兼收并蓄，对维护封建统治特别有利的思想体系。它能够被封建统治者所采纳[3]。为什么这么说呢？中华民族的起源就是小农文明，以家庭为单位进行生产，农民对自然条件和年长的有经验的生产者有依赖性，自然而然地形成了对权威的依赖心理，需要甚至是喜欢被集中有序的管理，后来催生出了尧舜禹、周天子与诸侯，再到后来持续几千年的封建君主统治，都与中华民族潜意识里的集体依赖心理有关。而儒家强调分明的等级秩序，要人们恪守自己的社会本分，从而使社会安定，我认为这种主张其实是顺应了人们的依赖和保守心理，按照儒家说的，人民只需要听从上层阶级的安排就可以安居乐业，他们认为何乐而不为呢？然后，儒家认为人性本善，要人们仁义、与人为善，这种主张在一个集体社会中是很实用的，因为它可以很大程度的避免冲突、纠纷和战斗，符合中华民族温顺的爱好和平的性格。要求崇敬祖先、守孝悌也迎合了中华人民对"根"的执着，不愿意轻易迁移，看重家族和集体的联系。再看墨家、法家过于激进，有些看法比较绝对，并且维护的是某个特定的阶层或是集体的利益，不考虑其他人的需求；道家又不爱"管事儿"，中国人多，各人的需求和利益或有不同，太过绝对的具体主张都不适用于中华民族，最好的就是有个像儒家这样观点温和、应变性强（可以根据不同时间、不同情况调整）的学说，能够很好地涵盖大多数人的意愿和利益，那么它就能被大众接受，就能成主流文化。

参 考 资 料

[1] 黄萍华. 论西汉从"黄老无为"到"独尊儒术"的转变[J]. 龙岩师专学报，2000（4）：49-51.

[2] 姜继为. 百家争鸣对后续中国之影响及其成因初探[J]. 中华文化论坛，2003（1）：69-72.

[3] 雅斯贝尔斯. 历史的起源与目标[M]. 魏楚雄，等译. 北京：华夏出版社，1989.

语言文学篇

A Comparative Study of the Word-formation between English and Chinese Netspeak Lexicons

魏钰芬

摘　要： 网络的迅速普及产生了一种新的"语言"——网络语言。这篇论文以词汇学作为理论基础，以近年来的英汉两种语言的网络词汇为语料，对其构词法进行了研究。通过比较两种语言的网络词汇的异同点得出以下结论：英汉网络语言产生的社会背景基本相同，在构词方式上都具有随意性，都出现了大量语义变化的词语；整体来说，英汉网络构词法均以传统构词法为基础，但在具体的构词方式上也有很大不同，英语的网络构词法和传统方法区别不大，但是汉语网络构词法中出现的独特的构词方式较多，比如汉语的网络语言中存在更多的谐音词和外来词等。此外，汉语网络词语中出现了大量的鄙俗语，这使得净化网络环境、规范网络用语势在必行。

关键词： 构词法；网络用语；对比；相同点；不同点

Abstract: The widespread use of Internet has generated a new language – Netspeak.Based on the theory of lexicology and the data of English and Chinese netspeak words, the thesis attempts to analyzethe word-formation of English and Chinese netspeak and make a comparison between them. Through the analysis, we can find their similarities and differences. The similarities are as follows: Firstly, both English and Chinese netspeak words are originated from the same social and cultural background. Secondly, both of them are free on word formation and have semantic changes. On the whole, the methods of netspeak word-formation are based on the traditional ones. However, there also exists major differences in some specific methods. The most conspicuous is that Chinese netspeak include more partial tone words and loan words. Besides, among Chinese netspeak exists many euphemistic expressions of vulgarism, which makes it imperative to purity the network environment and standardize the netspeakwords.

Key Words: Netspeak, Word-formation, Comparison, Similarities, Differences

Chapter 1　Introduction

1.1　Purpose of research

Language of human beings has the design feature of creativity. With the approach of Internet, it has been a tendency to use netspeak. A netizen may have difficulty in communication with others online or understand of the information without following the pace of this new emergence. (Wei L, Wenyu L 2014)

This paper has mainly two purpose. Firstly, in order to know the characteristic of netspeak word-formation, we need to collect typical and latest netspeak words. Secondly, the comparison of word-formation between English and Chinese netspeak can give us an understanding of the universal and unique features of netspeak.

Therefore, this paper, with quantitative dada, will aim to give people a clear picture of netspeak word-formation between English and Chinese and analyze the similarities of differences between them.

1.2   Previous studies of netspeak

The netspeak (or Internet slangs) on Wikipedia is defined as: Internet slang (Internet shorthand, Cyber-slang, netspeak, or chatspeak) refers to a variety of slang languages used by different people on the Internet[①]. It comes out thick and fast in these years.

Comparatively speaking, the study on netspeak started earlier abroad. In 1997, University of Hartford held a conference on "Internet and Language". Many famous scholars are involved in this and they discussed the status of the English in netspeak, education by Internet and so on. Six years later, another netspeak-study conference was held in Spain. These two conferences are the landmarks of research on netspeak in linguistic circle. In 2001, David Crystal, one of the world's foremost authorities on language and the editor of Cambridge Encyclopedia of the English Language, published the book titled Language and the Internet. (赵永丰，2007) In this book, he defined netspeak as: A type of language displaying features that are unique to the internet, and encountered in e-mail, chat group, virtual world and World Wide Web, arising out of its character as a medium which is electronic, global, and interactive. (David Crystal, 2001：18)

The study on netspeak began thirteen or fourteen years ago in China. It develops quite fast. The number of the books and articles about netspeak is increasing dramatically. The representative work on netspeak *An Introduction to netspeak* (于根元, 2001) displays a systematic analysis of the lexical features of Chinese netspeak. In recent years, an increasing number of scholars and graduate students start to analyze and compare the netspeak between English and Chinese. In the thesis The Study on the Word- formation Commonality of Network Languages both in English and Chinese (刘智慧，2011), the author summarized some similarities and features of English and Chinese netspeak. And the thesis titled A Comparative Study of Netspeak Neologisms between English and Chinese written by Zhao Yongfeng made a more thorough study on netspeak word-formation. From the formation to the feature as well as the comparison, we can have a clear understanding of these new netspeak words.

From things been said above, it can be seen that all these have made a contribution to the research on netspeak. Nevertheless, we find it not convincible enough for the words studied by them easily get obsolete as the use of netspeak words changes rapidly. For this reason, this paper tries to collect as top and latest netspeak words as possible. Hope this paper could make some contribution to further studies of netspeak word-formation.

---

① https://en.wikipedia.org/wiki/Internet_slang

1.3　Layout of the paper

The main content of this paper includes four parts. The first part is a general introduction to this paper. The second part mainly studies the process of word-formation between English and Chinese. The third part, the heart of this paper, presents the comparison of word formation between English and Chinese netspeak and the last part is the conclusion of this paper.

Chapter 2　The Process of Word-formation

2.1　The Process of Word-formation of English netspeak

According to the Wang Rongpei's (2002: 21) view on English word-formation, there are three major ways, i.e., derivation, compounding and conversion. Besides, there are abbreviation (including clipping, initials, and acronyms and blendings), back-formation and onomatopoeia; however, the quantity in word-formation of netspeak words are different from traditional methods.

Table 1　Classification of word-formation process of English netspeak

	Number	Percentage
Compounding	45	45%
Abbreviation	28	28%
Existing word form with new meanings	10	10%
Other word-formation processes	10	10%
Derivation	6	6%
Conversion	1	1%
Total	100	100%

2.1.1　Compounding

Compounding is a word-formation process consisting of joining two or more bases to form a new unit, a compound word. (张韵斐, 2004: 35) It is the most productive way of creating netspeak. From the data collected, as shown in Table 1, it can be calculated that compounds constitute 45% of all the top 100 netspeak. The formation of compounding words can be analyzed from the perspective of word class and syntax. Grammatically speaking, there are mainly three kinds of compounds.

1. Noun Compounds:

1) Noun + noun: flash mob

2) Adj. + noun: black fax

3) Verb + noun: desire line

4) Noun + adj.: doorknob rattling

2. Verb compound

Noun + verb: text-walk

3. Adjective compound

1) Adj. + adj.: Blue-hot

2) Verb + noun: Post-gay

3) Noun + p.pr: Vote-shaming

2.1.2 Abbreviation

Abbreviation can also be called shortening, as the name says, it produces the words in shorter forms. In Computer Mediated Communication (CMC), people often shorten the words for the purpose of fast typing. These shortened words include not only blending and clippings, but also initialisms and acronyms.

1) Blending

Blending is the combination of clipping and compounding in which new words are created by the overlap of words or fragments of existing words. (赵永丰，2007) There exists seven kinds of blends.

1) Head+ word: testilying= testifying + lying

2) Word +head: dadbod= dad + body

3) Head + head: nico-teen= nicotine + teenager

4) Head + tail: fappy= fat + happy

5) Word + tail: brandscape= brand + landscape

6) Tail + word: camgirl= Webcam + girl

7) Others: fandom= financial + domination

2) Clippings

There is only one word genariancreated through clipping, which is from septuagenarian or octogenarian, means an elderly person.

3) Initialisms

Initialisms is a type of shortening, using the first letters of words to form a proper name, a technical term, or a phrase; an initialism is pronounced letter by letter. (张韵斐，2004: 72) There are some in the following: BYOD from bring your own device and CPA means continuous partial attention

4) Acronyms

Acronyms are abbreviations that are pronounced as if they were words. Among the data collected, there are only two acronyms: BANANA means build absolutely nothing anywhere near anyone (anything) and GOOMAY means get out of my back yard.

2.1.3 Existing word form with new meanings

There are 10% words are given new meanings to be used by people as a new word. For example: Dipstick usually means a long, thin stick for measuring the amount of liquid in a container, especially the oil in a car engine while in netspeak, it means to take the measure of a person or a situation.

2.1.4 Other word-formation process

Apart from all the words mentioned above, there are still some words that are difficult to define their ways of word-formation. Many of them consists of more than three words or even a sentence.

For example: Dog that caught the car refers to a person who has reached their goal but doesn't know what to do next.

2.1.5　Derivation

Derivation or affixation is generally defined as a word-formation process by which new words are created by adding a prefix, or suffix, or both, to the base. (张韵斐，2004: 42) Comparing to the traditional words, this way in the word-formation of netspeak is decreasing.

1) Prefixation: miso: misophonia

retro: retrosexual

2) Suffixation: ist: deathist

ocracy: narcissocracy

2.1.6　Conversion

Conversion means that the form of the word keeps unchanged but the class of the word changes. For example: Google means to search for information on the website, especially on the search engine Google.

2.2　The Process of Word-formation of Chinese netspeak

Chinese word-formation is more complex than English. Generally we can classify it into two types: simple words and compound words. But usually the word-formation refers to the formation of compounds. There are mainly three ways. The first is compounding, including the combination of morphemes, one morpheme modifies another part of morpheme, two morphemes have a V-O relation, two morphemes have a Predicate complement relation and two morphemes have an S-V relation. The second is affixation, involving prefix, infix and suffix. And the last is reduplication. (姚乃强，贺季萱, 1982)

After careful studies of the word forms and sources of neologisms in Chinese netspeak, the researcher summarizes nine types of word-formation in Chinese netspeak(Table 2).

Table 2　Classification of word-formation process of Chinese netspeak

	Number	Percentage
Abbreviation	22	22%
Partial tone words	19	19%
Hard to define	19	19%
Old word with new meanings	16	16%
Loan words	12	12%
Compounding	4	4%
Metaphor or metonymy words	3	3%
Reduplication	3	3%
Onomatopoetic words	2	2%
Total	100	100%

2.2.1 Abbreviation

Convenient and timesaving, abbreviation have been the most productive way in creating Chinese netspeaks. Definitely, many netizens prefer to use these shortened words in CMC. For example: 不明觉厉（bùmíngjué lì, it seems to be great although one cannot totally understand）; 注孤生（zhùgūshēng, it's destined to be lonely whole life）.

2.2.2 Partial tone words

It is widely admitted that intonation plays a very important role in distinguishing the meanings of words in Chinese. However, pursuing speed and limited by the input conditions, netizen find it difficult to bring the role of intonation into play. Thus a large quantities of words with partial tone are produced. There are mainly two types:

1) Chinese words: 蛇精病 (shé jīng bìng, lunatic); 涨姿势（zhǎng zī shì, to know some new knowledge）

2) English word: 狗带（goudài, go die）; 亦可赛艇（yikěsàiting, exciting）

2.2.3 Other word-formation processes

Among the top 100 Chinese netspeaks, there also exists a large proportion of words that cannot be defined exactly in which way they were formed. For example:

撕逼 (sībī, quarrel fiercely)

洪荒之力 (hónghuāngzhīlì, prehistorical powers)

2.2.4 Existing word form with new meanings

With the advanced development of society, some old concepts and social phenomenon even daily stuffs capture netizens' attention so that they give them the new meaning. For instance: 醉了（zuìle, someone gets drunk, now it means speechless）; 有毒（youdú, poisonous, now it means bad fortune or soothing inevitable）

2.2.5 Loan words

In order to express the new things and concepts, Chinese Netspeak has been borrowing words from dialects and other languages, especially English and Japanese.

1) Loan words from Englis:弯的 (wānde, gay)

2) Loan words from Japanes: 宅男 (zháinán,for men with obsessive interests that leave no time for normal life outside the home); 魔性 (móxìng, from Japanese 魔ま性しょう, greatly temptation)

2.2.6 Compounding

Compounding is no longer a major way of word-formation in netspeak words. Here are some examples: 颜值 (yánzhí, apperance); 心塞 (xīnsāi, gloomy)

2.2.7 Reduplication

Netizens are used to creating new words by the means of reduplication to express intimacy such as "萌萌哒 (méngméng da, cute and sweety)" and "分分钟 (fēnfēnzhōng,a fraction of a minute)."

This kind of words usually to intensify rhetoric.

2.2.8　Metaphor or metonymy words

In these years, some metaphor or metonymy words have become new favorites of netsizens especially the youngsters.

2.2.9　Onomatopoeic words

Duang (to add some special effects); 么么哒 (me meda, to kiss someone)

3　Comparison of Word-formation in English and Chinese Netspeak

3.1　Similarities

3.1.1　The social and cultural background

1) Constantly developing cyberculture

The theme of cyberculture is social economic life, which contains different aspects, such as politic, economy, entertainment, science and technology, education and so on. (姜莉，2014) Due to the rapid development of society, netspeak as a result of the digital revolution and the subsequent wave of CMC technologies that have been incorporated into society and our daily lives. Whether in domestic regions or at abroad, the open internet environment can be integrated with different cultures. The cyberculture becomes increasingly international and diversified. All of these contribute to the formation of netspeak.

2) Fast-paced life

One of obvious features of netspeak words is convenience. People use quantities of compounds and acronyms even some special symbols to communicate with each other online. The main group of cyber netizen is young adult. They believe that inputing a complete sentence or word will be a waste of time.Under such circumstance, netspeakwords are used in a large scale so as to promote the efficiency of communication on the Internet as well as make the conversation more interesting. For instance, in English, people often use "LOL" to replace "laugh out loudly", use "BTW" to replace "by the way". In Chinese, the word "不明觉厉 (bùmíngjuélì)" represents the sentence "It sounds great although I don't understand what you are talking about. "

3.1.2　The features of English and Chinese netspeak

1) Both English and Chinese netspeak words are created at will.

Netspeak words is the language of a virtual world with various forms owing to the open environment. Unlike literary and colloquial words, this new language cannot restrained by the traditional grammatically function. As an open platform, the Internet gives the equal speech right to every netizen. Thus everyone can create his/her own words on the premise that everything word is understandable. This phenomenon is the same to both English and Chinese netspeak. Examples abounded in life. In English, "text-walk" means to conduct a text message conversation while walking while in Chinese, "捉急 (zhuoji)" is equal to anxious.

2) Both English and Chinese netspeak words have semantic changes.

Some old-established words take on additional shades of meaning as a result of the diversity of culture in some certain occasions. These words often follow certain well-marked tendencies: specialization, generalization, amelioration and pejoration. Besides, some words totally change the original meaning. For example, "dipstick" in English means a graduated rod dipped into a container to indicate the fluid level while in netspeak, it means to take the measure of a person or a situation. "打酱油" in Chinese now means someone is indifferent to something.

3.2   Differences

1) Loan words

The number of loan words in Chinese netspeak is extremely large, taking 12% while in English is no loan words according to the data collected, which is the mostconspicuous difference. Most of these loan words are Japanese. Having advanced economy and developed animation industry, Japan, as our neighboring country, has a great influence on our own culture. In recent years, Japanese carton has been a new favorite for young adults. Thus many Japanese words are transliterated into Chinese such as 皆さん（minasan）meaning everyone. Apart from Japanese, English also plays an important role in creating netspeak words such as "弯的 (wan de)" which means gay.

2) Partial tone words

Partial tone word is a unique feature of word-formation in Chinese netspeak. As Chinese syllables are comparatively simpler, the tone has played a very important role in distinguishing word meanings. It is also one of the realization of recursiveness in Chinese. Chinese character has four tones, and each tone can correspond to several Chinese characters. Nevertheless, some of these partial tone words are euphemistic expressions to abuse someone or laugh at someone, some of them even kind of vulgar, which may have a negative effect on teenagers. At the same time, it sheds lights on the necessity of cultivating good manners when a netizen use netspeak words. It's time for government to purity the network environment and standardize the netspeak words.

3) Metaphor or metonymy words

There exists a great discrepancy referring to the meaning of "dog". In Chinese netspeak, some words related to "dog" become young adults' favorite. In western culture, dog has a commendatory sense, symbolizing loyalty and wisdom. People regard them as their friend. For example: Love me, love my dog. He is an old dog, etc. In contrast to western culture, the interpretation of the dog always hold derogatory meaningin Chinesesince thousands of years ago. The idioms such as "狼心狗肺" means that someone be as cruel as a wolf while "狗急跳墙" means a cornered beast will do something desperate. In modern society, the meaning of dog has a diachronic change. It becomes a more neutral word than a derogatory one and it has been an image for young adults to poke fun at themselves. On the one hand, the young generations are under great pressure for the confusion about their future. On the other hand, they are in the beginning stage of their career and have not acquired a higher position so they use the word "dog" to represent their social status.

4　Conclusion

Through a contrastive analysis of word-formation in English and Chinese netspeak, we draw the conclusion that new words are also governed by the formation rules. From the study, this thesis summarize seven types of English netspeakword-formation, which are almost the same as traditional ones. The compound words and blending is the most important way in creating words. Compared to English netspeak, Chinese netspeak have nine types of word-formation, among which include both the traditional types and the unique ones brought into being by the Internet era, especially the abbreviation and partial tone words.

The emergence of informal and colloquial netspeak words is the product of the modern society. The arbitrariness of creating words and the tendency of abbreviation and old word with new meanings in both English and Chinese shed light on netizens' psychological factors. The netspeak in both English and Chinese reflect the social and psychological attributes of language, while the differences between them result from the language discrepancies and cultural background.

With the continuous development of society, the number of English and Chinese netspeak words will be on the rise. The study of netspeak needs further observation and insightful research in the future.

References

[1] David Crystal. Language and the Internet [M]. Cambridge: Cambridge University Press, 2001.

[2] Wei Liu, Wenyu Liu. Analysis on the word-formation of English netspeakneologism[J], Journal of Arts & Humanities, 2014.

[3] https://en.wikipedia.org/wiki/Internet_slang

[4] http://spacekid.me/internet-slangs/

[5] http://www.wordspy.com/

[6] 刘智慧. 英汉网络语言的构词共性研究[J]. 湖南师范大学社会科学学报，2011，40（5）：119-122

[7] 汪榕培，卢晓娟. 英语词汇学教程[M]. 上海：上海外语教育出版社，1997.

[8] 姚乃强，贺季萱. 汉英构词法异同刍议[J]. 解放军外国语学院学报，1982（3）：2-8.

[9] 于根元. 网络语言概说[M]. 北京：中国经济出版社，2001.

[10] 赵永丰. 英汉网络语言对比研究[D]. 大连海事大学，2007.

[11] 张韵斐. 现代英语词汇学概论[M]. 北京：北京师范大学出版社，2004.

Triple Images of Hester Prynne in *The Scarlet Letter*

张　蕊

摘　要：《红字》是一部由美国著名作家霍桑创作于 1850 年的小说。这是一部反映女主人公海斯特在清教主义的影响下所发生的重大人生的改变。到现在，已经有大量的学者深入地研究了《红字》，其中包括研究它的象征主义、主题、心理学、人物等各类话题。但从小说所反映的历史语境出发，以清教主义对女性的道德操守的规范以及塑造和以作者霍桑的女性观以及对于清教的解读这两个角度来分析女主人公的研究却不太多。因而，本篇论文会着眼这个话题，着眼海丝特这一人物形象展开分析。正是因为清教主义里严格的规定，才使得海丝特的努力如此困难和有意义，从而让海丝特学会成长，让读者学会谅解，同时也使得《红字》更有价值。

关键词：海丝特；霍桑；清教主义

Abstract: *The Scarlet Letter,* written by American renowned author Nathaniel Hawthorne, is a 1850 work of novel in a historical setting.This is amasterpiece depictingthe great change of the protagonist, Hester Prynne under the influence of Puritanism. Until now, a variety of scholars have deeply researched *The Scarlet Letter*, whose topics are its symbolism, themes, psychology, characters and so on. But only few of them focus on Hester Prynne both from the Puritan perspective of women in that historical context and from the Hawthorn's standpoint of women and Puritanism. Therefore, I will concentrate on this angle of view to analyze it and express my own understandings. Owing to the harsh requirements in Puritanism, Hester's struggle is so difficult but meaningful, which consequently contributes to heroine's growth, ultimately enlightens readers to forgive, and therefore renders *The Scarlet Letter* more meritorious.

Key Words: Hester, Hawthorne, Puritanism

Chapter 1　Introduction to *The Scarlet Letter*

The Scarlet Letter is Nathaniel Hawthorne's masterwork. It is considered toinitiate a distinctive American literary tradition. *The Scarlet Letter* is made up of a long prefatory named The Custom-House and 24 chapters.Set in Boston, Puritan Massachusetts Bay Colony, New England, it tells us the story of Hester Prynne, who conceives a daughter through an affairand has to wear the scarlet letterAwhich stands for Adulteress forever but struggles to create a new life of dignity, even making the scarlet A mean Able and Angel. In this novel, there are four main characters. They are respectively Hester Prynne, Arthur Dimmesdale, Roger Chillingworth and Pearl. Hester Prynne is the most vital character in this novel. Arthur Dimmesdale is a young and handsome clergyman. Though he is admired by the local people, he committed adultery with Hester and he is not brave enough to stand out and take his responsibility. Therefore, he experiences many tortures and he brands the Scarlet Letter A in his chest. At last, he died but he told the truth in public, saving his soul. Roger Chillingworth is the husband of Hester Prynne but he hides this fact from others to get rid of her shame. What's worse, he is pretty cruel and ruthless. He takes revenge on Chillingworth, even doing something bad. Pearl is the daughter of Hester Prynne and Arthur Dimmesdale. Pearl is a elf-child and she brings much happiness to Hester. What's more, Pearl is a pretty, cute, brave and innocent girl. In the end of the story, she leads a happy life.

Nathaniel Hawthorne (July 4, 1804 - May 19, 1864), the author of *The Scarlet Letter*, was born in Salem, Massachusetts, which was also the place where this story happens. Both William Hathorne and John Hathorne were his ancestors. William Hathorne was a Puritan and the first of the family to emigrate from England to Salem. As an important member of the Massachusetts Bay Colony, he was notorious for his harsh sentencing. And John Hathorne was the only judge involved in the Salem witch trials who never repented of his actions. In order to dissociate himself from his infamous forebears, Hawthorne probably changed his name in his early twenties. From these, we can see that Hawthorne has a complex feeling towards Puritanism. To some degree, *The Scarlet Letter* also shows his attitude towards Puritanism.On the one hand, he appreciates the Puritan thoughts and values that attach great importance to self-perfection and the social development. Puritanism helps build the American culture and give rise to the Individualism. Deeply rooted by Puritanism, he believes in the inherent evil, original sin. On the other hand, he condemns the negative impacts of Puritan society on people's spirit. Also influenced by European Renaissance and humanism, Hawthorne criticizes the stern religious principles, strict moral rules and hypocrisy of the Puritans. Edgar Allan Poe once wrote,"The style of Hawthorne is purity itself. His tone is singularly effective—wild, plaintive, thoughtful, and in full accordance with his themes ... We look upon him as one of the few men of indisputable genius to whom our country has as yet given birth."(McFarland, 88–89) And *The Scarlet Letter* is written in Hawthorne's late years, which nearly is the most thoughtful.

As for the historical background of *The Scarlet Letter*, it centers on New England and features moral allegories with a Puritan inspiration.As a literature masterpiece,*The Scarlet Letter* mirrors the history and culture of Boston in the 17th century. When reading this book, I totally enjoy the author's vivid and detailed description, which places me in that specific period of history and culture though it is far away from us. The book says, "THE grass-plot before the jail, in Prison Lane, on a certain summer morning, not less than two centuries ago, was occupied by a pretty large number of the inhabitants of Boston; all with their eyes intently fastened on the iron-clamped oaken door. Amongst any other population, or at a later period in the history of New England, the grim rigidity that petrified the bearded physiognomies of these good people would have augured some awful business in hand."(Hawthorne 40) As we can see, the story happens in New England, Boston. With regard to its time, it takes place in the 17th century, there are lots of famous figures during the 17th century used in *The Scarlet Letter*, such as Governor Bellingham, the eldest clergyman of Boston John Wilson and so on. Richard Bellingham actually did serve as governor of the Massachusetts Bay Colony on multiple occasions: 1641 to 1642, 1654 to 1655, and 1665 to 1672. For John Wilson, he immigrated to Massachusetts in 1630 and became a priest in a Boston church. These were historically real person, helping make the book seem real and the influence of Puritanism seem real. During that period, Puritanism has an abominable influence on this place, for example, "But, in that early severity of the Puritan character, an inference of this kind could not so indubitably be drawn."(Hawthorne 41) And knowing the things above lays the foundation of my understanding and analysis.

Chapter 2   Hester in *The Scarlet Letter*

The analysis of this section below will be divided into three parts. Initially, from Puritan perspective on women in historical context, Hester is judged as a sinner. However, based on traditional interpretation of this novel, the author, Hawthorne, is considered to throw a different light on heroine and actually sympathize with Hester who is regarded as not a sinner but a victim. But under my scrutiny, Hester projected by Hawthorne is not only a victim but actually stand out as a hero in that community.

To begin with, I will explain the specific terms using frequently in this thesis. Puritanism is the beliefs and practices of the Puritans.The Puritans were originally the members of a Protestant group of Christians in England in the 16th and 17th centuries who wanted to worship God in a simple way but still retained much of its Roman Catholic doctrinal roots. As for Puritans, they accepted the doctrine of predestination, original sin and total depravity, and limited atonement through a special infusion of grace from God. According to historical data, in the early 17th century, thousands of English Puritans settled in North America, mainly in New England. And "Non-separating Puritans" who did not advocate setting up separate congregations distinct from the Church of England, which made up most Puritans and were different from "separating Puritans", played leading roles in establishing the Massachusetts Bay Colony in 1629. Nowadays, it is widely accepted that the cultural form of Puritanism has a major influence in the development of New England. Puritanism influences American culture profoundly and *The Scarlet Letter* pictures it a lot.

2.1   Hester, A Sinner

In *The Scarlet Letter,* Puritans took Hester as a sinner. Let's see how these people say about Hester,"It would be greatly for the public behoof, if we women, being of mature age and church-members in good repute, should have the handling of such malefactresses as this Hester Prynne. What think ye, gossips? If the hussy stood up for judgment before us five, that are now here in a knot together, would she come off with such a sentence as the worshipful magistrates have awarded?" (Hawthorne 42) Even one female shouted, "This woman has brought shame upon us all, and ought to die." From these words and more, we can see that the society loathed Hester and she was considered to be extremely sinful of guilt and shame. "The age had not so much refinement" (Hawthorne 41), this meant the Puritanic code of law was severe. With no tidings of her husband, Hester fell in love with Arthur Dimmesdale. After people found Hester betray her husband, she was sent into jail and was forced to wear the scarlet A at her bosom. Traditionally, Christians emphasized such moral principles as duty, discipline, thrift and hard work, and sex was considered to be the original sin. Some religious sects even regarded sex as the root of all evils and practiced strict celibacy, less alone adultery.

2.2　Hester, A Victim

However, according to Hawthorne's perspective, he did not regard Hester as a sinner, instead, he took Hester as a victim. The book wrote,"Her husband may be at the bottom of the sea - they have not been bold to put in force the extremity of our righteous law against her. The penalty thereof is death." Even if Hester escaped from death, her misery did not end, she was excluded and marginalized from the mainstream sphere of that social activity which already marked the lifestyle of the emigrants. And the society was sensitive about her sin, even the children of the Puritans mocked at Hester,"Behold, verily, there is the woman of the scarlet letter; and, of a truth, moreover, there is the likeness of the scarlet letter running along by her side! Come, therefore, and let us fling mud at them!"(Hawthorne 89) In addition, due to Hester's sin, some of the Puritans wanted to deprive Hester of her child Pearl. The stern magistrate said,"Woman, it is thy badge of shame! It is because of the stain which that letter indicts, that we would transfer thy child to other hands."(Hawthorne 96) From these pictures, we can see clearly that Hester was leading a terrible life that she did not deserve. The punishments of Puritans on her were beyond her sin. She was more of a victim than a sinner from the author's perspective. As far as I am concerned, Hester represented Hawthorne to some degree. Hawthorne was deeply rooted in the atmosphere of Puritanism. He approved of the positive effect of Puritanism upon boosting the social development. However, through protagonist Hester, the victim of Puritanism, Hawthorne also criticized the harsh religious principles and hypocrisy of the Puritans. For example,"The discipline of the family, in those days, was of a far more rigid kind than now. The frown, the harsh rebuke, the frequent application of the rod, enjoined by Scriptural authority, were used, not merely in the way of punishment for actual offences, but as a wholesome regimen for the growth and promotion of all childish virtues"(Hawthorne 78), but Hawthorne did not agree with this kind of teaching model.

Furthermore, according to Holy Writ (Bible), Hester also could not get rid of horrible treatments. The Ten Commandments include "You shall not commit adultery" or "You shall not covet your neighbor's wife". Herefrom, we can see clearly that Ten Commandments were aimed at men. And adultery was a malicious sin. But in history it was always women that were punished. They were humiliated in public and were stoned to death. It reminded me of the general situation of women in the ancient times of China. Men could marry more than one woman simultaneously but women couldn't. And women mustn't betray their husbands. Otherwise, they would be soaked in the "pig cage" and drowned to death. As we can see, women were imprisoned in the strict rules and harsh requirements in the ancient times. Similarly, Hester was also a pitiful victim under the control of Puritans. In the author's eyes, Hester was not the sinner, but a victim of that particular society.

2.3　Hester, A Hero

At last, it does not suffice to conclude the image of Hester merely with a word "victim" in

Hawthorne's opinion; in his heart Hester symbolizes more of a hero than just a pitiful victim. When Hester first appeared in *The Scarlet Letter*, the author described Hester in this way, "She repelled him, by an action marked with natural dignity and force of character, and stepped into the open air, as if by her own free will"(Hawthorne 43) and "The young woman was tall, with a figure of perfect elegance on a large scale... Those who had before known her, and had expected to behold her dimmed and obscured by a disastrous cloud, were astonished, and even startled, to perceive how her beauty shone out, and made a halo of the misfortune and ignominy in which she was enveloped."(Hawthorne 44) From these sentences, I think the author described Hester admirably. Besides, Hester was determined, brave and strong. In New England, during that period, the residents' thinking was dominated by Puritanism, but Hester rebelled it. She wanted to obtain True Love, so she challenged the authority though she was trapped in that particular society. And no matter how difficult the situation was, she did not speak out her lover's name even if he was a hypocrite. The love between Hester and Arthur Dimmesdale couldn't be tolerated by the society. Hester shouldered the responsibility and became a victim under this circumstance who was transformed into a hero gradually. In the Chapter V named Hester at Her Needle, Hawthorne showed his sympathy and admiration deeply and clearly. After Hester came out of the prison, she made a living by needlework. Her needlework was so proficient that her handiwork became the fashion. Nevertheless, from the tone of the sentence "Her skill was called in aid to embroider the white veil which was to cover the pure blushes of a bride. The exception indicated the ever relentless vigour with which society frowned upon her sin", the author expressed his sympathy in that way. From the word "frown", the author showed his concerning emotions. Besides, though males dominated the society where she lived and she was despised by others, she was an independent woman, making a living by her excellent handiwork. Her courage was uneasy and inspiring. Luckily, through her efforts, Hester changed the meaning of the scarlet letter A and people's ideas, "The letter was the symbol of her calling. Such helpfulness was found in her - so much power to do, and power to sympathise - that many people refused to interpret the scarlet A by its original signification. They said that it meant Able; so strong was Hester Prynne, with a woman's strength."(Hawthorne 141)

What's more, despite of her adultery, Hester did not flee though she could but chose to stay, like the book said, "It may seem marvellous, that this woman should still call that place her home, where, and where only, she must needs be the type of shame"(Hawthorne 68) In the end of the story, Hester still came back to New England for there was a more real life here, "Here had been her sin; here, her sorrow; and here was yet to be her penitence."(Hawthorne 227) Even the motto on her tombstone was: —"ON A FIELD, SABLE, THE LETTER A, GULES."(Hawthorne 228) Hester was a victim in *The Scarlet Letter*, but she was saved in the end of the story. She raised her daughter by herself and changed people's opinions in the end, making them accept her step by step. It somehow represented that she broke the limitation on female's role and tried to start a new era of life with freedom, self-esteem and independence. After reading this book, I was totally convinced by Hawthorne's description on Hester that actually she was even a hero in this community.

Chapter 3　Conclusions

The novel *The Scarlet Letter* was composed in 1850 when Hawthorne had established a mature outlook and obtained an insight into the world as well. By reading this book, we will have our own understandings. And there is no doubt that *The Scarlet Letter* has its far reaching significance beyond time and space, which has been proved by the fact that there have been continuous studies on this novel. Whether Hester is a sinner, a victim or a hero, we will have our own views after reading this book. So, through the analysis of the protagonist in this book, Hester Prynne, we can have a better view on how to look at things. We should not be limited by one opinion. If we try to think more, sometimes things will be more meaningful.

Furthermore, I'd like to summarize my thoughts on *The Scarlet Letter.* Firstly, I think that Hester was a sinner to some degree. Obviously, she did something wrong, she committed adultery. Even today, we still usually blame mistresses. Secondly, from the specific period, she was also an victim because she could have had a good way to deal with her love and marriage. But the reality was that she experienced many miseries. Finally, she became a hero and proved her self-value. From this book, I came to realize that we should look at things from more angles.

In addition, Hester believed "At some brighter period, when the world should have grown ripe for it, in Heaven's own time, a new truth would be revealed, in order to establish the whole relation between man and woman on a surer ground of mutual happiness."(Hawthorne 228) But with the development of the society, the relation between men and women is becoming more and more reasonable. I believe that day will come also in the Earth.

To sum up, I firmly hold the view that I have learned much from *The Scarlet Letter* and this analysis.

References

[1] Alden T. Vaughan. The Puritan Tradition in America: 1620-1730[M]. New York: Harper & Row, 1972.

[2] Brodhead, Richard. The school of Hawthorne [M]. New York: Oxford University Press, 1986.

[3] Foster, Stephen. The Long Argument: English Puritanism and Shaping of New England Culture1570-1700. Raleigh: The University of North Carolina Press, 1991.

[4] Hawthorne Nathaniel. The Scarlet Letter. Reed & Fields, 1850.

[5] Henry James. On Hawthorne. London: Macmillian Press, 1979.

[6] Roland Joffé (director). The Scarlet Letter (film). America, 1995.

[7] Zaine Ridling, Ph.D.ed. The New Revised Standard Version. Division of Christian Education of the National Council of the Churches of Christ in the United States of America, 1989.

Gloom to Blossom: A Narrative Psychological Interpretation of Female Black's Subjective Construction in *Beloved*

秦佳音

摘　要：20 世纪 70 年代以来，美国黑人女性作家及其作品在美国乃至世界文坛上引起极大反响，由此引发了对黑人女性主义文学批评及研究的蓬勃发展，其中，黑人女作家托尼·莫里森的多部作品都对人们反思黑人群体历史，尤其是黑人女性地位，为黑人文化新的发展之路做出了巨大贡献，《宠儿》更是使其摘取了诺贝尔文学奖的桂冠。通过将心理学与文学结合，从叙事心理学的角度分析《宠儿》中黑人女性主人公赛丝、丹芙、贝比·萨格斯在奴隶制时期前后的主体意识建构过程，可以发现《宠儿》中的创伤叙事非常必要且极具治愈力量。黑人群体尤其是黑人女性必须勇敢直面残酷的历史，通过自爱和获得黑人群体的支持，才能走出过去的心理阴影并拥抱美好的未来。

关键词：《宠儿》；叙事心理学；黑人女性；主体意识建构

Abstract: Since 1970s, some prominent African-American female writers and their works have received wide attention and discussion in American, even worldwide literary field, facilitating the rise and booming development of black feminist literature criticism and research. Toni Morrison and her works are typical, making enormous contributions to reflecting the tragic history of black community, especially theunvalued status of black females, exploring a new way out of the black culture. This thesis will focus on her masterpiece, *Beloved*, which made her the first African-American Nobel Laureate for literature. By combining psychology and literature and interpreting the struggling during and after slavery in constructing subjective consciousness of three heroines sethe, Denves, basy suggs in Beloned from the perspective of narrative psychology, the conchision can be drawn that narrative therapy is necessary and healing. The black community, especially the black females must take the courage to face up to the painful past. Only by loving themselves and getting supports of both the female and male compatriots, they can get rid of the psychological shadow and embrace a brilliant future with growing independence.

Key Words: *Beloved*, Narrative psychology, Black females, Subjective consciousness construction

Chapter 1　Introduction

1.1　Toni Morrison and *Beloved*

Toni Morrison, the first African-American Nobel Laureate for literature, also one of the greatest contemporary novelists in the African-American history. As the Nobel committee holds, she is an outstanding novelist who "gives life to an essential aspect of American reality" and one who "delves into language itself, a language she wants to liberate from the fetters of race" (1993). She has written nine novels to date and made great contribution to American literature, culture and ideology. From the perspective of a black female writer and literary critic, she is dedicated to probing into the possibility of constructing the viable identity for the marginalized black community, especially the struggling life and experience of black women. The central issues in her novels are mainly "race, class, gender" and she adopts an artistic vision that encompasses both a private and a national heritage.

Most of Morrison's works are about love and the loss of love. The preface of *Beloved* says:"*I will call them my people, which were not my people; and her beloved, which was not beloved.*"Woman is the carrier of culture and mother is the bridge who conveys the culture. Thus, maternal love is an indispensable and main story line in *Beloved*. The special cord is exclusive to woman and makes females' awakening subjective consciousness more powerful.*Beloved* is Morrison's fifth novel, also the most controversial and successful one. The novel *Beloved* is like a journey about the construction of black community's identity, especially the construction of female black's subjective consciousness. Beloved was based on a real story of an African-American slave mother on a newspaper clipping, Margret Garner, killing her two-year-old daughter to avoid her being recaptured. Her Infanticide was seemingly brutal and inexplicable at that time, however, in *Beloved*, Toni adopted the powerful fictional style and multiple narrative techniques to rebuild this past horrifying event, exploring the root cause of oppression and revolt of slaves and their traumatic spiritual life. By depicting the devastating impact of slavery on these black female slaves' postbellum life, Morrison stated their predicament. Though free physically, they still try desperately to reclaim their identities and the painful past prevents them enjoying the present, let alone pursue a brilliant future. As the novel goes: *"freeing yourself was one thing, claiming the ownership of that freed self was another."*

1.2　Research Background, Motivation and Objective

The title of the term paper is Gloom to Blossom: A Narrative Psychological Interpretation of Female Black's Subjective Construction in *Beloved*.Personal reason of focusing on Toni Morrison's *Beloved* is that in recent years, women's rights have been greatly promoted and feminism has gained enormous attention from the public. Thus, a large number of literary work related to the feminism were again studied by many scholars. As a female and a citizen of the world, the author of this thesis is interested in the marginal group and tried to research their status.

Nowadays, black females as the marginal group are still struggling in the multiple predicaments: ignored and undervalued by the white Americans, black males. They are excluded from the mainstream of American society. It is almost impossible to utterly forget the painful physical and psychological trauma. Most importantly, by narrating the traumas in their mind, they can reconstruct the 'self' and confidence, further achieving the function of healing and getting out of the historical shadow.

The thesis will mainly explore questions as follows: How the multiple predicaments are embodied in the characters in *Beloved*? How they lose their identities and then reconstruct their subjective consciousness?

How the narrative therapy is employed to heal their traumas? Based on the closing read of the text and the theory of narrative psychology proposed by Theodore R. Sarbin (1986), the thesis aims to analyze the process of the female black characters' subjective construction in *Beloved*, putting forward the identity construction embodied in the novel, hopefully initiating new inspirations for people that take interests in it.

Chapter 2　Literature Review and Theoretical Framework

2.1　Literature Review at Home and Abroad

Since its publication in 1987, Beloved was regarded as a masterpiece and milestone of African-American literary history. Meanwhile, it exerts a far-reaching influence on the real life of African Americans with more learned scholars and readers giving critical appreciation. Various narrative voices and techniques also provide critics with different facets to analyze this novel. In China, academic studies about black females' works fell behind. Domestic academic studies mainly focus on the maternal love and symbolism of characters. From the late 1980s and the early 1990s, Toni Morrison's works have gained increasing critical appreciation. As for *Beloved,* its research perspectives have gone through different stages. Most of the early studies engaged in the political and postcolonial aspects. Cultural and aesthetic aspects can refer to various themes, such as feminist criticism, maternal love, reader's response, symbolism, etc. Some other critics, like Dominick LaCapra, Barbara Hill Rigney, pondered over the historical trauma and the process of spiritual healing of the characters from the psychoanalytical perspective. It is the complex multiplicity that endows *Beloved* with various themes. In all, the voices and status of black females still lack attention in current researches at home and abroad.

2.2　Theoretical Framework— Narrative Psychology

Based on above literature reviews, the author of this thesis wonders whether there exist new perspectives and further connotations to explore in *Beloved*. Then it turns out that few people have explored the novel from the narrative psychology, especially from black females' perspective.

Narrative psychology is a perspective within psychology concerned with the "storied nature of human conduct". Namely, human beings deal with experience by observing stories and listening to the stories of others.

The term 'narrative psychology' was introduced by Theodore R. Sarbin in his 1986 book *Narrative Psychology: The storied nature of human conduct*, in which he claimed that human conduct is best explained through stories and that this explanation should be done through qualitative research. Then, Jerome Bruner explored the "narrative kind of knowing" in a more empirical way in his 1986 book *Actual Minds, Possible Worlds*. The narrative approach was also furthered by Dan P. McAdams, who put forward a life story model of identity to describe three levels of personality, leading to explorations of how significant life transitions are narrated and how the "self and culture come together in narrative."

Narrative psychological approaches have become influential in research into the self and identity, as analyzing life stories can explore the "unity and coherence" of the self, helping people reconstruct identities to some extent. In *Beloved*, there exist two main ideas about reconstructing subjective consciousness in narrative psychological way. First, a person's life story becomes a form of identity as how they choose to reflect on, integrate and tell the facts and events of their life. People gain the coherence by thinking and reflecting. Once the 'unity and coherence' was interrupted for somehow psychological traumas, theindividuals would suffer self-loss and lose their bearings in real life. For instance, Sethe and Baby Suggs refused to leave the haunted house and keep contact of outside world after the slavery. Second, individuals can choose to narrate elaborate and selective life experiences, helping listeners and themselves find identities, even reconstruct identities. They can draw strength from these totally new and positive stories. The principles of narrative psychology well interpret the process of constructing black females' subjective consciousness during and after the slavery period in *Beloved*.

The final goal of narrative psychology is to seek understanding.That's also why Morrison created *Beloved*: to find understanding and support from the compatriots and the white people for many miserable women like Sethe, Baby Suggs and Denver.People could not accept Sethe's infanticide behavior,especially during the darkest slavery period. Seeing Sethe'sdisesteem, Baby Suggs felt desperate and finally knew that the bodies of black neverbelong to themselves. Since then, she gave up the enthusiasm towards life and chose to lie in bed to wait for death. As a black male who worked with Sethe and loved her silently, Paul D also could not understand Sethe's merciless. Sethe's only daughter Denver had become deaf out of fear since she knew her mother's violent past. It can be seen that all people around Sethe never try to accept and listen to her as her compatriots and families. Besides, though slavery abolished, the black community still lived under the control of white-dominated culture and lost in past traumas. The most frightening thing is thatthey rather blamedthe broken family on themselves than the white people. They accept distorted 'self' images subconsciously and lack the confidence to build a new home. The basic principle of narrative psychology is that "people understand and define themselves by verbal media, speaking or writing and continuously participating in the process of defining themselves." However, the black females are excluded from the right of speech. In addition, their bitterly painful memories prevent them voicing the selves. Thus, how do they reconstruct their subjective consciousness, namely, seek 'self' is the most urgent problem.

2.3 The definition of 'self' in narrative psychology and *Beloved*

In narrative psychology, narration is based on time dimension. One's behavior is connected by a series of things may happen in the past, at present or in the future. It is this coherence that shapes a person. Usually, I-self (subject) creates Me-self (object) to tell stories. The "self" in narrative psychology can be multi-faceted, multi-characterized and multi-identified. It can be both the narrators and listeners.

In *Beloved*, the third-person narration is the I-self (subject) and the representative of the black female. It replaces the black females to narrate the stories during and after slavery.The characters in *Beloved* such as Sethe, Baby Suggs, Paul D, Denver are Me-self(object). Meanwhile, the third narration person(subject) here represents people who own the same painful past like Me-self(object). Their life experiences in the novel could becoincided in real life.

Stories themselves reflect the process of individuals' mental development and change and the process is unfolded by narrating.

Chapter 3　The Self-loss and Subjective Consciousness Reconstruction of Black Females in *Beloved*

From the novel, it can be seen that black people's identities mostly are defined by the white people, their slave owners. They can be tortured inhumanly in mental and physical. Women's condition was worse, they were defined as sexual tools and breeding stock during the slavery. They are deprived of social status, the right of speech and basic human rights.

As Bell hooks said, "black identity has been specifically constructed in the experience of exile and struggle." In this chapter, the author intends to analyze the destruction and reconstruction of three heroines' subjective consciousness from narrative psychological interpretation.

3.1　Sethe's Self-loss and Reconstruction

Sethe, the protagonist, is a black female and slave who is dependent and brave. In her childhood, she witnessed her mother's being maltreated and died before her.In her adolescence, she worked in the Sweet Home and her masterMr. Garnerwas relatively kind. However, she was scarcely literate and actually has little knowledge of identity. Then the master died and the new master 'schoolteacher' tookover the plantation.The nightmares began. First, the schoolteacherinsulted them and defined them as 'animals'. Then his nephew assaulted Sethe sexually and stole her milk for her children. Sethe decided to escape and went to Cincinnati at all costs. There she only enjoyed 28 days' warm of the black community. The school teacher came and reclaimed her and her children as his property. In desperation, Sethe killed her daughter in order to free her from being a slave again. That's the beginning of Sethe's awakening subjective consciousness.

After the sentence of destroying others' property was over, Sethe should have gained the freedom, whereas lived numbly with her youngest daughter Denver.She was indulged in the sorrowful past: the dead daughter named Beloved who she killed by herself during the slavery. Besides, her dead daughter's ghost always haunted the spiteful house and seemingly requested her maternal love. The whole community rejected Sethe's familyand her daughter was also disturbed by Sethe's 'ruthless'. In all, Sethe gradually lost her identity during the slavery and couldn't rebuild her life after the slavery. Until the appearance of Paul D brought her memory back. No doubt Paul D is important to help Sethe's reconstructing her subjective consciousness.

I got a tree on my back and a haunt in my house, and nothing in between but the daughter I am holding in my arms. No more running--from nothing. I will never run from another thing on this earth.(Beloved,p18)

This excerpt best explained Sethe's situation at that time. She rather lived in the spiteful 124 than busy escaping all the time. Then Beloved, her dead daughter came back. She also functioned as a key role to Sethe' reconstruction. As storytelling becomes a way to feed Beloved，Sethe seems to heal herself in this way

"Because every mention of her past life hurts" "Everything in it was painful or lost... the hurt was there—like a tender place in the corner of her mouth that the bit left" "But, as she began telling about the earnings, she found herself wanting to, liking it... in any case it was an unexpected pleasure."(Beloved, p69)

By narrating her painful past, Sethe finally felt relieved. She regained the power of loving, as a mother and a woman.

3.2   Baby Suggs' Self-loss and Reconstruction

As the representative of the first generation, Baby Suggs is a typical black female in the slavery period: deeply maltreated as a breeding stock. Although her white masters beat, hurt, damage her physically, sexually and mentally, she never thought about rebelling and tried to define herself as a human being.

To Baby Suggs, six white men father her eight children. What she prayed was one of her white masters not to make her pregnant. But the wish never came true. Besides, the marriages between black slaves were nothing but animals' mating to white slave masters. Baby Suggs suffered a great deal of the pain in most of her life. Among many children of her, only Halle was allowed to be with her. Under the oppression of slavery, Baby Suggs never enjoyed the right as a mother and a wife, let alone defined herself as a human being.

Though without many descriptions, Morrison has portrayed a vivid image of Baby Suggs. Her first awakening subjective consciousness is renaming herself. After she gets the freedom, she discards the name "Jenny" given by her master, instead of "Baby Suggs". By insisting on self-naming, she keeps her emotional connection with her husband and takes the first step in striving for self-definition.

The second try is after she gained freedom, she became a spiritual leader in the local black community.

"Because slave life had busted her legs, backs, head, eyes, hands, kidneys, womb and tongue, she had nothing left to make a living with but her heart—which she put to work at once." (Beloved, p102)

Baby Suggs not only defines her self-value, but also inspires everyone in her community to appreciate and value themselves. It is quite a great stride to help rebuild the confidence of black people.

However, she failed to avoid white people's voice and others' opinions. Schoolteacher's destruction of her family and Sethe's infanticide, she totally gave up the hope. She refused to recall her past and to preach the world again. Her final years were spent in a lifeless way mediating the color.

In narrative psychology, without storytelling and the coherence of constructing herself, Baby

Suggs could not heal the pain and find a way to survive. Her subjective consciousness just sprouted, however, ruined by the slavery and others'prejudices.

3.3 Denver's Self-loss and Reconstruction

As the youngest generation, Denver represents black female after the slavery. Their situations can best show the impact of slavery on black females. Living in the fear of her mother's ruthless and grandmother's numbness, Denver was always alone in this haunted house without a friend to play with in real life. What she experienced shows Morrison's thoughts of awakening black females' consciousness: confront and fight.

It is difficult for a little girl to struggle for her self-identity. But Denver indeed tried hard to awaken her subjective consciousness. She repeatedly asked her mother about her birth and the history of her mother in the slavery. What she wanted was that Sethe could be a normal mother. She made great efforts to make her mother happy and got out of the past anguish by narrating it. However, *"to Denver's inquiries Sethe gave replies or rambling incomplete reveries."(Beloved, p69)* That's why Denver could not behave like a normal kid. As a child, she was brave enough to help drive the ghost away, but still not enough to face the bloody family history. The appearance of Paul D and Beloved brought her hope as well.

"Denver was seeing it now and feeling it—through Beloved. Feeling how it must have felt to her mother. Seeing how it must have looked." (Beloved,p92)

By hearing and retelling the stories of Sethe, she knew a lot about slavery and her mother's bitterness. In observing the chaos at home and hearing Sethe's explanation to Beloved, Denver understands her mother's infanticide more deeply than ever. Meanwhile, she knew that it is her responsibility to protect her mother from harm in the future. She had already awakened and owned her subjective consciousness.

From above analyses, we can see black females are violently deprived of the dignity and right as a mother and woman. Only by narrating can they redefine the lost selves. Some tried and succeeded while others failed. It is definitely a tough journey for them and there is still a long way to go.

Chapter 4　Narrative Therapy in Narrative Psychology and the Application in *Beloved*

4.1 Necessity of Narrative Therapy for Black Females.

Narrative therapy is a form of psychotherapy that seeks to help people identify their values and the skills and knowledge they have to live these values, so they can effectively confront whatever problems they face. This chapter is about the necessity of narrative therapy for black females. It refers to Toni Morrison's reflection of slavery in American history. She felt shocked about this kind of national amnesia (Taylor-Guthrie 257): "It is both a painful past for black people and bloody history for the white people." (Morrison, 1992) Only by externalizing the trauma and finding the power of reconstruction through narrating can the black people construct their identities and confidence.

4.2　The Embodiment of Narrative Therapy in *Beloved*

The victims usually refused to rememorize the painful past. Morrison didn't emphasize too much about the slavery. She returned the right of speech to the slaves themselves.

In *Beloved*, the theory of narrative therapy was embodied as follows: counter-culture narration, narration of painful history, narration of traumatic aftermath.

4.2.1　Counter-culture narration

The white people and black males are usually regarded as mainstream to the black females. That's why counter-culture narration is special and typical in *Beloved*. Taking Sethe's infanticide for example, in schoolteacher's eyes, Sethe is nothing but a crazy woman. He used humiliating "nigger" to describe her and regarded her as an animal while in the coworker, a black male slave Stamp's view, Sethe did not deserve being a mother and wife. He was shocked to tell Paul D about Sethe's abnormal behavior. However, in Sethe's eye, it is the great maternal love. The counter-culture thought reflected the miserable situation and narrative therapy of black females.

4.2.2　Narration of painful history

For instance, it tells the origin and development of black slave trade. After the new sea- lane was opened up by the European colonizer in 16th, they start to snatch land from Indian, they trade Negro as merchandise. They even cited reasonable proof from the Bible and the definition of private property.Many plots in Beloved reflect Morrison's imagination and fiction to reshape historical context, reappear historical memory. The whole novel can be seen as a literary work and the history of slavery.

4.2.3　Narration of traumatic aftermath

After experiencing the emotional and physical traumas, individuals will fall into two extreme states: amnesia or re-experience. Therefore, they are numb sometimes while out of control sometimes. Fragment narration and flashback are main types in narrative psychology. The whole novel was unfolded in this fragment structure and the narration perspectives varied all the time. Sometimes, victims chose to forget and avoid retouching things connected with traumatic experience. For instance, the selective amnesia of Paul D, the meditation on colors of Baby Suggs, the deafness of Denver all represent traumatic aftermath.

4.3　Significance of Narrative Therapy

It goes without saying that narrative therapy is healing and powerful. The influence of narrative therapy of black females in *Beloved* can be achieved in four aspects: deconstruction of the mainstream culture, externalization of traumas, identity reconstruction, witness the change.

Under the control of white people, the normal desires of black females such as marriage, knowledge are forbidden. However, through narrative therapy in *Beloved,* they achieved the desires.

For instance, Baby Suggs renamed herself and loved her husband until death. Sethe regarded her marriage with Halle as a solemn ceremony rather than a simple mating. She specifically designed her 'wedding dress'. Being a slave did not deprive her of hope towards the ideal life. The relationship between Sethe and Denver, Paul D is also moving. Sethere gained the ability to love as a woman and mother in the end. Denver took the courage to go out of the house to seek help from other people in the community for her mother. Paul D shouldered a man's responsibility to take care of his beloved one, the total new family. The ending is full of hope and warm.

"Sethe," he says, "me and you, we got more yesterday than anybody. We need some kind of tomorrow." (Beloved)

Chapter 5   Conclusions

The thesis has analyzed the struggling process of black females' constructing subjective consciousness in *Beloved* from the perspective of narrative psychology. As an outstanding African-American female writer, Toni Morrison cherishes strong nationality sense and owns sharp observations. She could perceive the traumas buried in the bottom of black females' hearts that have already became their obstacles to new life.

The self-identity was tarnished by the bitterly painful past and the voices of white people. However, the white people don't blame the traumatic aftermath on themselves. It turned out just the opposite that black females themselves mistakenly shoulder these heavy mental burdens and historical responsibilities. They can't build confidences to start a new life and see the energy hid in their body. They pessimistically fall in the double tortures of guilty and shame.

Morrison integrated these fragments of memory of black females' traumatic experiences by telling stories. The life experiences of heroines in *Beloved* all show their rebel against unfair slavery, their enthusiasm and pursuit towards love and freedom, the constant struggles of healing traumas. In a word, from gloom to blossom requires supports of both the female and male compatriots.The novel *Beloved* provides the whole black community, especially black females, with a chance to narrate their bitterly painful life stories, seek understanding and support by storytelling in order to externalize the traumas, finally find the power to solve difficulties in real life, discover themselves and reconstruct their subjective consciousness.

References

[1] Aoi Mori. Toni Morrison and Womanist Discourse[M]. New York: Peter Lang Publishing Inc, 1999.

[2] Gloria Naylor. Conversation with Toni Morrison[M]. Mississippi: University Press of Mississippi, 2008.

[3] Bouson, J,Brooks. Quiet asit kept: Shames, Trauma and Race in the Novels of Toni Morrison[M]. Albany: State University of New York Press, 2000.

[4] Lee D, John. Life and Story: Autobiographies for a Narrative Psychology[M]. Westpoet, Conn: Praeger, 1994.

[5] Sarbin, Theodore R. The Storied Nature of Human Conduct[M]. New York; Praeger, 1986.

[6] Harris, D.S. Narrative and Community Crisis in *Beloved*. [J]. Melus, 2001, 26（4）：153.

[7] 托尼·莫里森. 宠儿[M]. 北京：人民文学出版社，1996.

[8] 唐红梅. 种族、性别与身份认同[M]. 北京：民族出版社，2006.

[9] 王玉括. 莫里森研究[M]. 北京：人民文学出版社，2005.

[10] 唐陶华. 美国历史上的黑人奴隶制[M]. 上海：上海人民出版社，1980.

[11] 施铁如. 自我的社会建构观与叙事辅导[J]. 心理科学，2005（28）：189-191.

Research on the Gothic Elements in Literature

彭诗祎

摘 要： 哥特，原指欧洲"后古典文明时期"居住在北欧地区的一个未开化的民族，公元 5 世纪后"哥特"一词被打上了血腥、残暴和黑暗的标签。哥特一词最早被用于形容中世纪独特的建筑风格，到了 18 世纪中后期逐渐成为一种新的小说体裁。本文通过对哥特起源的探究，可以探明其产生和发展的社会背景以及哥特内涵的转变过程。通过对具体哥特小说，即《简·爱》和《呼啸山庄》中哥特元素的分析，找寻其继承的规律以及不断创新的部分。最后，通过对当代哥特小说的研究，通过对比其与传统哥特小说的异同，揭示社会心理的变化及未来发展的趋向。

关键词： 哥特；传统；文学；复兴；小说

Abstract： Gothic, which originally referred to the uncivilized Germanic tribes in Northern Europe, had been labeled with savage, fatuity and darkness. As British society had been through dramatic revolution from the 17th to the 18th, the denotation of Gothic changed a lot, which embodied that the European world launched a social revival opposing the prevailing rationalism during the Movement of Enlightenment and then spread to the America. From then on, the Gothic Tradition began to form in the fields of literature and architecture. It brought the dark sentiment presented during the Middle Age back to life. This article aims to unveil the social and cultural background of Gothic elements. By probing into literary field which is relevant to Gothic with typical specimens, we figure out how Gothic is presented in literature and what major theme it has. With a view to the history of Gothic, we find out the evolution of it and comparisons are made to clarify this process.

Key Words: gothic, tradition, literature, revival, fiction

Chapter 1　Origin of Gothic

1.1　Origin of the Word

Goth originally refers to the tribes living in Northern European who belonged to Teutonic tribes. Since the 3rd century, Teutons started to flood into the Southern Europe. During this ethnic migration which altered the history of Europe, impetuous Goths played a role of the pillar in fighting against Romans. After conflicts and invasion lasting for several centuries, Teutons finally cracked down the Western Roman Empire and Goths began to establish their realms in Italy, Spain, South of France and Northern Africa.

Goths disappeared as an ethnic in about the seventh century, however, their bellicosity and aggression left Southern Europeans with indelible impression stimulating hatred and horror emotions. After the time when Western Roman Empire had perished, an Italian named Vasari unearthed the word Gothic to embody an architectural style of the Middle Age which was distasted by Renaissance thinkers.

This architectural style prevailed in Europe from the 12th to the 16th. It was widely applied in churches and castles. The steep reef, thick stone walls, tinted glass and dim corridors perfectly illustrated its meaning—the so-called Dark Ages which replaced the Roman time. Under the guidance of Renaissance thinkers, Gothic was endowed with interpretations of darkness, blood, uncivilization and mystery.

It was not until the middle of the 18th century that Gothic became a sort of novel. This kind of novel usually developed stories happened in deserted castles or ruins in the past. They embraced with murder, violence, horror, revenge, rape and even supernatural power. This kind of writing style was filed to gothic was due to a pioneer named Horace Walpoles, whose novel *The Castle of Otranto* subtitled by *A Gothic Story* was regarded as the first gothic novel in the history. Its roaring success brought a wave of gothic writing. With *The Mysteries of Udolpho* written by Ann Radcliffe and *The Monk* written by Mathew Lewis, gothic novel began to form into structure in Britain and spread to other countries.

The gothic movies appeared in modern society with the first monument built in 1931. It was once in fashion before the wartime. After the war time, it was declined for the audience were in need of reliving comfort to soothe their pain in mentality. It was in the 1990s that Gothic movies came back to our sight and hit our box office. The gothic elements in movies were no longer limited to the traditional impression of the Middle Age. Gothic intermingled with other elements and extended its theme and range, producing more omnifarious effects.

1.2 The Gothic Revival

The context of Gothic was the "rule of thirds" which used to divide our history into the ancient time, the middle time and the modern time. From the 12th century to the 15th century, the humanists refused to be connected to the middle age, for their consistency lay in the ancient time and the current era. In this condition, the middle age was a tenebrous gap. Gothic architecture was considered to be undesirable creation for barbarians, utterly opposed to the trend. But some contemporary scholars raised the idea that gothic was closely related to scholasticism and the renaissance. In the event of scholasticism, rationalism was subordinated to relief.

It was English people that first viewed Gothic in the esthetic perspective and restored its value. Around 1740, the English person, Thomas Gray (1716—1771) had highly remarked the gothic beauty of Reims Cathedral. In 1772, Goethe (1729—1832) complimented on Strasbourg Cathedral as if it were a "tree from heaven".

The Gothic Revival generated from Britain in the 18th century. It might be involved in a new esthetics movement and development of romanticism. This led people to reconsider the value of the middle age. The derogation of Gothic was to blame for the essence of overwhelming rationalism and classism. It was hard for people growing up in this cultural environment to accept the mysteriousness, depression and lack of proportion. However, people tended to show interest in those fields of the esthetic in the 18th. The era of rationalism revealed with escalating sharp confrontation as this ruling theory went to extremes. Unsurprisingly people realized their limitations. As a country boasted its valuable historical heritage and conservative tradition, Britain had more link to the old age. And for the sake for its geographic feature, the French Revolution sparked less flame here. Gothic was prevalent in the middle and later period of the 18th . It was universally reckoned as prologue of romanticism.

1.3　Social Environment of Britain (18A.D—19A.D)

Gothic elements appeared in literature work in Britain in 18 A.D. At this time, France was stormed by its French Revolution which reframed its society dramatically. This event led many experts to the conclusion that gothic literature was the production of French Revolution. Reasonable cause as it was, it is of more significance for us to look into the comprehensive environment in Britain.

After the Battle of Culloden, rebellion of Stuart Dynasty was sentenced to failure. However, conflict for kingship had never come to an end. On the one hand, George ? who was on behalf of royalty and nobility, reinforced king's power in disguise of the initial—patriotic and loyal to the throne. On the other hand, political elites who represented the emerging bourgeoisies consistently promoted democracy under the guidance of man's nature right. Afraid of chain reaction brought by French Revolution and War of Independence, George ? governed Britain with repressive rules. Not only did he eliminate democratic officials in army, but also arrested the London mayor who held the opposite attitude. At the same time, many writers, publishers or merchants who were in favor of democracy were put into prison with the crime of defamation and treason. These actions made Bill of Rights a piece of blank paper.

Faced with intensive political conflicts and violence, the British middle class had the complex political mentality.For one thing, they just sprang up from the Industrial Revolution and won their economic independence, looking forward to further ascend of political status. Naturally they advocated the reforms put by emerging bourgeoisies while they felt the prospect was perplexed. For another thing, out of their class specialty, which meant they, unlike royalty and nobility, could never count on their blood carrying precedent benefits and guarantee for safety. They obeyed principles of caution, prudence and tolerance. Radical revolution would never be their preference when dealing with social changes. Based on this kind of identity, the middle class recognized and complimented the cultural value of royalty and nobility existing in the Middle Age, for these feudal heritage worked as gears in society. All in all, living in this rapidly transforming industrial society, they began to discover their ascending conditions and history with extremely complicated mentality.

The prominent figure who took specific position on social reforms were personalized in Gothic novels. Edmund Burk (1729—1797)wrote *Reflections on the Revolution in France.* This book was thought to be a mirror of the middle class social mentality. He highly praised chivalrous culture and gothic politic structure succeeded from the Whigs. According to his interpretation, Britain's ultimate ideal for civil was absolute freedom, based on which chivalrous culture could not be erased because it symbolized the glorious tradition and experience of Britain. Unlike Burk, Mary Wollstonecraft (1759—1797) proposed a different opinion as a radical liberal. Her book *A Vindication of the Rights of Men* illustrated negative effects of chivalrous culture to defy Edmund Burk. As is mentioned above, the anxiety and uncertainty about politic path perplexed the majority of British society and sometimes it was even dominant. "Revolutionary politicization, counter revolutionary nostalgia, and prudent escapism are all possible reactions, and are presented in different ways in Gothic literature. The unusual significance of Stoic Philosophy—sometimes more precisely the prospect of failure Philosophy—the vast majority of people in order to cope with the fierce change, may not conform to the trend of the Gothic features."

Chapter 2   The Gothic Elements in Literature

2.1   The Classic Gothic Works

The first gothic novel was born in Britain named *The Castle of Otranto,* written by Horace Walpole (1717—1797). His father was the first prime minister of Britain. Because of his family background, Horace gave up further education in Cambridge University and stepped into politic as a party member of the Whigs. Unfortunately, lack of sophistication, father's leave and a chain of punch withered away his patience. 1747, He bought a cottage in Twickenham and named it as Strawberry Hill and rebuilt it as a gothic architecture after 13-year construction. It was undoubtedly a successful design and recreation of Gothic which was modeled after by many other architects.

What made Strawberry Hill fabulous lay in its symbolic meaning. Horace almost built it in the way of clip and paste. In the castle, the gothic meaning subversive—it no longer stood for violence, darkness and depression; on the contrary, it unrevealed vigor, initial, courage, bizarre, fantasy and romance. His first gothic novel was bred in this castle.

In his prologue in rendition, Horace made it clear that he intended to " fuse two legends; that is ancient legends and modern legends." On the one hand, imagination should be fully inspired and more fascinating scenario was supposed to come up; on the other hand, people in the novel should act as normal as people in the real world. His book perfectly accomplished this task. Evocative simplicity, appropriate paces and natural actions reminded us of masterpieces written by Fielding and Defoe. Dramatic conflict and tempestuous plot echoed Aristotle's the Three Unities. The bright and dark line took turns pushed forward. Superpower elements which expressed by old prophet were also added into it. Cursed was the Manfreds', they themselves witnessed cruel fate progress in front of their eyes. Even his character became affected by supernatural power. Unlike writers such as Defoe or Fielding, he put emphasize on protagonist's confrontation with fate.

The publication of *the Castle of Otranto* drew enormous attention, most of which were supportive while neoclassicists strongly criticized it, saying it against the traditional rule of novel writing. As a respond to this remark, in a letter to Madame Dudeffand, he expressed his faith that he didn't base his novel on the era which left nothing except rationalism. He wrote this book to despise those regulations, rationale and philosophy.

At the same time, many great historical gothic novels sprang up. Horace Walpole innovated the style of historical gothic novels. Countless writers such as Clara Leaf, Sophie Lee, William Beckford, Charlotte Smith, Madame Harry and etc. Ann Radcliffe was gifted in writing romantic gothic novels and also she was a poet. She was hailed as "the first female poet who wrote fictional romantic novels". Her works intermingled scaring and suspensive plot with romantic sentiment. Her representative works were *Some of the forest* (1791), *The Mysteries of Udolpho* (1794). Her first gothic novel was greatly shadowed by Horace's works. It described a castle ruled by a "usurper", a "Manfreding" tyrant, a surrealistic "ghost" and a blueblood adolescent. From the time she wrote her second book *The Legend of Sicily,* she gradually established her own style and added much innovative design. The sacred and fairy scenes, sentimental character, unique story structure and explanatory supernatural enabled her to be well-known by following novelists.

Other novels like *Secret Room* written by Sophia Lee, *Maria* written by Elizabeth Blower and *Helena* written by a Jane Doe all more or less made improvement and were added more contemporary elements. Mary Shelly's *Frankenstein* reached the peak of gothic novels in 1818. Gothic novels started fading in the 1840s. Nevertheless, the tradition bred up short ghost story in Victoria's era and greatly influenced America novels writing. Edgar Allan Poe (1809—1849), Washington Owen (1783—1859) and Nathaniel Hawthorne (1804—1864) were on behalf of the writers at this time.

2.2   Gothic Elements Analysis—Taking *Wuthering Heights* and *Jane Eyre* as Examples

Emily Bronte's(1818-1848) *Wuthering Heights* was the most typical gothic novel at her time. It portrait Heathcliff and Katherine's desperate love story and ruthless revenge taken by Heathcliff. It was considered controversial because its depiction of mental and physical cruelty was unusually stark, and it challenged strict Victorian ideals of the day regarding religious hypocrisy, morality, social classes and gender inequality. The English poet and painter Dante Gabriel Rossetti, reffered to it as "A friend of a book—an incredible monster […] The action is laid in hell, - only it seems places and people have English names there."

Charlotte Bronte's (1816—1855) *Jane Eyre*follows the   emotions and experiences of its eponymous heroine. In its internalisation of the action- the focus is on the gradual unfolding of Jane's moral and spiritual sensibility, and all the events are coloured by a heightened intensity that was previously the domain of poetry—Jane Eyre revolutionized the art of fiction. It depicted a girl who was ordinary-looking, impoverished, rebelling and dared to love or die met with Mr. Rochester who also had a strong will to fight against old rules and their tortuous road to pursue love. These two works were both abundant in romantic tint and gothic feature.

2.2.1   Characterization

In the perspective of characterization, characters in the novels were mysterious. Heathcliff in *Wuthering Heights* came from "Villain Hero" from gothic tradition. Villain hero was generated from gothic literature. This form of literature inclined to shape a character who seduced other people, at the same time he sufferedfrom destiny. This kind of character tended to be both evil and charming. Heathcliff was impetuous, arrogant and depressed, which resulted in his love and family's ruined. In spite of his evil actions, we should take the exterior environment into consideration. He wasn't born to be a villain, on the contrary, his personality was suppressed by social reality for quite a long time and disordered. Even if he reflected the malicious side of humanity with his brutal murder, his love for Katherine was pure, clean and enthusiastic, which revealed the glorious side of humanity. That made us come to a point that, until today, we are still pathetic about him. We stand by his side in a gloomy way to resist other devil characters. In this sense, he played the part of both a persecutor and a victim, which is unquestionably a villain hero.

Mr. Rochester in *Jane Eyre* is also a typical villain hero. He has a four-square figure and changeable character. He seemed doomed to be solemn. He married his wife without true love and sought for indulgence in an unethical way. Locking his wife up in the attic, he showed no care for her. His evil was indirectly appointed in the text. He was more of a victim who was hurt by feudal society—without either free will to chase love or legitimate right to succeed family property. His life was miserable even with money covering its essence. Readers easily shed compassion for him. We cannot ignore that he still held his passion for life after his suffering in the fire. He represented miscellaneous humanity when faced with ups and downs in life.

2.2.2 Atmosphere Rendering

In perspective of atmosphere rendering, these two works were filled with horror and tension. In Wuthering Heights, terror kept hovering above the village. The story displayed the wired gothic weather in the county of Yorkshire. With howling wind and thick snow all year round, Wuthering was a special word in this novel. Except for the weather, all the surroundings were in gothic style. Outside the villa was a boundless grey plain. Inside the villa was dark for the lack of light. *Jane Eyre's* beginning set a gloomy tone for the whole book. The writer described several strange giggle and fire to create a scaring scene. To provoke conflict, Charlotte narrated Jane's nightmare and the vampire in it. This paved the path for Bertha's entrance. Without the settings of horrific elements, Jane's leaving would be unreasonable and maniac wife would be unexpected.

2.2.3 Theme

In perspective of theme, the revenge and confrontation for property of *Wuthering Heights* is traditional gothic theme. Author Joyce Carol Oates sees the novel as "an assured demonstration of finite and tragically self-consuming nature of "passion". It has several major elements which are related to gothic.

Even though the noel is a great romance, the author doesn't follow the strict guidelines of the genre: the revenge plot is just as powerful- if not more so- than the love that pulls Catherine and Heathcliff together. Without revenge as such a predominant theme, Wuthering Heights would just be another thwarted love story. When Heathcliff can't have the woman he loves, he turns his attention to getting revenge on his childhood tormenter, Hindley. The fact that Hindley already drinks life a fish and gambles to excess makes Heathcliff's vengeance all the easier.

Jane Eyre also has the same features however it has the relatively gentler density in extravagance. Charlotte intended to take gothic as a preliminary instrument to criticize the inequality in society and praise the ideal and romantic feelings of humanity. The novel goes to a bright end eventually. There is strong gothic imagery in this novel. For example, the red-room is dark like blood.

It emits strange noises and has a large mirror that distorts Jane's appearance. All these elements—a dark and foreboding room where a family member died, the color red, ghosts and phantoms, and the romantic gothic scene of rain on the moors—are Gothic and predict future Gothic locales and themes in the plot. The gothic features in Jane Eyre are mainly externalized through the gothic imagery.

Chapter 3　The Gothic Evolution in Modern Literature

3.1　General Overview on Gothic Evolution

In the 1960s, gothic literature revived in Britain and America. *Rebecca* written by Daphne du Maurier brought gothic novel back to life. The early gothic novels were in stereotype, gradually losing its innovative. A castle with ghost shadow, the "chase-run-chase" plot between a fairy pale maiden and cold-blooded killer was inevitable. In the early 19th century, a renew gothic mode which was not restricted to village setting and stereotypical structure was born. It simply showed spirit, ghost death and such supernatural themes. Under this condition, horror fiction appeared.

In the 1960s, Victoria Halt's (1906—) first novel *Mistress of Mellyn* lifted the cushion of the development of gothic novels in the 1960s. Gerald Gross, editor of the Ace Books named this type of books with mysterious and romantic features provided for women as gothic fiction. From then on, this concept had been recognized by critics and writers. Despite that gothic fiction was invented in the 18th.

Century, modern publishers prefer to use "romantic suspense fiction" rather than gothic fiction to name the female works.

During the forming process of gothic fiction, horror fiction, romantic fiction and historical fiction usually interfered with it. Therefore, critics used to classify gothic fiction into horror gothic, romantic gothic and historical gothic. From the 1960s until today, gothic fiction had dramatic development in America. Comparing to that in Britain, American gothic fiction had more innovative breakthrough and thematical difference.

3.2　New Characteristics

In the series books of *Twilight*, the writer displays a vampire family in which everyone has the unique supernatural ability. She also constructs a binary world in which vampires live with human beings. The character of vampire, unlike that in the old gothic fiction, varies as much as human. They are no longer the representative of violence, fruity and darkness. They are living creatures who possess same feelings as human do. What's more, the romantic elements play a significant role in this work, making it attractive to young readers. Edward and Bella' love crosses the boundary between two species. This unconsciously satisfies our inner greed for legendary love. As for the theme, the writer conveys some positive belief to us through this gothic story. Justice will never be defeated by devil and true love will be the colossal weapon we can use to fight against darkness.

Chapter 4　Conclusions

"The State is an imagined community." Fiction reflects the mentality of society to a great degree otherwise it is generally utilized to assert the hinted opinion people hold about the society. Looking back to the evolution process of gothic fiction, we figure out that its political function gradually faded. In the past, especially during the Middle Age, it was the symbol of dark realities and unequal treatment which was programmed by satire and critic. With the evolution of society, Britain and America are walking on the democratic and industrialized path. Domestic conflicts are smoother a lot than the early time. Citizens' aesthetical tendency also changes with their mentality, guiding the Gothic analysis to a different aesthetic perspective. Gothic started to join the mainstream of literature work in universal judgement and ultimately derived its branches and systems. Now people prefer wonderful, romantic gothic story than those which filled with anxiety and tension without referring to their political intentions. This phenomenon not only reveals the transformation of gothic fiction, but also implies that the function of literature varies according to the social changes.

References

[1] Bloom Horold. Marry Shelly. New York: Chelsea House Publishers, Inc, 1985.

[2] Varma D P. The Gothic Flame. Metuchen: The Scarcecrow Press, Inc, 1987.

[3] Heather, Peter. The Goths. Cambridge: Blackwell Publishers Inc., 1996.

[4] Spingam, J.E. Critical Essays of the seventeenth century. Gloucestershire: Clarendon Press, Inc, 1909.

[5] Varma, Devendra P. The Gothic Flame Being a History of the Gothic Novel in England: Its Origins, Efflorescence, and Residuary Influences. Metuchen and London: Scarecrow Press, 2007.

[6] 黄禄善. 革命、焦虑和哥特式表现[J]. 外国文学评论，2009（1）：31-46.

[7] 黄禄善. 哥特身份和哥特式复兴——英国哥特式小说的"哥特式"探源[J]. 外国文学研究，2008，30（1）：108-118.

[8] 刘新明. 拂拭历史的尘埃，重现艺术的光彩[J]. 上海师范大学学报，1994（1）：35-45

[9] 万俊. 关于美国当代哥特小说[J]. 外国文学研究，2000（1）：111-113.

[10] 肖明翰. 英美文学中的哥特传统[J]. 外国文学评论，2001（2）：90-101.

[11] 朱振武，王子红. 爱伦坡哥特小说源流及其审美契合[J]. 上海大学学报（社会科学版），2007，14（5）：92-96.

[12] 陈晋华. 哥特小说在英美文学中的演变[J]. 赤峰学院学报，2011，32（6）：121-122.

Analysis on the Minor Character
——Mrs. Henry Dashwood in *Sense and Sensibility*

冯　静

摘　要： 在《理智与情感》中，简·奥斯汀塑造了近20个有闲阶级的先生、夫人和小姐。除了对主要人物的生动描写外，一个个次要人物，即使着墨不多，无一不是精心雕琢，活灵活现，有血有肉。对次要人物的描写也是这部小说获得成功的重要因素之一。从人物刻画角度来看，对于次要人物如亨利·达什伍德夫人描写较多且描写角度较多。而目前对《理智与情感》中人物描写的研究主要集中于男女主人公和他们之间的爱情发展。次要人物在小说中，对丰满故事和推动情节发展也具有重要的作用，但目前的研究却比较少。该小说中具体的描写亨利·达什伍德太太的文段为研究对象，着重从该人物本身所体现的特征和形象，和其在该小说中的作用和影响两个方面来探讨该人物，通过细读文本分析该次要人物的形象和作用，可以得出以下结论：亨利·达什伍德太太虽本身具有一定的局限性，但也有其可取之处，与当时普遍的母亲不同，她不以金钱和地位为标准为女儿选择丈夫，而以女儿自身幸福为中心。在当时的社会背景下也算是一个心态较为开放和包容的理想性母亲。此外，她虽然是一个次要人物，但其仍具有饱满的性格和形象。

关键词： 理智与情感；次要人物；人物特征；人物形象；亨利·达什伍德太太

Abstract: In *Sense and Sensibility*, Jane Austen created nearly twenty gentlemen, ladies and misses from the leisure class. Except the vivid description of the main characters, the secondary characters are also carefully crafted vividly and substantially, even if the content is not much.. The description of the minor characters is also one of the important factors in the success of this novel. From the characterization point of view, the secondary figures such as Mrs. Henry Dashwood described much more than other minor characters from various angles. At present, the researches on the description of characters in *Sense and Sensibility* mainly focus on the main characters and their love stories. Minor characters in the novel play an important role in enrichingthe novel and promote the plot, but the current researchesare relatively few in this aspect. In this paper, the contents of Mrs. Henry Dashwoodare the object of study, focusing on the features and image embodied in the character herself and herfunctions and influences in the novel. By reading the novel to analyze the image and the role of Mrs. Henry Dashwood, finally draw the following conclusion: Although Mrs. Henry Dashwood has some limitations, she also hasmerits.During that time, unlike the major mother, she did not take the money and status as a standard for daughters to choose her husbands, her daughters' happiness was the imperative condition. She was an ideal mother with an open-minded and generous characteristics. In addition, although she is a minor character, she still has the round characteristics and image.

Key Words: *Sense and Sensibility,* minor character, character feature, character image, Mrs. Dashwood

Chapter 1   Introduction

Jane Austen is skillful in formulating characters by from different devices and angles. The number of minor characters are apparently more than the protagonists even they are they occupied most contents of a novel. However Jane Austen can use accurate description to disclose the merits of them. It is a vital component for the success of Jane Austen's novels. The legendary English writer E·M·Forster has said that the characters in Jane Austen's novels are round not flat. *Sense and Sensibility* as the world around popular novel has employed many minor round characters. In *Sense and Sensibility*, the minor characters appear in most episodes and have the interactions with the main characters to influence the main characters' emotions and the development of its plot, so analyzing the image and characteristics of the minor characters has imperative way to understand the meaning of this masterpiece. .

Mrs. Henry Dashwood is the minor character that I choose to analyze her functions in the novel. She is a minor character who harbors much more description than most other minors. There has sufficient conversations and direct an indirect descriptions to discover her characteristics. She also a typical one who can influence others especially one protagonist—her second daughter for their similarities. She possesses most of the functions as a minor character due to her special identity—two protagonists' mother.

Because most study are focusing on analyzing the protagonists' characteristics and image and their love, there are not many people analyzing the minor characters in *Sense and Sensibility*. The importance of minor characters functions has been eclipsed by the conspicuous protagonists.

With the concrete example of Mrs. Henry Dashwood , the image and functions of minor characters can be well demonstrated in how her image is formed by analyzing the different devices used to describe the Mrs. Henry Dashwood and how Mrs. Henry Dashwood functions in different perspectives.

The purpose of this paper is to give an all-round analysis on the minor character—Mrs. Dashwood in *Sense and Sensibility*. Through this detailed study, this paper presents a systematic analysis on what the image contributes and how it functions.

Chapter 2   The Image of Mrs. Henry Dashwood

This chapter will be divided into two parts. First part will discuss the background of Mrs. Henry Dashwood in this novel. Second part will discuss the formulation of Mrs. Henry Dashwood's image by different devices that the author used in detail respectively.

2.1   The Background of Mrs. Henry Dashwood.

Mr. Henry Dashwood' s uncle passed away, and left his large estate and fortunate. His will was read. He left his estate from his nephew, but he also required that after Mr. Henry Dashwood passed away, the estate should give to his son who was the child of his former marriage. For the sake of it,

Mrs. Dashwood and their three daughters did not have the right of inheritance. Soon after his uncle's death, Mr. Henry Dashwood passed away, so his son and his family moved in to the Norland Park. Because his son and his son's wife was very selfish and narrow-minded, and betrayed his promise to his father that he would take good care of his mother-in-law and his three sisters. Mrs. Dashwood could not bear the attitude of her daughter-in-law to her and to her first daughter's affection to Mr. Edward who was the brother of her daughter-in-law.

At that time, Mrs. Dashwood received a letter from her relation, so she decided to move out and started a new life in Barton Cottage. Her daughters agreed.

From then on, they lived in Barton Cottage and the story was revolved around the love stories of her daughters.

Mrs. Dashwood is a mediocre housewife, affectionate, stupid. The mother's most prominent character is too romantic, even though she is the mother of three children. For her, the common sense, the care, the cautious, all submerged in her subtle romantic character. She did not actively embark on the future of life, after the death of her husband, but indulged in the endless mourning. She was unconscious about the financial straits of their life after leaving the Norland Park. No matter the family trivia or survival plan need the help and guidance of her eldest daughter Elinor.

2.2   The Devices of Shaping the Character

This part will be divided into two parts, one is about the direct descriptions which include the conversations and the author's narrations which are largely employed in this novel, and the other is about the indirect descriptions which include the others' comments and the attitudes to Mrs. Dashwood, her comments and attitudes to others. This chapter will revolve around these specific aspects.

2.2.1   Direct Descriptions

In Jane Austen's novels, she seldom used the appearance description. She preferred use the vivid conversation and interesting plot to formulate the characters.

Conversation is a direct way to show the speaker's feelings, especially, Mrs. Henry Dashwood, a very emotional and romantic woman. Besides showing her feelings, she is also excellent in magnifying them.

An example from the novel:

One day, Elinor talked about the difference between Edward and his sister, which arose Mrs. Henry Dashwood's interesting.

"It is enough," said she; "to say that he is unlike Fanny is enough. It implies everything amiable. I love him already."

"I think you will like him," said Elinor, "when you know more of him."

"Like him!" replied her mother with a smile. "I can feel no sentiment of approbation inferior to love."

"You may esteem him."

"I have never yet known what it was to separate esteem and love." (*Sense and Sensibility*, 13)

Actually, before this conversation, Mrs. Dashwood was in such affliction as rendered her careless of surrounding objects. She saw only that he was quiet and unobtrusive, and she liked him for it. Just because Elinor's positive comments and her dissatisfaction to her daughter-in-law, Mrs. Henry Dashwood over appreciated him and she began to catch every change to get acquainted with him. From this point, we can see that Mrs. Dashwood is quite easy to be charged by her emotions not the wise. She is a superficial and thoughtless person.

An example from the novel:

No sooner did she perceive any symptom of love in his behavior to Elinor, than considered their serious attachment as certain and looked forward to their marriage as rapidly approaching.

"In a few months, my dear Marianne," said she, "Elinor will in all probability to settled for life. We shall miss her, but she will be happy."

"Oh! Mama, how shall we do without her?"

"My love, it will be scarcely a separation. We shall live within a few miles of each other and shall meet every day of our lives. You will gain a brother, a real, affectionate brother. I have the highest opinio in the world of Edward's heart."

In this conversation, Mrs. Henry Dashwood showed her nosy and urgent to her eldest daughter's marriage. Actually, before her assertion, Edward and Elinor had never talked about the affection to each other. What's more, Edward was a coward man and Elinor is a wise and sense woman. Just because of some behaviors that perceive some symptom of love to Elinor, she affirmed that they would soon got married in several months, however, they just knew each other for several weeks. Her blind confidence just showed her stupid and poor ignorant. At the same time, her subtle romantic that was accustomed to magnify her emotion was revealed. In some extents, she loved it.

Another device that Jane Austen often employed in this novel is the narration from the perspective of God. From this angle, it can help readers to understand the character easily, and promote and indicate the following plot naturally. The author can formulate and shape all the things in the novel easily and freely. From this perspective , the novel will become more clear in many details and the whole content will become opener.

An example from the novel:

Some mother might have encouraged the intimacy from motives of interest, for Edward Ferrars was the eldest son of a man who had died very rich; and some might have repressed it from motives of prudence, for except a trifling sum, the whole of his fortune depended on the will of his mother. But Mrs. Dashwood was alike uninfluenced by either consideration. It was enough for her that he appeared to be amiable, that he loved her daughter, and that Elinor returned the partiality. It was contrary to every doctrine of hers that difference of fortune should keep any couple asunder who wad attracted by resemblance of disposition; and that Elinor's merit should not be acknowledged by everyone who knew her, was to her comprehension impossible. (*Sense and Sensibility,* 12)

From the direct description of Mrs. Dashwood's attitude to Elinor and Edward's love, we can see that Mrs..Dashwood deeply loves her daughter,hopes them can find the person they love and love them. It is quite different with the common standard about marriage at that time. Most people in that period, thought money is the first thing in choosing the wife or husband. She just cared about her daughters' happiness in marriage. The reasons for her attitude to encourage and support her daughters to persue their true love are about the characteristics of herself and her own experience. We have already know that she was a romantic and emotional woman. Because of this, she believed in love. Once, Marianne was desperate about her marriage and worried about that she could never find a man she loved and lived her. At that time, Mrs. Dashwood comforted her with her own experience, she said: " Remember, my love, that you are not seventeen. It is yet too early i life to despair of such an happiness. Why should you be less fortunate than your mother? In one circumstance only, my Marianne, may your destiny be different from hers!"(*Sense and Sensibility*, 14) From this, we can get a conclusion that Mrs. Dashwood had a perfect marriage. It gave her the confidence that her daughter would find their true love like her. This narration has revealed that Mrs. Dashwood is a kind, mercy and considerate mother with romantic imagination and huge confidence to her daughters' marriage, even if she had many disadvantages in her characteristics. From this aspect, she could be called a competent mother.

An example from the novel:

Their visitors, except those from Barton Park were nor many; for in spite of Sir John's urgent entreaties that they would mia more in the neighborhood, and repeated assurances of his carriage being always at their service, the independance of Mrs. Dashwood's spirit overcame the wish of society for her children; and she was resolute in declining to visit any family beyond the distance of a walk. (*Sense and Sensibility*, 31)

This narration has revealed that even if their life was quite different from before in Norland Park, she did not want her three daughters and herself lost the manner and decency. She ached her daughters for that they had to walk to visit someone far away. She persisted not to use Sir John's carriage and it was a disclosure of her self-esteem. These showed Mrs. Dashwood was a good mother who deeply loved her daughters and did not want them to suffer. In other aspect, she also had strong self-esteem.

From the conversations we find that Mrs. Dashwood has many disadvantages like stupid, ignorant and etc. But from the narration, the author wants to tell us even if she is not perfect but she also has some good characteristics especially as a mother. She cares about her daughters' everything and encourages them to marry with love not money and status of a man possessing. From this direct description, Mrs. Dashwood is a innocent woman with some limits. Her image is round and real. Human is complex being in characteristics. Everyone has merits and shorts.

2.2.2 Indirect Description

In *sense and sensibility*, there are also some others comments to Mrs. Henry Dashwood and her comments to others also can reflect what kind of a person she is.

An example from the novel:

Mrs. Dashwood is busy in move out Norland Park and transporting her furniture to Barton Cottage.

"It chiefly consisted of household linen, plate, china, and books, with an handsome pianoforte of Marianne' s. Mrs. John Dashwood saw the packages depart with a sigh: she could not help feeling it hard that as Mrs. Dashwood's income would be so trifling in comparison with their own, she should have any handsome article of furniture.(*Sense and Sensibility*, 18)

From Fanny's comment to Mrs. Henry Dashwood showed that she had a great taste and an exquisite life. In other people's eye, Mrs. Dashwood could be a elegant woman. Actually, these exquisite households were expensive, it alluded that Mrs. Dashwood had a rich life and she was generous to buy these things to meet her family's use. The comparison between the two woman, we could find that Fanny did not have that kind of taste and she was chinchy even she had much more money and she did not have the hobby and pleasure of life. From this angle, Mrs. Dashhood's image has become more positive.

Mrs. Dashwood's comments to others can also reveal her characteristics. People will tend to approve one's behaviors or words that correspond to his or her own value and tend to disagree something that betrayal their own perspectives.

An example from the novel:

The contempt which she had very early in their acquaintance felt for her daughter-in-law was very much increased by the further knowledge of her character, which half a year's residence in her family afforded; and perhaps in spite of every consideration of politeness or maternal affection on the side of the former, the two ladies might have found it impossible to have lived together so log had not a particular circumstance occurred to give still greater eligibility, according to the opinions of Mrs. Dashwood, to her daughters' continuance at Norland.

Mrs. Henry Dashwood's scorn to her daughter-in-law reflected her value that she looked down upon the narrow-mined and selfish person and alluded that Mrs. Dashwood was a open-minded and upright person. Because in this novel, Fanny was a negative character, the comparison between the two women, foil the Mrs. Dashwood's positive aspect of her characteristics.

The image of Mrs. Henry Dashwood is a positive character in generally speaking. Even if she had some disadvantages that mentioned in the foregoing parts. In that period, women did not receive much education, and the shorts could be regarded as the limits that that generation endowed to her. Her love and her value to marriage could be a ideal model which corresponded with the author. In Jane Austen's many novels, mothers were not such a positive image. Mrs. Dashwood could be a ideal mother and her merits had surpassed her shorts.

Chapter 3   The Functions of the Character

From the foregoing analysis, the image of Mrs. Henry Dashwood could be pictured in our mind. And we has a general impression about what a person she is. The following chapter will discuss the functions of the minor character—Mrs. Dashwood in this novel. Its functions focus on four parts. First is to promote the plot. Second is to enhance the theme. Third is to foil the protagonists and fourth is to highlight the Jane Austen's writing skills.

3.1   To Promote the Plot

Because Mrs. Dashwood was a open-minded mother. She only cared her daughters' happiness.

It paved the way for the girls to persue their love without the obstacles from their own mother. What's more, they could receive the encouragement from their mother and the person they loved can also gain Mrs. Dashwood's pleasure. She gave her daughter the freedom to choose their marriage took their feelings as the center. It is quite precious for her daughters in that generation. Her positive attitude promoted the development of the plot. If Mrs. Dashwood was a woman like other mothers taking the money and status as the most important things in a marriage. They may not be that lucky to find their true love and get married finally. She was a pusher to make the love stories toward the good direction.

3.2   To Enhance the Theme

There were a sentence in the novel: "the resemblance between her and her mother was strikingly great." (*Sense and Sensibility*, 6) The "her" there presents Marianne. From the background of the novel, Marianne is the embodiment of sensibility. So it showed that Mrs. Dashwood was also controlled by the sensibility and her emotion. She is also a embodiment of the sensibility, according the that sentence in the novel. Jane Austen's intended to tell the women that they should use the sense to treat their affection. Mrs. Dashwood is a typical woman who used her emotion to treat things in her life. So she was easy to be emotional and desperate about the sorrow and be over-happy about the common things. It would apparently show her ignorant and stupid characteristics.

3.3   To Foil the Protagonists

Her eldest daughter is the embodiment of sense, as we have mentioned in the foregoing part, Mrs. Dashwood can be regarded as the embodiment of sensibility. Her ignorant and stupid shorts is to to foil her daughter Elinor's advantages. The novel has mentioned that: "Elinor, this eldest daughter whose advice was so effectual, possessed a strength of understanding and coolness of judgment which qualified her, though only nineteen, to be the counsellor of her mother...and her feelings were strong; but she knew how to govern them: it was a knowledge which her mother had yet to learn." (*Sense and Sensibility*, 5-6) From this aspect, we can know that Mrs. Dashwood is used to foil her eldest daughter.

Chapter 4   Conclusions

By carefully studying the minor character—Mrs. Henry Dashwood, we can pictured a vivid image of a mother and her functions in the whole novel.

After analyzing the different devices used to picture the Mrs. Dashwood's image, we can find that when Jane Austen formulated the character, she seldom directly depicted their appearance and psychological activities. She used the conversation to to display the characters and used the narration to compensate the other parts of the characters that did nor show in the conversation and plot. According to her unique writing skill, the character are round not flat .they were like the true peoson around us.

The analysis of Mrs. Dashwood has found out that she is not only a simple and flat minor character who was thoughtless, ignorant, superficial, reckless, emotional and irritable, she also a generous, open-minded, elegant and polite woman, which was mentioned in the novel. She could be a ideal mother in that period. She did not care about the fortune and status, and only focused on her daughters' happiness.

Mrs. Dashwood is a successful minor character in this novel. We can analyze her from many different angles and find out different features compared with other mothers in Jane Austen's novels. Mrs. Dshwood is a ideal woman and mother even if having the limits of that generation.

References

[1] Austen Jane. Sense and Sensibility. Shanghai: Shanghai World Publishing Corporation, 2007.

[2] Li, An. Sense and Sensibility (film). Columbia Picture, 1995.

[3] ClueBot, NG. Senseandsensibility. June 2017. <https://en.wikipedia.org/wiki/Sense_and_Sensibility> 02 Jul. 2017.

[4] 简·奥斯丁. 理智与情感[M]. 孙致礼译. 南京：译林出版社，2000.

[5] 杨钰. 简·奥斯丁小说中母亲形象分类研究[D]. 华中师范大学，2010.

Analysis of Chokecherry Tree in *Beloved* from the Perspective of Archetypal Criticism

朱珈璇

摘　要：1987 年《宠儿》由托尼·莫里森完成至今已有 30 年时间。期间，学者们对这本著作从各个方面进行了分析，中外的研究成果更是数不胜数，但是少有仅仅只对文本中出现的某一单一事物进行分析研究。本论文借助诺思罗普·弗莱《批评的解剖》中原型批评的理论从象征（symbol）、写实（Representation）和"逼真"（Lifelikeness）和原型隐喻（Archetypal Metaphor）三个角度分析主人公塞丝身上的树状伤疤。通过这三个不同角度来分析得出伤疤的内在含义，可以揭示黑奴所受的创伤和当时残酷的社会现实。

关键词：苦樱桃树；原型批评；黑人奴隶

Abstract: It has been thirty years since Toni Morrison finished her masterpiece—*Beloved*. During the thirty years, there have been a great number of scholars doing research on this novel from different perspectives. And there also has been uncountable analysis about it. But there have been few researches about a single issue in this novel. This paper analyzes the tree-shaped scar on the protagonist—Sethe's back from three aspects which are the symbol, the representation or "lifelikeness" and the archetypal metaphor from the perspective of archetypal criticism. This paper tries to get the inner meaning of the scar, related the trauma that the African Americans suffered and the crucial reality of that time.

Key Words: chokecherry, archetypal criticism, African Americans

Chapter 1　Introduction

1.1　Introduction to *Beloved*, Chokecherry Tree & Archetypal Criticism

Beloved is a 1987 novel by the American writer Toni Morrison. The novel is about the story that the African American woman, named Sethe kills her daughter who is a crawling-already girl on the way of escaping slavery. Because she doesn't want her daughter to be recaptured and take back to the place where she lives as a slave. And eighteen years later, a girl presumes to be her daughter, called Beloved, returns. And all the things start to become different. The novel won the Pulitzer Prize for Fiction in 1988 and was a finalist for the 1987 National Book Award.A New York Times survey of writers and literary critics ranked it the best work of American fiction from 1981 to 2006.(Wikipedia)

Chokecherry is a species of bird cherry, native to North America; the natural historic range of P. virginiana includes most of Canada, most of the United States and northern Mexico.(Wikipedia)

Chokecherry was the vehicle of scar on Sethe's back in *Beloved*. On her way to escaping slavery, a white girl named Amy who helps her when she gives birth to her daughter interprets the scar on her back as a chokecherry tree. Sethe is willing to accept the interpretation of the scar. After that, she calls it a tree or chokecherry tree.

Archetypal literary criticism is a type of critical theory that interprets a text by focusing on recurring myths and archetypes in the narrative, symbols, images, and character types in literary work. As a form of literary criticism, it dates back to 1934 when Maud Bodkin published Archetypal Patterns in Poetry. Archetypal literary criticism's origins are rooted in two other academic disciplines, social anthropology and psychoanalysis; each contributed to literary criticism in separate ways, with the latter being a sub-branch of critical theory. Archetypal criticism was at its most popular in the 1940s and 1950s, largely due to the work of Canadian literary critic Northrop Frye.(Wikipedia)

1.2　Research Background

Chokecherry is the huge scar on Sethe's back on her way fleeing slavery. She knows the tree-shaped scar from a white girl, named Amy. To comfort Sethe and to release Sethe's physical pain, Amy beautifies the scar on purpose which makes Sethe accept the description and remembered the "chokecherry tree" on her back forever. In this situation, "chokecherry tree" becomes the important metaphor in the text and it has special degree of symbolism.

For Sethe, "chokecherry tree" symbolizes the physical pain that she suffers. "Choke" is the description to the first part of her life. And the physical pain can be cured as time goes by while the psychological pain may be with Sethe for her whole life. Toni Morrison, the author, tries to use the physical scar to cover the psychological pain—the remorse and regret after killing her daughter by herself. Further more, "chokecherry" is also the symbol which reflects the pain that African-American suffered in the history. "Tree on the back"is the spiritual burden. And in some degree, it relates to the reasons why African-Americans are poor and violent,and there is always a high crime rate in their society. (中国作家网）

1.3　Research Motivation, Methodology

The research motivations of chokecherry in *Beloved* can be recounted as follow: first, Beloved is a masterpiece of Toni Morrison and the theme of it is more related to American southern Gothic. And it is abnormal that someone's scar is likened to the chokecherry tree. So the novel has great attraction for me. Second, there are a great number of critics giving interpretation on this novel from different perspectives. Few critics have analyzed the chokecherry in the novel from the perspective of archetypal criticism.. Third, the research can offer us ways to solve the problem that the psychological pains that Chinese suffered from the Great Proletarian Cultural Revolution when we discuss the method to deal with the African-Americans' psychological pain.

Based on these facts, the paper is applicable to analyze the chokecherry tree from the perspective of archetypal criticism and it is fitting to say that archetypal criticism is a helpful and effective way to study the novel by analyzing chokecherry tree.

Chapter 2　The Archetypal Criticism of Chokecherry Tree

2.1　The Symbol of Chokecherry

When we read something, it is easy to find out that our attention moving in two directions at once. One direction is outward or centrifugal,in which we keep going outside our reading, from the individual words to the things they mean, or, in practice, to our memory of the conventional association between them. The other direction is inward or centripetal, in which we we try to develop from the worlds a sense of the larger verbal pattern they make. In both case,we deal with symbols. (Frye 73)

Chokecherry tree is a suckering shrub or small tree growing to 4.9 m (16 ft 1 in) tall. The leaves are oval, 3.2–10.2 cm (1 1/4–4 1/32 in) long, with a coarsely serrated margin. The flowers are produced in racemes 38.1–76.2 cm (15–30 in) long in late spring (well after leaf emergence). They flowers are always white and the fruits are about 1 cm (3/8 in) in diameter, range in color from bright red to black, and possess a very astringent taste, being both somewhat sour and somewhat bitter. The very ripe "berries" (actually drupes) are dark in color and less astringent and more sweet than when red and unripe. Chokecherry is toxic to horses, moose, cattle, goats, deer, and other animals with segmented stomachs (rumens), especially after the leaves have wilted (such as after a frost or after branches have been broken) because wilting releases cyanide and makes the plant sweet. About 10–20 lbs of foliage can be fatal. Symptoms of a horse that has been poisoned include heavy breathing, agitation, and weakness. (Wikipedia)What's more, the juice of it's flowers, branches, bark and fruits of chokecherry is easy to make animals or human beings which or who eat it become sleepy and unconscious. (360 百科)

According to Freud, the "depression, unsociability, and tedium vitae" are all the reflection of hysterical symptoms. In the novel, it is quite obvious to find out that these hysteria symptom in Sethe.

At the begging of the novel, the narrator introduces the living situation of her house—124: 124 WAS SPITEFUL. Full of baby's venom... (Morrison 1) But by 1873 Sethe and her daughter Denver are its only victims. Two boys flies away. And her mother-in-law is dead. Except working, Sethe always stays at home without letting Denver going outside too. These symptoms are the manifestation of trauma and the reflection of the harmful effects originated from the white dominated slave system. As a result, she is unable to develop as a self because of the harm to her and fixes on the "memories" that hold terrible and unspeakable secrets.

Sethe's childhood memories about her mother's mark pain, sexual trauma and her experiences that she went through during her old days under the slave owner's control are the causes of hysteria. At the same time, Ihold that Sethe's infanticide, which she did in confrontation with the slave owner's capture, also plants a traumatic seed for her later hysteria. The presentation of her aitiology is in effect the dark history in American reality and the reliation of Toni Morrison's writing intention. After she accepts Amy's interpretation of the scar, it becomes the symbol of "chokecherry tree" and the image of blooding life and fertility. When she suffers from hysteria, the chokecherry tree can be regarded as the symbol which is the start of the hysteria. And chokecherry's "juice" of flowers, branches, bark and fruits begins to influence her, making her sleepy and unconscious.

Chokecherry tree is a very important symbol in the novel. When we see the world--chokecherry, we will image the appearance of it and things related to it, which can be considered that our attention moves in the outward direction. And we we relate it to the whole context, we may regard it as the potential cause of hysteria in Sethe,which can be considered that our attention move in the inward direction.

2.2　The Representation and "Lifelikeness" of Chokecherry Tree

In most cases, when readers pick up a novel, our immediate impulse, a habit forested in them, is to compare it with "life". In this way, the works can strikes a chord with them. In literature, the emphasis in both practice and theory has been on representation or "lifelikeness". (Frye 134) In this novel, chokecherry tree was one kind of representation or "lifelikeness".

2.2.1　The Cause for Chokecherry

Chokecherry tree, the scar, appears on Sethe's back after the school teache's two nephews find that she tells Mrs. Garner on them that they hold her down and take her milk which belongs to her daughter. As an outsider of what happens to Sethe, we can understand why she is so angry. First of all,She is a mom, she wants to protect her girl and things belongs to her, especially when it comes to the point which relates to her girl's life. Second, she wants to be self-respected as a human being. Breast is a very private part of female. What the school teacher's nephews do to her can be regarded as sexual trauma. And the behavior of the boys really do offend. After knowing that Sethe tells on the boys, schoolteacher makes one of the boys open up Sethe's back, and when it closes , it makes a tree. It grew there still. (Morrison 17)The period when the background is settled is actually the time when lots of African Americans were under the slave owners' control and suffering their oppression and exploitation of labor. Or more even, the slave owners regarded them as the livestock which could be used cowhide on. And it was a common phenomenon that they beat the female slaves when they were pregnant and then took their milk.

2.2.2　The Description of Chokecherry

In this novel, the author mentions chokecherry eight times in total. The first place where the context generates the detail description of the chokecherry tree, is when Sethe is on her way of escaping slavery and she meets the white girl, Amy.

In the silence of an Amy struck dumb for a change, Sethe felt the fingers of those good hands lightly touch her back. She could hear her breathing but still the white girl said nothing. Sethe could not move. She couldn't lie on her stomach or her back, and to keep on her side meant pressure on her screaming feet. Amy spoke at last in her dream walker's voice.

"It's a tree, Lu. A chokecherry tree. See, here's the trunk — it's red and split wide open, full of sap,and this here's the parting for the branches. You got a mighty lot of branches. Leaves, too, look like, and dern if these ain't blossoms. Tiny little cherry blossoms, just as white. Your back got a whole tree on it. In bloom. What God have in mind, I wonder. I had me some whippings, but I don't remember nothing like this..." (Morrison 79)

Amy's worlds describe a beautiful scenery. She beautifies the scar. And it is easy to know the sentence "Tiny little cherry blossom, just as white" refers to Sethe's hurt which was suppurating. To comfort Sethe , Amy beautified the scar on purpose which makes Sethe accept the description and remember the metaphor—chokecherry tree forever. It is nature that human beings release their pain by choosing a objective concept to represent a negative issue. When Paul D rubs his cheek on her back and learns that way Sethe sorrow, he will tolerate no peace until he had touched every ridge and leaf of it with his mouth, none of which Sethe could feel because her back skin has been dead for years. Sethe can't feel the hurt and the emotion change which should exist. But Because Sethe wants to forget the old days on purpose, Paul D hear no sigh or see no tear coming fast.

2.3   The Archetypal Metaphor of Chokecherry Tree

Archetypal metaphor involves the use of what has been called the concrete universal , the individual identified with its class. (Frye 124)

Each of these three categories, the city, the garden and the sheepfold is by the principle of archetypal metaphor mentioned before and which we remember is the concrete universal, identical with the others and with each individual within it. Hence the divine and human worlds are,identified with the sheepfold, city and garden, and the social and individual aspects. Thus, the typical world of Bible presents the following pattern:

divine world   =   society of gods   =   One God

Human world   =   society of men   =   One Man

Animal world   =   sheepfold   =   One Lamp

The chokecherry tree on Sethe's back indicates readers the illusion to the Biblical Tree of life that in Revelations 22: 2 overshadows death, especially as Sethe herself blooms with life in the middle of the ravages of slavery as she faces her death.

Amy is the message of God. She interprets the tree-shaped scar as the chokecherry tree, while the school teacher is the representative of oppressors and exploiters. And his and his nephews' crucial behavior to Sethe actually means the castigation of civilization to her who was barbarous. The conflict between civilization and barbarism is represented by the tree-shaped scar. What's more, the function of the chokecherry tree is emphasized. In Bible, in the Paradise which is created by God, there are two trees. One is tree of life and the other is tree of wisdom. The tree-shaped scar—chokecherry tree on Sethe's back can be considered as the two trees. The reason why it is the tree of life is that the scar is opened by one nephew of school teacher who is angry that Sethe tell on them that they take her milk for her baby who isn't born. It is the symbol of reproduction and continuation of African Americans' lives and culture. It is the symbol of eternal life. The reason why it also can be regarded as the tree of wisdom is that it is the symbol that the school teacher who represents "civilization" uses cowhide on her. He imparts the so called knowledge of civilized era with his cultural hegemony. As a result, there is a chokecherry tree on Sethe's back, which is the mark of sadness and humiliation of African Americans. The scar combines both depression and hope.

It links the main characters in this novel: Sethe, Denver, Baby and Paul D. And it makes the theme of the novel more specific.

To sum up, the tree-shaped scar on Sethe's back is the witness to the civil of slavery. It witness the humiliation Sethe gets from her master and it records her painful past. It has been an indispensable part of her life.

Chapter 3　Conclusions

Generally speaking, there are lots of issues we can analyze from the chokecherry tree from the archetypal criticism. When we analyze it from the symbol, it can be regard as the potential cause for hysteria in Sethe. The detailed description and the reason for thought of Sethe that she wants to her past days under the slave owner's control make the chokecherry tree representational and lifelike. From the archetypal metaphor aspect, the chokecherry tree can be regarded as the tree of life and the tree of wisdom in Bible. The chokecherry tree is the depression and the hope for Sethe. And the pain that Sethe and other African Americans can be healed with the help of their communities.

References

[1] Frye Northrop. Anatomy of Criticism. Shanghai: Shanghai Foreign Language Education Press, 2009.

[2] Morrison Toni, Beloved. Beijing: Foreign Language and Research Press, 2006.

[3] Wikipedia. Archetypal Literary Criticism. 15 June, 2017. https://en.wikipedia.org/wiki/Archetypal_literary_criticism 16 June 2017.

[4] Wikipedia. Beloved. 12 June, 2017. https://en.wikipedia.org/wiki/Beloved_(novel) 16 June, 2017.

[5] Wikipedia. Prunus virginiana. 18 May, 2017. https://en.wikipedia.org/wiki/Prunus_virginiana 16 June, 2017

[6] 360 百科. 苦樱桃树. 2015 年 4 月 10 日． http://www.baike.com/wiki/苦樱桃. 2017-06-18.

[7] 张静君. 重获心灵的自由——圣经原型解读托尼·莫里森的《宠儿》[D]. 河南师范大学，2012.

[8] 中国作家网. 托尼莫里森《宠儿》后背上的那棵树. 2013-07-10. http://www.chinawriter.com.cn, 2017-06-17.

A Research on Shortness of Feminism in *Jane Eyre*

谢倩倩

摘　要:《简·爱》历来被学者们推崇为女性主义的扛鼎之作, 坚韧自强的主人公简爱以弱势的女性处境从小开始反抗人生的不公正, 以自己的自尊自爱赢得了平等幸福的爱情。波伏娃的《第二性》被誉为 "有史以来讨论妇女的最健全、最理智、最充满智慧的一本书", 作者以丰富渊博的知识论证了女性在社会上所处的劣势地位, 并从历史、精神分析学和生物学的角度分析其原因, 是研究女性主义的必读书目。学者们对《简·爱》中体现女性主义的部分进行了数不胜数的研究, 但是以波伏娃《第二性》的部分观点为指导, 我们仍然可以发现作品中女性主义彰显得不足。文章主要通过对里德太太的人物塑造, 罗彻斯特和柏莎的结局差异以及简·爱最后通过继承遗产以回归家庭的剧情设定三方面结合《第二性》中后母和母亲形象、通奸以及婚姻和家庭的相关观点进行分析论述, 从而讨论研究《简·爱》这部女性主义代表作中的女性主义彰显的不足之处。通过对这些不足之处的研究和学习, 人们可以更全面地理解学习这部经典之作, 从而增强对女性的正确认识, 并且能意识到当代社会中潜在的女性压迫, 并予以反抗。

关键词:《简·爱》;《第二性》; 女性主义不足

Abstract: *Jane Eyre* has been widely acknowledged as one of the most representative work of feminism, which characterizes a highly self-esteemed and independent heroine —Jane, who fought against the unfairness and oppression towards women courageously, and never became subjugated to the destiny. *The Second Sex* is the most well-known classic of feminism as well, written by encyclopedic Simone de Beauvoir, which analyzes and explores the disadvantageous situations of women and the reasons from history, psychoanalysis and biology. Countless scholars have done the research on the feminism in *Jane Eyre*. However, if we study it carefully and deeply under views of step-mother and mother image, the private ownership, the marriage and family in T*he Second Sex*, we can still find some shortness of feminism in the book even it has been greatly manifested. This paper is going to discuss the parts of characterization of Mrs. Reed, the endings of Rochester in adultery and Jane's inheritance of heritage to return to family to explore the shortness of feminism to shed new light on the work. Besides, we can have a clearer cognition of feminism, be aware of the hidden oppression in contemporary society and revolt against it.

Key Words: *Jane Eyre, The Second Sex,* shortness of feminism

Chapter 1　Introduction

Jane Eyre has always been appreciated and praised highly by countless scholars because of its outstanding description and manifestation of the independent and resistant woman —Jane, which also makes *Jane Eyre* the representative masterpiece of feminism. The heroine Jane, who stood in the extremely disadvantageous female position—the situation of all the women in that time, was an orphan because of her mother's chase of true love and the rebellion against the convention. Then Jane rebelled the ruthless aunt Mrs. Reed and cousin, fought against the hypocritical headmaster Mr. Brocklehurst of Lowood, left Mr. Rochester after knowing his marriage and refused John River's proposal because of her " strive to achieve Selfhood all her life."(Liu Jing, 2008: 16) Thus through her consistent struggling and endeavor, she gained an equally romantic relationship and her independent identity just like Jiang Ling argued that "the main theme of *Jane Eyre* is the deconstruction of woman's otherness and their pursuit of independent identity". (Jiang Ling, 2005: 02) *The Second Sex,* written by the French existentialist Simone de Beauvoir, in which the author deals with the treatment of women throughout various subjects such as history and biology, is regarded as the most brilliantand supreme work of modern feminism, the most thorough, reasonable and intelligent masterpiece of female and the "bible " of women. The Second Sex came up with the theory of " otherness "— "Thus humanity is male and man defines woman not herself but as relative to him." (Beauvoir, 1949: 7) There are a tremendous amount of scholars having researched about the feminism parts in *Jane Eyre,* however, if we study the masterpiece in the direction of the views in *the Second Sex,* we can still find that there are some shortness of feminism which are determined by the historic restrictions. And these shortness are always rooted in subconsciousness and inevitable. This paper will analyze the three parts of characterization of Mrs. Reed, which is related to the analysis of mother and the characterization of women, the ending of Rochester in adultery which is related to adultery under private property and Jane's inheritance of heritage to return to family which are related to the family bound and restrictions of women in *The Second Sex.*Consequently, through the research and study on the shortness of feminism —the shortness of feminism of the masterpiece which has already been manifested a lot, we can shed new light on the work and have a clearer cognition about situations of women and how the history determines it, besides, we can be aware of the hidden oppression in contemporary society and revolt against it.

Chapter 2   Shortness of Feminism in Mrs. Reed

2.1   Step-mother and Mother Images in *the Second Sex*

Beauvoir points in her book that "It was as Mother that woman was fearsome; it is in maternity that she must be transfigured and enslaved". (Beauvoir, 1974: 189) Because of the admiration of mother's magic of reproduction, man honored Mother and endowed them with heathenism but because of their "otherness ", they also held their fear and hidden detest. " The source of these terrors lies in the fact that in the Other, quite beyond their reach... woman retains many of the disquieting power she possessed in primitive societies." (Beauvoir, 1974: 190) "The respect that haloes the Mother, the prohibition that surround her, suppress the hostile disgust that is mingled spontaneously with the carnal tenderness she inspires. " (Beauvoir, 1974: 191) Therefore, they show the cruelty of maternity by characterizing the image of step-mother as a step-guardian in myth and legendary. "In every country tales and legends have similarly incarnated the cruel aspect of maternity in the stepmother. It is her stepmother who would have Snow White perish. In the figure of the wicked stepmother —like Mme Fichini, whipping Sophie through Mme de Segur's books — survive the antique Kali with her necklace of severed heads." (Beauvoir, 1974: 191) Like a tradition, in massive novels, the heroine is always abused by her step-mother after their blood-mother died.

Besides, Beauvoir reveals mothers' control on their daughters, because they regard their daughters as their "alter ego" and when they want to be independent, they think they are "ungrateful". "The little girl comes nearer to being wholly given to her mother... in her she seeks a double. She projects upon her daughter all the ambiguity of her relation with herself; and wen the otherness of this 'alter ego' manifests itself, the mother feels herself betrayed." (Beauvoir, 1974: 496) After that, envy will come up, especially in the relationship between their husband and their daughter. " The jealousy is at first concerned with relations between the little girl and her father... Frequently, the oldest girl, the father's favorite, is the special object of the mother's persecution." (Beauvoir,1974: 497) Beauvoir argued that "it seems to her mother that she is robbed of this future which opens before her daughter. " and finally they even grasp their husband's love which is the most essential for them while they are already less competitive. They cannot tolerate any woman stealing their husband's love even their daughters so they are incline to be hostile to these kind of young females.

2.2　Characterization of Mrs. Reed in *Jane Eyre*

The character of Mrs. Reed is a remorse and hypocritical woman who has no mercy on Jane. Features of the character are mainly manifested through her behaviors, utterance and the reasons behind them.

Mrs. Reed is a wealthy widow guardian to Jane and the wife of Jane's dead uncle. She was bound by a deathbed promise to her husband to raise and take care of Jane. However, Mrs. Reed doesn't like Jane at all. She made discriminatory regulations on her kids and Jane "Me, she had dispensed from joining the group; saying, She regretted to be under the necessity of keeping me at a distance", (Bronte, 1951: 1) and ignores her children's abuse on Jane and even helps them when Jane gives a rebellion " Mrs. Reed was blind and deaf on the subject: she never saw him strike or heard him abuse me, though he did both now and then in her very presence, more frequently, however, behind her back." Jane's obedience to all the unfairness and gratitude for her raising are always wanted. Reed John said that "You ought beg ... and wear clothes at our mama's expense." (Bronte, 1951: 1) The maid also said that " You ought to be aware that you are under obligations to Mrs. Reed: she keeps you; if she turns you off ,you would have to go poorhouse." "You ought not to think yourself on equality with Misses Reed and Master Reed, because they kindly allows you to be brought up here." (Bronte, 1951: 2) When Jane reveled Mrs. Reed's guilt, she felt terrified so she tries to slander the little girl in front of the headmaster Mr. Brocklehurst to keep her hypocrisy. Even when Jane grew up and returned to see her in her last illness when Jane took the initial step to forgive her, she didn't turn a pleased and tolerant face to Jane. "Again she regarded me so icily, I felt at once that her opinion of me—her feeling towards me—was unchanged and unchangeable. I knew by her stony eye—opaque to tenderness, indissoluble to tears—that she was resolved to consider me bad to the last; because to believe me good would give her no generous pleasure: only a sense of mortification." (Bronte, 1951, 21) Through these lines, a typical ruthless guardian to young child is shaped which is like the role of step-mother who makes a hero's pitiful childhood.

Apart from this, the reason behind the merciless woman is worthy of exploration. Mrs.Reed's detestation may come from Jane's mother. " I had a dislike to her mother always; for she was my husband's only sister, and a great favourite with him: he opposed the family's disowning her when she made her low marriage; and when news came of her death, he wept like a simpleton. He would send for the baby; though I entreated him rather to put it out to nurse and pay for its maintenance." "In his last illness, he had it brought continually to his bedside; and but an hour before he died, he bound me by vow to keep the creature. I would as soon have been charged with a pauper brat out of a workhouse: but he was weak, naturally weak. "(Bronte, 1951: 21) We found that even in the her last time, Mrs. Reed even didn't feel ashamed towards Jane which we can interpreted as her stubbornness over her dignity (Bao Xiuwen,1999: 01) but we cannot deny that from these lines, we know that Mrs. Reed is jealous of her husband's preference to Jane's mother and Jane who is the typical woman character with envy of other women because of man's love.

2.3   Shortness of Feminism in Mrs. Reed

From what we have discussed above, we can find that Mrs. Reed is the very image of step-mother who envies of the young girl because of her rebelled quality and another man's love. But what this paper wants to point out is that the characterization of Mrs.Reed is just man's domination on woman. Because man's scare of woman's reproduction magic, they defend mothers by shaping the evil step-mother when they honor mother. They make it a tradition in literature, so readers have the established prejudice on step-mother and the author are more inclined to shape an evil aunt rather than an evil uncle. In addition, Mrs.Reed's jealousy on Jane proves woman's otherness because they count on man's attention and are hostile to another good young woman who even has the man's love. As a result, the characterizing of Mrs. Reed reflects the man's dominating views in people's subconsciousness and woman's hidden subordinating intention.

Chapter 3   Shortness of Feminism in Ending of Rochester in Adultery

3.1   Adultery in *The Second Sex*

Beauvoir pointed out that after the private ownership came out, women were totally be subjugated by men. "Private property appears: master of slaves and of the earth, man becomes the proprietor also of woman. This was 'the great historical defeat of the feminine sex'." (Beauvoir, 1949: 4) Subsequently, Beauvoir hit the nail on the head that people hold more tolerance towards men than women in adultery in patriarchal society. "Martial infidelity in our civilization still seems much more heinous for the wife than husband. Montaigne remarks: 'the severity of our decrees makes the addiction of woman to this vice a sorer fault than its nature warrants.' Woman's adultery risks bringing the son of a stranger into the family, and thus defrauding legitimate heirs ; the husband is master, the wife his property. " (Beauvoir, 1974: 480) Actually, polygamy has been transmitted for long history and still exists in many countries. Even in some countries, monogamy is settled as a law. However, because men take the dominate role of their property and society, so the society is still more tolerant to man's adultery and just consider it as a issue of morality.

3.2   Ending of Rochester's Adultery

Rochester is the hero of the book who is the most important to the heroine. However, he is a typical symbol of patriarchal oppression towards woman. We can see from his words to Jane "Do you agree with me that I have a right to be a little masterful, abrupt; perhaps exacting, sometime, on the grounds I stated; namely that I am old enough to be your father, and that I have a varied experience with many men of many nations, and roamed over half the globe, while you have lived quietly with one set of people in one house? " (Bronte, 1951: 20) Besides, Rochester is also a terrible patriarchal oppression to Bertha didn't utter a word at all because of her loss of discourse right. Her image is shaped by Rochester "Bertha Mason is mad; and she came of a mad family; idiots and maniacs through three generations!" "Bertha, like a dutiful child, copied her parent in both points. I had a charming partner- pure, wise, modest: you can fancy I was a happy man. I went through rich scenes! " (Bronte, 1951: 26) Bertha is Rochester's legal wife, but he still has love affair with Jane and want to got remarried. There is no doubt that he has an adultery, but he asserts him as a victim of a woman who he get married with to get a big fortune. " That is my wife, 'said he.' Such is the sole conjugal embrace I am ever to know—such are the endearments which are to solace my leisure hours! And this is what I wished to have." (Bronte, 1951: 26) However, things may don't go like what he claimed. Maybe like in *Wide Sargasso Sea*, (Jean Rhys,1966) Rochester was extremely merciless to drive her crazy. However, they have totally different endings. Bertha died because of her wishes to escape from the cruelty; while, even Rochester sacrificed to save Bertha but finally reunited with his beloved Jane. However, if we see thoroughly, we can find that the pitiful abandoned woman died with the cruel man who committed the adultery gaining his love.

3.3   Shortness of Feminism in Ending of Rochester's Adultery

The author tries to create a happy ending for the hero and heroine which is also a lot of readers' wish. But we see from the start to the end. We found Rochester is much more a beneficiary even he committed the adultery. Even though Jane left at the first time, but after the plot of his salvation which is also made Bertha—the obstacle dismissed, she finally get married with the patriarchal figure, while the victim of the adultery died silently. It greatly manifested the tolerance the patriarchal society gives to man which doesn't care woman's right and fairness.

Chapter 4   Shortness of Feminism on Marriage and Family

4.1   Marriage and Family in *The Second Sex*

Marriage is regarded as the " destiny traditionally offered " of a woman in *The Second Sex* "For girls marriage is the only means of integration in the community, and, if they remain unwanted, they are socially viewed, so much wastage." (Beauvoir, 1974: 417) Women are incomplete in society where they cannot function because the patriarchal systems and only through their marriage with a family, her territory where she can be the master. Actually, woman's work in family is less valued than man's creative work. " The same cause which had assured to woman the prime authority in the house – namely, her restriction to domestic duties – this same cause now assured the domination there of the man; for woman's housework henceforth sank into insignificance in comparison with man's productive labor – the latter as everything, the former a trifling auxiliary." But, the established view of "a good marriage counts more than their effort for women" is transmitted through generations of women and thus is consolidated. As a result nearly all the women are taught to set a good marriage as their life purpose rather than strive and work by themselves even if they have the same talents and ability. This will make them pay more attention to attract and cater to men, be a good hostess and less to develop themselves to compete with men, which will strengthen their inequality in return. Beauvoir insists in *the Second Sex* that women can change their conditions, but most women mistakenly look for salvation in love. In the book, Beauvoir conjures up an image of " independent woman" who wants to be active, a taker, and refuses the passive man means to impose on her. The modern woman accepts masculine values; she prides herself on thinking, taking action, working, creating on the same terms as man. (Beauvoir, 1974: 674-675) Beauvoir means that women should make efforts to be independent, rather than seek salvation in marriage and make themselves confined to family.

4.2　The Plotting of Inheritance and Return to Family

Jane said she didn't want to play the role of "doing pudding, knitting socks, playing the piano, and sewing the embroidery pocket " before. (Bronte，1951: 17) Actually, she has her own ability to earn her own life and to explore the outside world. But the author doesn't make Jane an independent woman in society too deeply. She just made her a plain governess and then a heiress of a big fortune which can provide her easy life with Rochester rather than a woman really enters the social economy and has her own career. On the contrary, after hearing Rochester's situation, she came back and bound herself to the marriage and family. Jane promises Rochester that "I will be your nurse, your housekeeper. " (Bronte, 1951: 30) She will take the responsibility to take care of Rochester and doing the laundry even she said she detest such roles made by men before . When she came back to Rochester, she even called him "dear master " which can also show her relying on the man. So we can see even Jane is independent to some degree, but she is still dependent in love and finally drawback to family to be a subordination of man. (He Xiaomei, 2015: 2) She aims no realizing her own value in the world but realizing her value as a wife. She cannot really be independent from man.

4.3　Shortness of Feminism on Marriage and Family

Because of the strict priest family and special life experience Charlotte received rigorous education and only contacted with a few men—her father, her brothers and her literature teacher Eger. (Marty, Martin E 1959: 22) So she always held the worship of men just like she said "If one

day I get married with my husband, I must admire him even I will be willing to die for him."
(Gaskell Elizabeth, 1999: 5) Therefore, she deems that the love of family and marriage is the most
important and a good destination for a woman is a good marriage. (Yang Jingyuan, 1983: 2) Actually,
in the Victorian age, woman's economic rights were ruthlessly deprived by the society while the
education for women is mainly aimed to develop more gentlewoman-like housewives. The life goal
of moat women in that time is to be " the angle in the house". (Ardis L, 1984: 3) Besides, Charlotte
belongs to the petty bourgeoisie, (Chen Huijun, 2012: 1) which has no much power to participate
and even interfere the social economy and politics, let alone the women of petty bourgeoisie, so she
has no idea about how to make fortune and have a better position in society so that she can only
inherit a heritage to fill the huge gap in class between Jane and Rochester. And only in this way, Jane
can get out from the labor of survival and concentrate on her own marriage and family. Nancy Pell
argues that "the legacy that Jane receives from her uncle in Madeira makes possible her reunion with
Rochester that also significantly redefines her relationship to patriarchal structures." (Nancy, 1977:
415) Actually, "marriage is and still will be a big load and shackle towards women". (Yang Jingjing,
2008: 2) Marriage will be a long—lasting trap for women to jump out no matter in contemporary or
in the future. Besides, this is a powerful proof to demonstrate the shortness of feminism in book
because of the author's life experience which is finally determined by history.

Chapter 5   Conclusions

Jane Eyre is a classic book of great significance about feminism. The great author Charlotte
Bronte presents ideas of women that are considered " indecent" and rebellious in that Victorian age.
But she undoubtedly throw light on women by fighting against oppressive patriarchal society bravely.
It is unprecedented and momentous towards development of feminism.The greatness of the heroine
—Jane affected a tremendous amount of women. A lot of women are enlightened by the great Jane
and become the new kinds of women like her. Apart from this, it also strikes the literature world for
its theme with everlasting and abundant meanings. Indeed, it's the treasure of the feminism literature.
However, " Humanity is not an animal species, it is a historical reality. " (Beauvoir，1949：4) every
person is a historical person, and there is no exception for the great author. So the masterpiece also
has its shortness of feminism which are determined by the historic situations. We discuss and explore
this deficiencies under the direction of another great work—*The Second Sex*, which is also the
prominent masterpiece. We discovered that setting Mrs. Reed as a stepmother image like many fairy
tales is actually one kind of man's intentional characterization to restrain woman, the forgiveness on
Rochester in adultery actually reflects society's better tolerance towards man's adultery and the
return to family and marriage of the heroine actually reflects woman's deep restriction and
dependence on marriage. So that we can learn the book and the feminism more deeply and more
thoroughly. After that, we can have the better recognition of our own situations in contemporary
society and we can apply our findings to revolt against oppression and keep advancing in feminism.

References

[1] Bronte Charlotte. *Jane Eyre.* CRW Publishing. 1951.

[2] Beauvoir Simone de. The Second Sex, Le deuxième sexe, 1949.

[3] Gaskell Elizabeth. The Life of Charlotte Bronte . London: Penguin Books, 1999.

[4] Marty, Martin E.A Short History of English Literature, Living Age Books, 1959.

[5] Rhys Jean. *Wide Sargasso Sea,* André Deutsch (UK), 1966.

[6] 鲍秀文. 简·爱中里德太太形象分析[J]. 浙江师范大学学报，1999（1）：56-57.

[7] 陈慧君. 论女性主义的彰显与不足——兼评《傲慢与偏见》《简·爱》《德伯家的苔丝》[J]. 湖北经济学院学报，2012，9（4）：117-118.

[8] 冯翠翠. "自我"与"本我"——简与伯莎·梅森关系的再解读[J]. 世界文化，2007（10）：7-9.

[9] 贺晓梅. 抗争与妥协——《简·爱》中女性意识的觉醒和缺憾[J]. 语文建设，2015（3）：46-47.

[10] 刘晶.《简·爱》的后殖民主义解读[D]. 曲阜师范大学，2008.

[11] 路甬祥. 简·爱的性格分析[M] 北京：北京大学出版社，2006.

[12] 吴朋.《简·爱》中简·爱的人格魅力[J]. 外语界学报，2001（8）.

[13] 王惠昭. 浅析《简·爱》中的女性价值观[J]. 外语与外语教学，2001（10）.

[14] 杨静远. 勃朗特姐妹研究[M]. 北京：中国社会科学出版社，1983.

[15] 杨菁菁. 重活话语权的第二性——《藻海无边》和《简·爱》比较分析[J]. 科技创新导报，2008（20）：147-147.

Contrast Analysis of Irony Between *Emma* and *Pride and Prejudice*

李　娜

摘　要： 反讽是一种文学或演讲常见的修辞手法，常常以一种与原义相反的表达来达到一种讽刺或者夸张的效果。反讽属于修辞学的一个重要组成部分，具有不同的类型：语言反讽、结构反讽、情境反讽和戏剧反讽。本篇文章将以 19 世纪著名小说家简·奥斯汀的两部著名爱情小说为研究文本来分析语言反讽和结构反讽的相同点和不同点。《爱玛》和《傲慢与偏见》正是结构反讽和语言反讽的典型代表。通过对比和分析作者在两篇小说两种不同的反讽手法，试归纳总结出结构反讽与语言反讽的不同作用和功能，通过对比的方式来突出差异，然后分析两种反讽手法在文本中具体体现的作用，从而得出结论。了解反讽修辞以及不同类型的反讽手法有助于我们更好地欣赏文学作品和体验修辞艺术的美妙。

关键词： 反讽；结构反讽；语言反讽；简·奥斯汀；《爱玛》；《傲慢与偏见》；修辞学

Abstract： Irony is a commonly rhetorical technique, mainly used in the literary or speech in order to achieve the purpose of satire or exaggeration, and irony as an important part in rhetoric could be classified different types. Such as verbal irony, structure irony, situational irony and dramatic irony. This paper mainly studies the similarities and differences between structure irony and verbal irony by the typical examples of *Emma* and *Pride and Prejudice* written by Jane·Austen in 19th century. Comparing and analyzing the way that the two types of irony is used and concluding what are different functions of these two different irony types. The methods in the paper are comparing and analyzing. The differences of two kinds of irony could be showed by comparing and analyzing, to conclude the specific functions of structure irony and verbal irony. It helps readers to appreciate the literature works better and taste the interests of rhetoric as a language art.

Key Words: Irony, structure irony, verbal irony, Jane Austen, *Emma*, *Pride and Prejudice*, rhetoric

Chapter 1　Introduction

Irony is a kind of language style which has opposite meaning with the literal surface to express and achieve a kind of ironic effect and critical purpose. Irony belongs to an important part of Rhetoric. For a long time, irony is the important object of study in philosophy, literature and rhetoric because of attractive communicative value as a part of rhetoric. Stepping into the 20th century, with the development of modern linguistics, especially cognitive linguistics and pragmatics, people found irony is challenge to the all kinds of explanation theories about language as a not straight language. Thus, the interest for studying irony has been strengthened day by day. So far, irony has become a dominant research topic crossing linguistic philosophy, psychology literary criticism, cognitive linguistics and rhetoric and so on. The rhetoric has become a complete system.

Meanwhile, romantic novels became popular in the 19th and Jane, Austen is a symbol of novelist makes a great contribution to apply and develop irony to describe love and marriages in her works. Emma and Pride and Prejudice are the two famous love novels of her works. But it's different in the characters and description devices in the two novels. In terms of irony, it mainly uses structural irony in Emma and there is a lot of verbal irony in the Pride and Prejudice. In Emma, the structural irony is showed by the unexpected plot development, and the protagonist, Emma's characteristics and character image could be seen from the changes of plots, such as self-assertive, incongruous with a lot of disadvantages, while Elizabeth in Pride and Prejudice is minded and independent by the means of conversations and actions of Elizabeth in the way of verbal irony.

Thus, this paper will focus on the different function between structure irony and verbal irony by analyzing these two texts. This paper mainly talks about structure irony and verbal irony by comparing the two different novels.

Firstly, this paper will mainly narrative the stories of Emma and Pride and Prejudice. Telling the main characters and the plots.

Secondly, this paper will analyze the irony in this two different texts, to explore what's the difference between two types of different irony in this two novels and what's the functions of using different irony and how to help the writer to develop articles.

Thirdly, trying to conclude what the different and similar functions have between structure irony and verbal irony.

Fourthly, this paper will analyze why the author so knee to use irony in her works according to writer's own experience. Why the writer use different types of irony in two novels with the similar theme. Is it acceptable that changing the irony methods or exchanging each other's the irony methods between two novels? If not, what's the reason for it.

It is helpful to be familiar with irony specifically and know more about the Jane Austen's works.

Emma is regarded as the symbolized novel in irony and is a sublime position in the history of literature.Pride and Prejudice is another famous novel about women's love and status and there are a lot of irony figures of speech to shape the characters in it. Comparing to the similarity and difference of irony in Emma and Pride and Prejudice, which is helpful to distinguish the functions of irony and appreciate the literature works. We can see how to adopt to the irony in writing and we also could learn how to appreciate the satire literature. What's more, irony is a kind of language art and has its unique aesthetic value. Handling the skills, we could make our speech more vivid and more powerful. We could feel the interest fantastic of language.

Chapter 2　Brief Introduction to Irony

2.1　Definition of Irony

Irony, as an art form, has a long history of evolution. It comes from the Greek, which means that falsehood is thought to be true. In the Lecture on the History of Philosophy written by Hegel, he thought: Irony is infinite and absolute negation. (索伦·奥碧·克尔凯郭尔, 225) This notion is the definition of irony in philosophy and this paper won't discuss too much details about it . However, there is no unified definition of irony because its meaning and the use are more extensive than the Chinese meaning.The word in the paper is used as a rhetorical device, with the meaning of "sarcasm". Irony is a kind of language style which has opposite meaning with the literal surface to express and achieve a kind of ironic effect and critical purpose. (苗琴, 14) In a previous study, comparing the different irony and finding that there are at least five elements. It should (a)be evaluative. (b) be based on incongruence of the ironic utterance with co-or context. (c)be based on reversal of valence between literary and intended meaning. (d) be aimed at some target.(e) be relevant to the communicative situation in some way (Burgers, Van Mulken, & Schellens, 2011) By the early 19th century, the meaning of irony expanded further and it was widely used as an artistic technique.

2.2 The classification of Irony

Generally, the irony is classified as classical irony, romantic irony, cosmic irony, structural irony, verbal irony , situational irony, dramatic irony and tragic irony. However, the myriad possible communicative goals of ironic comments indicate that irony can be used in a various way. So scholars suggest that irony has various subtypes. (Christian Burgers, 291)

2.3 The Structural Irony and Verbal Irony

2.3.1 The Structural Irony

According to the M.h.Abrams' definition: "Structural irony is that an innocent protagonist or an innocent narrator, and she or he cannot overcome own shallow- brained and follows his/her own bigoted course. But the reader could realize the mistakes and share the author's views in the behind of the simple character. What's more, the readers could correct the mistakes under the requirement of the writer." The structural irony depends on the reader could share the ironic intention from the writer, actually, which is a kind of compliment to the reader's intelligence. So what's the key is creating a stupid hero and sharing the truth with the reader and writer together. (刘丹翎, 146)

2.3.2 The Verbal Irony

In recent years, the most influential study of irony from the pragmatic perspective is Sperber interpretation and Wilson's echoic interpretation theory of irony (Sperber and Wilson, 1981, 1986; Sperber, 1984; Wilson and Sperber,1992). They creatively the concept of"each" and define verbal irony as a variety of echoic interpretive use, in which the speaker dissociates himself/herself from the opinion echoed with accompanying ridicule or scorn. Therefore, for the identification of verbal irony it is essential to find the echoic quality of the utterance and the speaker's attitude of dissociation towards this utterance. (Hong zhao, 176)

2.4 The Irony in 19th Century and Introduction of the Author

The 18th century is an important age in the history of England, and the literature in this time is named by the historian: "the Augustans", which means it is similar with the Augustan age in ancient Rome with the stable society and a lot of poets, novelists and essayists. The characteristic in this time is epic ,rural and ironic. And this age also named : a great age of irony. (刘丹翎, 145)   In the 19th, romanticism springs up and the Augustans is still continuing. Jane·Austen (1755—1871)   is born in the end of 18th, and lives in beginning of 19th. Thus, irony has an affect on her works to a great extent.

Chapter 3   The Irony in the Novels

3.1   The Summary of Emma and Pride and Prejudice

3.1.1   The Main Idea about Emma

Although convinced that she herself will never marry, Emma Woodhouse, a precocious twenty-year-old resident of the village of Highbury, images herself to be naturally gifted in conjuring love matches. There are two new visitors in Highbury—Frank Churchill and Jane Fairfax. The story happens among the young men and women in this town. She makes her friend- Herriet Smith break up with Robert Martin, a well-to-do farmer for whom Harriet clearly has feelings, and Herriet Smith becomes infatuated with Mr.Elton under her encourages. But Elton likes Emma. And then she makes a match between Mr Frank and Herriet. Meanwhile, she thinks Jane will fall in love with her brother-in -law and treasured- friend—Mr.Knightley. At last, she found she and Knightley love each other and Frank has been secretly engaged with Jane. Besides, Herriet accepted the second proposal from Robert Martin.

3.1.2   The Main Idea About Pride and Prejudice

The story is surrounded by a family of Benet with five daughters and their marriages. A young man named, Bingley moves into Netherfield and becomes their neighbor. He falls in love with the biggest daughter—Jane. Meanwhile, Mr.Bingley's friend, Darcy loves the second girl—Elizabeth. In fact, Elizabeth loves Bingley, too. But she believes in the calumny to Bingley from Wayne and has the prejudice to him. Furthermore, Darcy is pride of his wealth and status. So she refused the proposal from Darcy. In the end, the misunderstanding is eliminated the two persons change the pride and prejudice towards each other and they get married.

3.2   The Structural Irony in Emma

Emma is regarded by some literary critic as the maturest work in artistic technique in the Austen's works. (刘丹翎, 146) And Dr.Kettle thinks this novel is the greatest and the most representative work during the Austen's life. Furthermore, the structural irony is the symbol of characteristic in *Emma*. The specific analysis about structural irony in the text as the following.

3.2.1   The Reversal Between Emma's Expectation and the Reality:

Emma strongly breaks apart Herriet and Martin because she thinks Martin as a farmer   cannot deserve Herriet. So she wants Herriet to make friend with Elton. She think Herriet won't marry far away from her and she could take the control of Herriet In this way. But Elton likes Emma and marries another woman after accepting the refuse from Emma; She think Jane and Knightley will be a good couple and it turns out to be Jane and Frank have the engagement earlier. She swears she never gets a marriage while she finds she loves Knightley finally. All of what happened is totally out of the Austen's expectations, which confirms that how ridiculous Emma is.This is a kind of structural irony adopting to the plots. From the strong and ironic reversal between Emma's desire and the truth, we can see that Emma is arrogant and stubborn.

3.2.2　The Free Indirect Speech

In the novel, the write tells the story in the third person. More importantly, the free indirect speech is largely used in the text. The reader and the author are put together in this way, which likes the author is a friend who is telling a story she knows. The reader witness the characters' s mistakes as a calm spectator. In 1.3.1, we know about the structural irony is about creating a stupid hero and sharing the truth with the reader and writer together. Thus,Austen in *Emma* makes it.

Such as in the chapter 1 in *Emma*. There is a description about Emma "The real evils,indeed, of Emma's situation were the power of having rather too much her own way. And a disposition to think a little too well her self; Those were the disadvantages which threatened alloy to her many enjoyment." As we could know from the words, the author describes Emma's characteristics directly and tells the reader what's the person is .

In chapter 3. After meeting Herriet, Emma thinks of her that "the acquaintance she had already formed were unworthy of her. The friends from whom she had just parted ,though very good sort of people, must be dong her harm" Emma defines Herriet according to her assumption.　For the inner activity of Emma, Austen uses the free indirect to reveal, which makes the reader knows that what a ridiculous the image is! There are a lot of such description of Emma in the article, which makes the reader understands thoroughly Emma and enjoys the pleasure under the guide from the writer and the irony to the character.

3.2.3　The Protagonist as the Victim of irony

The protagonist Emma is shaped as a pride, self-conceit, selfish even stupid person in the novels. So Emma exits as an subject of satire. The character is a sacrificial lamb in the irony. The reader and the author are as the wise witness to watch the story. At last, the structural irony ends when Emma grows up and becomes mature.

3.3　The Verbal Irony in *Pride and Prejudice*

3.3.1　The Verbal Irony in the Conversations

The verbal irony in Pride and Prejudice is showed by the dialogues. In the first person and the direct speech, the characters are shaped in the novel. Such as a conversation between Mr. Benet and Mrs. Benet :

" Mr Benet, how can you abuse your own children in such way? You take delight in vexing me. You have no compassion on my poor nerves."

"You mistakes me ,my dear. I have a high respect for your nerves. They are my old friends."

As we can see from this, Mr. Benet didn't care about his wife's poor nerves because she mentions it for twenties years. But he tells her he respect it very much. The verbal irony in the dialogues occupies main location in the article, which makes the passage more humorous and the character more vivid.

3.3.2　The Echo in the Verbal Irony

The echo is frequent in the conversation, for example the conversations in the Mr. Bingley's house between Elizabeth and Darcy:

"Mr.Darcy is not to be laughed at."

"My temper would perhaps be called resentful: my good opinion once lost is last for ever."

"That is a failing indeed! Implacable resentment is a shade in a character. But you have choose your fault well. I really cannot laugh at it; you are safe from me."

Elizabeth mocks Darcy is a person that cannot be laughed, and then telling him I won't laugh at you. But in fact, she is laughing at him. The echo in the conversation shows the wisdom of Elizabeth and prejudice to Darcy.

Chapter 4　The Contrast of Structural irony and Verbal Irony

4.1　The similarity between Structural Irony and Verbal Irony

4.1.1　Shaping Characters

Irony is a good way to shape the characters. As we could know Emma is a beautiful, smart and wealthy girl but she is stubborn and illusioned in the structural irony. She takes actions according to her imagination and assumption. What she make the mistakes are showed by the structural irony; While Elizabeth is intelligent, capable, brave, independent, sincere and unit. She ignores the social customs and follows her own heart to pursue the freedom and happiness bravely. (苗琴, 15) And her such imagination is shaped by what she said and did in the dialogues. Because she has a kind of prejudice and misunderstanding for the Darcy's pride, her words mostly are ironic. So the verbal irony in her words expresses her intelligent, capable and brave characteristics.

4.1.2　Organizing and Promoting Plots

The structural irony in Emma is mainly used in the reversal of plots. Every reversal is a climax of the story. The story is pushed again and again through the changes of plots. The Emma realizes her mistakes when the structural irony stops and then the story ends. And the verbal irony express the action's of characters. Especially Elizabeth has prejudice to Darcy, so she has ironic words toward him.Gradually, she found she is wrong, and she changes her attitude and the verbal irony reduces. Irony implies the development of plots and reveals the development of plots.

4.1.3　Reinforcing the Theme

The theme in *Emma* and *Pride and Prejudice* is the marriage not only care about money but also love. In *Emma*, Emma thinks the marriage should be equal status and perfect match. Thus, she wants to arrange the people's marriage around her. However, she finds she is totally wrong by the structural irony. In the marriage, love is the base. Meanwhile, in Pride and Prejudice, Elizabeth doesn't accept Darcy' love. Because Darcy is pride of his wealth. So she pursues the marriage above the respect and love. In the beginning of the novel: it is a truth universally acknowledged, that a single man in possession of a good fortune must be in want of a wife. This sentence satires the social phenomenon that the marriage depends on the wealth.

4.2 The Difference Between the Structural Irony and Verbal Irony

4.2.1 The Object of Satire

In *Emma*, the object of satire is Emma.The structural irony is achieved by the showing Emma's defects in character. But in *Pride and prejudice,* the characters are the issuers showed by verbal irony. The reader will have a kind of feeling of through the global to read the story in a superior location in the structural irony as the wise. And the reader could feel the wisdom of characters and enjoy the charming of language.

4.2.2 Different Person Statements

In Emma, the author uses the third person and the free indirect speech to tell the story, which could put the reader into an objective perspective in the structural irony. The first person and the direct person is used in the verbal irony in Pride and Prejudice. It makes the characters in novels vivider and fresher.

4.2.3 .Different Character Images

Emma is a stupid person that is spoiled by her father and tutor. Thus, not only is she lively, but also she is stubborn and illusioned. Because the structural irony requires a such person to feel and share the presentiment between the author and the reader. Elizabeth is intelligent, capable, brave, independent, sincere and unit. Her image is shaped by the verbal irony in the conversations. So the two different irony shape two kinds of person. The character in structural irony is pejorative to some degree. And the verbal irony is a foil to image according the specific context.

4.2.4 Different Perspectives

In Emma, the writer and the reader explore the story in a objective view because of the adoption of third person. The audience knows what's wrong with the characters and have their own judgment. But in Pride and Prejudice, the author plugs the reader in the role of Elizabeth by using the first person. And the motion of readers is changeable with the mind of Elizabeth.

After knowing the differences and similarity between the structural irony and verbal irony, Let's suppose that whether exchange the type of irony between Emma and Pride and Prejudice? Obviously, no. Because the two characters are different totally. And the structural is suitable for *Emma* because Emma has the flaw. Elizabeth is a positive image that needs the verbal irony to shape.

Chapter 6   Conclusions

Above all, this paper explains the irony and distinguishes the structural irony and the verbal irony specifically. What's the irony in the literature and what are differences and similarities between two different ironies, and how to use them. By the case of Emma and Pride and Prejudice, this paper analyzes the functions of the irony in the literature as a kind of rhetoric. It is beneficial to better understanding and appreciate of Austen's favor style of writing: styles vary according to the extent to writer uses linguistically specific devices to constrain the hearer's choice of context, and the speaker chooses. But the paper didn't draws a regular rule about two kinds of irony. This paper just did a analysis according to the specific context. Hopefully, there are more researches about irony in the future.

References

[1] Jane Austen.Pride and Prejudice. Beijng: Central complication& Translation Press. 2012.

[2] Jane Austen. Emma. London: Penguin English Library, 1994.

[3] Miao qin, The Art of Irony in Pride and Prejudice [J]. 青春岁月，2013（7）：14-15.

[4] 简·奥斯汀. 爱玛[M]. 李文慧，等译. 北京：人民文学出版社，2005.

[5] 荣鹏涛. 简奥斯汀小说的讽刺艺术新探[J]. 语文建设报，2016（8）：56.

[6] 刘丹翎. 简奥斯汀的小说《爱玛》中的反讽艺术特色[J]. 西北大学学报，2003，33（3）：145-150.

[7] 索伦·奥碧·克尔凯郭尔. 论反讽的概念——以苏格拉底为主线[M]. 北京：北京大学出版社，2003.

[8] 王银萍. 论《爱玛》的反讽艺术[J]. 阜阳师范学院学报，2015（5）：41-44.

[9] 王红丽. The Image of Emma Shaped by Irony——On Jane Austen's Feminist Consciousness[D]. 郑州大学，2007.

[10] 王可. 论简·奥斯汀小说的讽刺艺术[J]. 芒种，2015（7）：127-128.

[11] 王晓越. Analysis on the Humor and Irony in Pride and Prejudice[J]. 校园英语，2016（3）：247-248.

[12] 肖铖. 分析小说《傲慢与偏见》在结构和人物性格中讽刺的运用[J]. 西藏大学学报，2002，17（2）：66-71.

Feminist Study of Mary Shelley's *Frankenstein*

李盈吟

摘　要： 在世界不断发展的过程中，女性主义这个话题愈发深入人心。女性主义不仅体现在各类女权运动中，还体现在人们对女性的认可与赞赏的态度，这是在以前男权社会绝对不会出现的情形。在女性解放运动中，一大波卓越的女性用自己的行动为全世界妇女同胞做了示范，特别是在文学领域，我们熟知的有西蒙波娃的《第二性》，罗斯玛丽的《女性主义思潮导论》，还有李银河的《两性关系》。但早在 19 世纪 20 年代，英国女作家玛丽雪莱就发表了对女权运动有极大推进作用的《弗兰肯斯坦》。《弗兰肯斯坦》被认为是世界上第一本真正意义上的科幻小说，书中所描述的资本主义与科学技术的发展、人类与自然的关系以及哥特风格都十分具有研究价值。而一些专家也指出，玛丽雪莱在《弗兰肯斯坦》中也向大家展示了她独特的女性主义思想。她的女性主义思想不仅体现在小说文本中，也体现在玛丽雪莱的人生经历中。在小说中，她将书中主要的女性角色塑造成完美天使，不仅拥有美好的面庞和独立自强，还拥有高尚的心灵和丰富的知识，这些女人也是书中男性所疼爱和需要的。她的这种安排似乎是在昭告世界她的女性主义观点：女人就该是独立且完美的。通过她命途多舛的人生经历，我们也能看出她对境遇悲惨，多磨多难的女性的态度：独立且自强。因为她自己就经历了足以让女人，甚至男人精神崩溃的丧母和丧子之痛。玛丽雪莱的《弗兰肯斯坦》对世界女权运动所起的作用是不可忽视的，而世界女权运动也在一定程度上将玛丽雪莱与《弗兰肯斯坦》推上新高度。

关键词： 女性主义；《弗兰肯斯坦》；玛丽·雪莱

Abstract: In the process of the world's civilizing and development, the subject of feminism has gained much more attention and popularity among people. Feminism, which can be found not only in various feminist movements but also in people's recognition and appreciation for women, was absolutely forbidden in the patriarchal society. In the world feminist movements, many remarkable women have had demonstration effect on feminist movements with their own efforts, especially in the field of literature. *The Second Sex* by Simone de Beauvoir, *Feminist Thought: A More Comprehensive Introduction* by Rosemarie Putnam Tong and *Sex Gender* by Li Yinhe are familiar to us. But as early as 1920s, an English female writer Mary Shelley has published her novel *Frankenstein,* which was regarded to have pushed world feminist movements forward greatly. *Frankenstein*, the world`s first science fiction, embodies the development of capitalism and science and technology, the relationship between human and nature and the Gothic horror factors, which was of significant research value. Scholars also found that Mary had added unique feminist consciousness to the book. Her feminist views exist not only in between the lines of the book, but in the research of the author herself. In the book, Mary described the major female characters as perfect angels who are in possession of not only pretty faces but also independent, gracious hearts and wide range of knowledge. These women in her book, are also cared and loved by men. Mary Shelley tries to convey her feminist consciousness that women are designed to be independent and perfect. In addition, through Mary Shelley's tough life experiences, her wishes to all the women who have suffered or not is that women should stay independent and strong on themselves, since she herself had suffered from the pain of losing her mother and her babies but she stills holds on to the life she had. Admittedly, Mary Shelley`s *Frankenstein* has promoted the feminist movements worldwide and in the meantime, feminist movements have guided Mary and *Frankenstein* to a new stage of history.

Key Words: Feminism, *Frankenstein,* Mary Shelley

Chapter 1   Introduction

This paper focuses on the great female writer Mary Shelley's world-renowned book *Frankenstein,* seen from the perspective of feminism. Mary Shelley writes a number of novels, stories, and journals. However, she is particularly famous for *Frankenstein,*or *The Modern Prometheus*, which is her canonical contribution to the literary world. She wrote the novel when she was only eighteen years old. As the first science fiction with high literary value, the novel gains timeless popularity. *Frankenstein* embodies elements of the Gothic novel and the Romantic movement. At the same time, it is an early example of science fiction. Brian Aldiss has argued that it should be considered the first true science fiction story because, in contrast to previous stories with fantastical elements resembling those of later science fiction, the central character "makes a deliberate decision" and "turns to modern experiments in the laboratory" to achieve fantastic results. It has considerable influence on literature and popular culture and spawned a complete genre of horror stories, films and plays. Seen from the perspective of feminism, Mary Shelley has described women in her book as angels who deserved men's care and love and she gives the main character an reflection of females. Also, she stressed that women's social function can not be ignored through the story of creating the female monster. In the meantime, Mary Shelley herself represented the ideal female image in her time when the society was dominated by men. Her parents were both outstanding at that time and her mother was a famous feminist. Because of her parents, she had the access to lots of distinguished guests who came to visit her father and she could read whatever she wanted to in her father's sanctum. In that way she met Percy B. Shelley, a great poet, who later became her husband. Her life experience made her to be extraordinary among her female peers. Thus *Frankenstein* came out and enjoyed long-term popularity. This paper will give a brief introduction of feminism, and secondly the author Mary Shelley's life experience associated with her feminist consciousness. Then most importantly, analyze the book *Frankenstein* from the perspective of feminism. Then the conclusion of the mutual promotion between feminism and Mary's *Frankenstein* and the importance of modern feminism will be drawn.

Chapter 2　First-Wave Feminism in the United Kingdom

2.1　Background Information

First-wave feminism was a period of activity during the 19th century and early twentieth century. In the UK and US, it focused on the promotion of equal contract, marriage, parenting, and property rights for women. By the end of the 19th century, a number of important steps had been made.

Between the 18th and 19th century, England prospered because of the development of science and technology during the Industrial Revolution. What's more, the theories of the Enlightenment renewed people's mind and broadened British citizens' horizon. In the trend of industrialization and political democratization, women walked out of their homes and joined the production link due to lack of labor after the great development of producing methods and soaring demand. Also in the process of political democratization, women were equipped with liberalism and egalitarianism, leading them to political groups and Chartism Movement. They even fought independently for voting rights, equal economic rights and social legislative power. Not only did they improve their own social status, but also they fueled the society with liberalism and pushed the political democratization in England forward.

In the early feminist movements in England, the great Mary Wollstonecraft and Mary Shelley were definitely heroines among the group of women in England. Mary Wollstonecraft was known as the "Pioneer of Modern Feminism" because of her views that women should be educated equally as men and that only in that way can gender equality be achieved. "Women ought to have representatives, instead of being arbitrarily governed without any direct share allowed them in the deliberations of government" (Wollstonecraft, 253). Instructed by her mother, Mary Shelley carried forward her mother`s feminist view and she, with the help of her renowned family background, her literary celebrity friends and her own sympathetic life experience, called for women to take up pens, weapons and knowledge like her to fight for the rights and respect they deserve.

2.2　Feminist Movements

The two great feminists did their best when feminism was first brought to people's mind in the world's industrialization and democratization. Mutually, they two have set a demonstration model for the world's feminist movements, or, in other words, they have accelerated the feminist movements. In the 1830s, the British government passed the *Custody of Infants Act 1839* which granted women the legal custody for their children under the age of seven after divorce. In Britain before 1857 wives were under the economic and legal control of their husbands, and divorce was almost impossible, but the *Matrimonial Causes Act of 1857* ended that unequal situation for women. Before 1870s, prostitution was regarded a horrible sin and in the 1860s, government passed the *Contagious Diseases Acts*, adopting the French way of handling prostitutes, which legalized prostitutes by granting them license and basic respect for their career. By the late 1860s a number of schools were preparing women for careers as governesses or teachers. The census reported in 1851 that 70 000 women in England and Wales were teachers, compared to the 170 000 who comprised three-fourths of all teachers in 1901.

A tremendous number of women have risen from their undervalued position to a comparatively equal and high social status since the 19th century. Undeniably speaking, the development of industry economy and the liberalization of traditional views resulted in the promotion of women`s social status. However, both Mary Wollstonecraft and Mary Shelley contributed to the feminist progress with their own way. Their contribution shall not be forgotten by the history. It can not be ignored that feminist movements and Mary's devotion impact each other with the mutual promotion between them.

Chapter 3   Mary Shelley's Feminist View

Technically speaking, there is no clear evidence that Mary is involved in feminist movements in the firsthand, but we can still find out some of her thoughts are similar to the essential part of feminism. Mary Shelley was born in August 1797 to Mary Wollstonecraft, the great feminist, and William Godwin, the political philosopher. Although she was the daughter of two distinguished celebrity of the time, young Mary never knew her mother because of Wollstonecraft's death. Thanks to her father's large collection of literary books, she could read whatever she wanted and she had the access to the main group of literary celebrities of her time. Many famous literary men frequented her father and in this way she met Percy B. Shelley whom she later married. Her desire for knowledge made her father to look at her in a totally different way. Her father described her as "singularly bold, somewhat imperious, and active of mind. Her desire of knowledge is great, and her perseverance in everything she undertakes almost invincible". (Johnson 1981, xii) Admittedly, Her family background and well-received education provided a foundation for her to become a woman writer.

In the 1920s, Mary finished the revolutionary *Frankenstein,* from the perspective of a woman in the patriarchal society. A lot of researchers have found that Mary is a feminist, to some extent. At that time, women were not allowed or appreciated to possess manly things, such as knowledge, reputation, or political power. But in Mary's family, things are different. Her mother Wollstonecraft was a famous politician and feminist. Wollstonecraft is best known for*A Vindication of the Rights of Woman* (1792), in which she argues that women are not naturally inferior to men, but appear to be only because they lack education. She suggests that both men and women should be treated as rational beings and imagines a social order founded on reason." With respect to women, when they receive a careful education, they are either made fine ladies, brimful of sensibility, and teeming with capricious fancies; or mere notable women" (Wollstonecraft, 142). She despised the unfair status women were in and she pointed out the truth of women's existence: "A man of sense can only love such a woman on account of her sex, and respect her, because she is a trusty servant."(Wollstonecraft, 143)

Under her mother's influence, there was no doubt for young Mary to develop concern for women. Moreover, she conveyed her feminist concern in her book *Frankenstein* by describing the four major women in the book as angels who deserved men's love and respect. Another reason for

these perfect women image is because Mary Shelley herself suffered great agony in real life, including the death of her mother, the bad relationship with her stepmother, the romantic affair with a married man, Percy Shelley and the death of her children. The sufferings hurt Mary both physically and mentally. Even though what Mary has gone through is unbearable at that time for a woman, she still lived with it and gradually she became so independent and so strong that the major four women in her book are the ideal female image whom she wants to become and that is her best wish toward women in her time. Women are supposed to be independent, confident, elegant and strong, in Mary's opinion.

Chapter 4   Feminism Reflected in *Frankenstein*

As we know, there are two stereotypical images of women in literature. In Sandra M. Gilbert and Susan Gubar`s famous book *The Madwoman in the Attic—the Women Writer and The Nineteenth-Century Literary Imagination*, they point out that there are often "the angel in the house" female image and "the mad woman in the attic" female image. (Gilbert, Gubar 186) In *Frankenstein*, through the male narrators` narratives, we can see that there are also two types of women—angelic women and female monster. So in this part, the feminism reflected in the book will be analyzed in two aspects, the angelic women image and the female monster image.

4.1   Angelic Women

In Frankenstein, Mary Shelley composed her novel in favor of men's interest in women. Although the story is written from the main character, a male's perspective, under the patriarchal social background, there are some women in the text, such as Frankenstein's future wife Elizabeth, his mother Caroline Beaufort Frankenstein, and the servant girl Justine.

Caroline Beaufort Frankenstein is a good example of women. She is a good daughter who nurses her dying father with the greatest tenderness; She is a perfect wife to Alphonse   Frankenstein; She is a model accepted by Justine and Elizabeth; She is a self-sacrificing mother who takes good care of her children and dies taking care of her adopted daughter. It is her dying wish that Victor and Elizabeth should marry. She represents the affectionate mother and loyal wife at that time.

Instructed by Caroline, Elizabeth is presented as another ideal feminine. When she is a little child, she is presented as a pretty present for Victor who treats Elizabeth as his promised gift.   She has learned well the lessons of submissiveness and devotion to others. She has no real dimension of her own and her life revolves around Victor and her family members.

Elizabeth is an angle in the eyes of men. Firstly, Elizabeth is an angle in this big family. She is portrayed as the perfect woman both physically and mentally, especially after the death of Frankenstein's mother Caroline. She takes the place of the mother figure in the household and acts as the comforter to the big family. Secondly, Elizabeth is an angle in the eyes of Frankenstein. "No word, no expression could body forth the kind of relationship in which she (Elizabeth) stood to me (Frankenstein), since till death she was to be mine only". (Shelley 58) Frankenstein treats her as his own possession. Their close relationship reveals that women are subordinate to men, or, women belong to men. Thirdly, Elizabeth is an angle who follows the standard of the patriarchal society. In the family, "the saint soul of Elizabeth shone like a shrine-dedicated lamp in our peaceful home" (Shelley 23). She does her duties to take care of her uncles and cousins; meanwhile, Elizabeth loyally waits for her lover Frankenstein and suffers loneliness. From one letter to Frankenstein, she clarifies her attitudes, "I confess to you, my friend, that I love you and that in my airy dreams of futurity you have been my constant friend and companion". (Shelley, 171) Elizabeth treats Victor as her absolute soul-mate, she also writes: "...if I see but one smile on your lips when we meet, occasioned by this or any other exertion of mine, I shall need no other happiness" (Shelley, 172). According to Gilbert and Gubar`s view, " If a woman is depicted as the angel in the house, she supposedly realizes that her physical and material comforts are gifts from her husband. Her goal in life, therefore, is to please her husband, to attend to his every comfort, and to obey him. Through these selfless acts, she finds the utmost contentment by serving her husband and children" (Gilbert & Gubar, 325). Elizabeth is such a lady. She is expected and also she is expecting to marry Victor. She is provided with the traditional duties that women are supposed to stay at home and look after the house. She conforms to the rules of society and she is doomed to be the female sacrifice of the patriarchal society.

The text is full of angles. Just like Gilbert and Gubar say: For the more secular nineteenth century, however, the eternal type of female purity was represented not by a Madonna in heaven but by an angel in the house. (Gilbert & Gubar, 21) They are presented as docile, sweet, happy, playful, affectionate, imaginative, delicate and beautiful. To some extent, their angelic images reveal the reality of women`s situation. They are habituated to be on the watch for every opportunity of doing good to others. (Ellis 1993: 1599) Those fictional female characters are composed to meet the society's wishes, what's more, to reveal the society's definition of women.

4.2　Female Monster

As there are angels in the book, there are also madwomen. In *Frankenstein*, the madwomen are mainly the two monsters which are the monster itself created by Frankenstein and the unborn female monsters.

Although the monster created by Frankenstein is universally believed to be a male for he desires for a female companion, but there is no clear evidence showing that the monster is a male in the text. Therefore lots of critics associate the monster with women because the two have something in common.

First of all, the monster has no name, no home and no legal rights, just like some women who are degraded if they are not defined as angels by men. Without a name, a person can not be recognized and accepted by the society. In the patriarchal society, women are in the inferior position compared to men so whether women can have names or positions are decided by men. And women have to fight for what is meant to be theirs: names, homes and legal rights. Secondly, women are the derivatives of the patriarchal society, so is the man-made creature. Only when women are needed by men, they can be seen and heard. In the story, the monster is created by Frankenstein to satisfy his scientific and chemical desire and in real life, women are seen as sexual playthings and personal slaves. However, when the creature finally came into being, Frankenstein, the creator, discarded it because of the ugliness and horrible appearance of the monster. If a women is ugly and seen as a potential menace to men, she will be absolutely discarded by men as well. To this point, the monster is the embodiment of women's social status.

Then there is an unborn female monster who would have been the monster's future companion. When the creature lived in the cottage, he read the book *Paradise Lost* and he compared himself to Adam who was also a created being but happy, prosperous and respected. Furthermore, Adam had a female companion, Eve, who could share his happiness and ease his sorrow. he complains " it was all a dream; no Eve soothed my sorrows nor shared my thoughts". (Shelley, 116) At last, He proposes his idea to Frankenstein, "you must create a female for me with whom I can live in the interchange of those sympathies necessary for my being". (Shelley, 130) So in the creature's thoughts, the female monster is his ideal companion who can give him comfort and care.

This is another example of women's social status, even if it comes out from a man-made monster's point of view that women exist only because they are needed by men.

Chapter 5   Conclusions

"A more subtle pleasure for the strong, the generous, the masterful, is pity for the wretched ... such sympathy for the humble, such 'pity for women' ". (Beauvoir, 218-219) Women have to and should solidarize to change their unfavorable position under the world's feminist movement background. On the one hand, Mary has done her best in redefining women's position and in promoting the early feminist movements. On the other hand, early feminist consciousness has helped Mary shape her new self-identity and her wishes for women reflected in *Frankenstein*. Feminism, through hundreds of years, has matured itself. The nearly perfect descriptions about women in Mary's work and Mary's personal experience as a woman in the patriarchal society doubtlessly fueled the development of feminism.

What is your first impression of *Frankenstein*? Is it horror or gothic? How about feminism from now on? As we can easily seen in the story, the female image in the book is the idealized women's social status. Women in *Frankenstein* are fragile, tender, considerate, courageous, intelligent, beautiful and charming, which is what women want in real life. They are taken good care of by men, they are respected by men, they are loved by men and they are worshiped by men to some extent. This book, along with its author Mary Shelley, plays an essential part in the progress of world feminist movement. What Mary Shelley did is not only composing a story, but also creating the ideal female image for women, for men and for the whole society. In addition, she gave the world a new impression of herself, who suffered great agony from a series of life tragedies but grew independent and strong on her own. Needless to say, just like her mother Mary Wollstonecraft, Mary Shelley is also the " Pioneer of Modern Feminism".

References

[1] "*Feminism in the United Kingdom*". https://en.wikipedia.org/wiki/Frankenstein. 16 Jun. 2017.

[2] *Frankenstein.* https://en.wikipedia.org/wiki/Frankenstein. 5 Jun. 2017.

[3] Glbert, Sandra M., Gubar, Susan. The Madwoman in the Attic: The Woman Writer and the Nineteenth-Century Literary Imagination. New Haven and London: Yale University Press, 2000.

[4] Gou He. Analysis of Frankenstein from The Perspective of Eco-feminism[D]. Harbin Normal University, 2013.

[5] Hadjetian, Sylvia. Mary Shelley's Frankenstein and Feminism. Grin Verlag, 12 Apr. 2008. (Seminar Paper)

[6] Li Gui Qiong. A Feminist Study of Mary Shelley`s Frankenstein[D]. Sichuan Normal University. 2016.

[7] Shelley Mary. Frankenstein. New York : Signet Classics, 2013.

[8] Simone de Beauvoir, Trans by H.M. Parshley. The Second Sex. London: Lowe and Brydone (Printers) Ltd., 1956. (Originally published in France by Librarie Gallimard in 1949 under the title Le Deuxiéme Sexe).

[9] Wollstonecraft, Mary. A Vindication of the Rights of Man and A Vindication of the Rights of Woman[M]. 北京：中国政法大学出版社，2003.

[10] 李倩. 她们的世界——英美女性科幻作家的独特写作[J]. 长春工程学院学报（社会科学版），2011，12（3）：119-121.

[11] 闵思思. 19 世纪英国女权主义思想研究[D]. 湘潭大学，2015.

[12] 潘迎华. 19 世纪英国的政治民主化与女权运动[J]. 史学月刊，2000（4）：85-92.

The Psychological Process of the Monster in *Frankenstein*

刘英子

摘 要：《弗兰肯斯坦》中，科学家弗兰肯斯坦创造了一个怪物，却因惊惧抛弃了他。怪物在离开实验室之后，为了成为人和融入社会，他曾经努力发展自己的认知、理性及爱的能力。可是由于自身及社会的原因，他最终沦为了精神进化过程中的失败者。要分析怪物的精神演化过程，可以从进化论和精神分析法的角度入手，同时这一过程主要分为精神进化和精神沉沦两个部分。

关键词：《弗兰肯斯坦》；认同；进化论；精神分析法；精神进化；精神沉沦

Abstract: In *Frankenstein*, Frankenstein, the scientist, created a Monster, but abandoned him because of fear. After leaving the laboratory, the Monster tried to develop his ability of cognitive, rationality and love. However, due to his own and social reasons, he eventually became a failure in the process of spiritual evolution.

This paper attempts to analyse the psychological process of the Monster from the perspective of evolution theory and psychoanalytic theory. And the process is mainly divided into two parts: spiritual evolution and destruction.

Key Words: *Frankenstein*, identity, evolution theory, psychoanalytic theory, spiritual evolution, spiritual destruction

Chapter 1   Introduction

Frankenstein, Mary Shelley's masterpiece, has long been hailed by Western scholars as one of the most outstanding Gothic novels and the first science fiction around the world. Some critics discuss it about the dangers of science and technology; some develop it from a feminist perspective. But I prefer to focus on the psychological process of the Monster created by Frankenstein.

The author mentioned in the preface, to write this story inspired by Darwin's biological research. In fact, the age of romanticism, the author lived, was based on the development of evolution theory. However, in that age, proposed before Darwinism, Lamarckism was more widely circulated. Jean-Baptiste Lamarck (1744—1829) believed that: In every animal which has not passed the limit of its development, a more frequent and continuous use of any organ gradually strengthens, develops and enlarges that organ, and gives it a power proportional to the length of time it has been so used. Moreover, many romantic thinkers pointed out that human spirit has been evolving too.

A lot of thinkers in the later generations accepted the idea of spiritual evolution. According to Erich Fromm(1960), an American psychoanalyst, "Human existence poses a question...he has awareness of himself, and this awareness of himself as a separate entity makes him feel unbearably alone, lost, powerless. The very fact of being born poses a problem. At the moment of birth, life asks man a question, and this question he must answer. He must answer it at every moment; not his mind, not his body, but he, the person who thinks and dreams, who sleeps and eats and cries and laughs - the whole man—must answer it. What is this question which life poses? The question is: How can we overcome the suffering, the imprisonment, the shame which the experience of separateness creates; how can we find union within ourselves, with our fellow man, with nature?" And then Fromm(1960) came up with the solution, "The question is always the same. However, there are several answers, or basically, there are only two answers. One is to overcome separateness, and to find unity by regression to the state of unity which existed before awareness ever arose, that is, before man was born. The other answer is to be fully born, to develop one's awareness, one's reason, one's capacity to love, to such a point that one transcends one's own egocentric involvement, and arrives at a new harmony, at a new oneness with the world." That is a positive and advanced way to spiritual evolution. However, chances are that man overcomes this sense of isolation by taking a negative, degraded approach, such as relying on an authority, or by degrading into a state of ideology that is not yet formed.

Frankenstein, to a certain extent, it is a novel reflected the process of spiritual evolution of human being. In *Frankenstein*, the Monster has no name, and just called him "the Creature"(Mary Shelley, 1818). It suggests that even if the Monster looks like a man physically, but has not evolved into a real "human being". Meanwhile, creature and creation are cognate words, which imply that the Monster is not only a creature created by Frankenstein, but also his second self. As for the Monster, in his short life, he experienced two extreme psychological processes—spiritual evolution and destruction.

Chapter 2   The Spiritual Evolution of the Monster

The spiritual evolution of human beings is a gradual process. For human beings, "existence" is to exist in a relationship between them and objects or others. To know the existence of men is to understand themselves and the world around them. Thus, The spiritual evolution of human beings often manifests as the identity for individuals to their own identities. Here, the "identity"(Erik H. Erikson, 1968), to answer questions such as "Who I am" and "What is my identity", refers to the identification of men to their own identities and roles.

The Monster's identity has always made him be in an awkward position. So did the author, Mary Shelley. Mary was got into the same trouble. She lived in a complicated family. Her stepmother disliked her and her father also gave her the cold shoulder. It was not until she grew up and met Percy Bysshe Shelley (1792—1822) that she got the chance to have emotional contacts with others. After that, Mary eloped with Shelley and gave birth to a baby. But at that moment, Sherry had not divorced with his wife, Harriet. It was in such a situation that Mary felt so deeply about the "Identity" issue. Therefore, when she wrote the Monster in Frankenstein, she mixed it up with her personal experience. As a result of it, the characters experience is often similar to the author's own experience. The Monster in the novel had been trying to build or find himself as an ordinary person. And this process of spiritual evolution can be divided into three stages: identity with nature, man and society.

2.1　Identity with Nature

Shortly after the birth of the Monster, he left the laboratory and came to the forest. The monster, at this time, his mental state is just like a child. For instance, "I gradually saw plainly the clear stream that supplied me with drink and the trees that shaded me with their foliage"; "I was delighted when I first discovered that a pleasant sound"; "I tried to imitate the pleasant songs of the birds but was unable". Then "My sensations had by this time become distinct, and my mind received every day additional ideas. My eyes became accustomed to the light and to perceive objects in their right forms; I distinguished the insect from the herb, and by degrees, one herb from another."

This is the Monster's identity with nature. Children love fairy tales since they consider themselves to be a part of nature, such as a rabbit or a lamb. So does the Monster. He is almost merged with nature.

However, he didn't realize that he was a "human being" at first, so he walked into the village. But when the villagers saw the Monster, they did the same thing like Frankenstein, screamed and ran away. However, the Monster was frightened too. And he suddenly realized that he could not be seen by the men. As we can see, at the beginning, the Monster was as docile as yeanling. Just like many other wild animals, he lived in the forest, or countrysides. He stole the villagers' food when he was hungry, like a mouse. In the Monster's personal statement, he also compared himself to the ass, which was in the French writer, Jean de la Fontaine's story named The ass and a lap-dog, "yet surely the gentle ass whose intentions were affectionate, although his manners were rude, deserved better treatment than blows and execration."

The monster has a natural affection and affinity with nature. In the first half part of the novel, there are a variety of narrations about how pleasant the Monster is when he enjoys the beauty of nature. Nevertheless, with the mental development of the Monster, just like many other people, the more he knows, the more disgruntled he feels. As Fromm(1960) said, "The tragedy of man is that he is in nature, yet he transcends nature."

2.2　Identity with Man

Since the Monster lived in a hovel adjacent to the family of De Lacey, he began to get touch with people. Through observation, he learned human language and common sense, even some noble behaviors of man, caused varieties of complex human emotions. "I felt sensation of a peculiar and overpowering nature: they were a mixture of pain and pleasure, such as I had never before experienced, either from hunger or cold, warmth or food..." Moreover, the Monster believed that the family of De Lacey was full of "superior beings", and in the Monster's imagination, "I formed a thousand pictures of presenting myself to them, and their reception of me. I imagined that they would be disgusted, until, by my gentle demeanour and conciliating words, I should first win their favour, and afterwards their love."

At this time, the Monster used to regard him as Adam, an average man. It is because he realized that he was a "human being", the Monster deeply knew the taste of loneliness.

Monster's thought and behavior are in compliance with requirements of being a man. Knowledge is just a passport in his imagination, because it breaks a more important rule, which has been agreed by everyone, he does not look like a "man". Thus, once he came to this world, he was labeled by "alien". With this label, he has long been deprived of the possibility of integration into the world.

2.3 Identity with Society

The Monster imagined that the family of De Lacey would accept him by his "gentle demeanour and conciliating words". These thoughts exhilarated him and led him to apply "with fresh ardour to the acquiring the art of language."

When Felix instructed Safie the book, *Volney's Ruins of Empires,* the Monster also learned it by eavesdropping on their talks. "Every conversation of the cottagers opened new wonders to me", and he began to understand "the strange system of human society", such as "the division of property, of immense wealth and squalid poverty, of rank, descent, and noble blood." Furthermore, he realized that "A man might be respected with only one of these advantages(high and unsullied descent united with riches); but without either he was considered, except in very rare instances, as a vagabond and a slave, doomed to waste his powers for the profits of the chosen few!"

The monster is fully equipped with the ability to communicate with people. For instance, when he persuaded Frankenstein to made a female companion for him, he demonstrated that his language competence and social ability was not inferior to his creator.

The Monsters even took part in social work, such as "during the night I often took his tools, the use of which I quickly discovered, and brought home firing sufficient for the consumption of several days". To his surprise, his human neighbours were totally amazed and thanked a lot to an invisible hand.

The "invisible hand" here is an allusion. According to Adam Smith(1776), "He generally, indeed, neither intends to promote the public interest, nor knows how much he is promoting it...he intends only his own gain, and he is in this, as in many other cases, led by an invisible hand to promote an end which was no part of his intention. Nor is it always the worse for the society that it was not part of it. By pursuing his own interest he frequently promotes that of the society more effectually than when he really intends to promote it." However, the monster done the works was not out of private interests, but the sympathy for De Lacey. He helped the De Lacey to gain their leisure time, and he could also learn to improve himself. In this way, the monster provided the most important help he could give to the poor.

The advanced stage of the spiritual evolution of human beings should be the identity of their own. In this stage, men discover their nature and infinite potential; form the independent self; recognize their own like God, heaven and earth as a whole; and do not need to rely on the approval of others to prove their value. Unfortunately, the Monster failed to evolve into this stage, so did the majority.

Frankenstein went astray with the establishment of his own subjectivity. He wanted to build his own subjectivity by mastering advanced knowledge. However, his motivation for creating life was selfish. Even worse, he tried to pose himself as a creator of life and everybody would be beholden to him. His selfish motivation doomed his failure. The monster basically stopped spiritual evolution after failed to integrate into society. He was in a desperate solitude, and later he identified with Satan, which was equal to betray God. Thus, the Monster did not have a home in spirit. Then, after repeated blows to his ideals, he chose a passive, degraded life strategy. He began his spiritual destruction.

Chapter 3　The Spiritual Destruction of the Monster

As Fromm (1960) said, "Birth is not one act; it is a process. The aim of life is to be fully born, though its tragedy is that most of us die before we are thus born. To live is to be born every minute. Death occurs when birth stops. Physiologically, our cellular system is in a process of continual birth; psychologically, however, most of us cease to be born at a certain point. Some are completely stillborn; they go on living physiologically when mentally their longing is to return to the womb, to earth, darkness, death; they are insane, or nearly so. Many others proceed further on the path of life. Yet they can not cut the umbilical cord completely, as it were; they remain symbiotically attached to mother, father, family, race, state, status, money, gods, etc.; they never emerge fully as themselves and thus they never become fully born."

In *Frankenstein*, after the family of De Lacey removed, the Monster was in the control of angry and decided to set the house on fire. This marked the plateau of the Monster's spiritual evolution, and began his destruction. Furthermore, there are some coincidences in the books picked up by the Monster in the forest. In the volume of Plutarch's *Lives,* Plutarch taught him high thoughts, "to admire and love the heroes of past ages". This book represented the supreme ideal of the Monster. In fact, he later rescued a drowning girl. And the book *Paradise Lost,* made the Monster identify with Satan, which set him up for the future revenge. Finally, the *Sorrows of Werter* was a sign of the Monster's eventual suicide.

In this book, knowledge is a disaster both for Frankenstein and the Monster. Specifically, the spiritual destruction of the Monster is manifested in the following three aspects: seeking protection from his master, taking revenge on the society; pursuing for death.

3.1　Seeking Protection from the Master

Seeking protection from others is a degradation. Since "many others proceed further on the path of life. Yet they can not cut the umbilical cord completely, as it were; they remain symbiotically attached to mother, father, family, race, state, status, money, gods, etc.; they never emerge fully as themselves and thus they never become fully born." (Fromm, 1960)

The Monster was deeply moved by the family of De Lacey. And he could not help to ask itself, "where were my friends and relations? " "I had never yet seen a being resembling me, or who claimed any intercourse with me"; and "what was I". After the family of De Lacey removed, it reminded the Monster of its creator, Frankenstein. And he claimed that "Remember, that I am thy creature; I ought to be thy Adam."

The monster wanted to have a female companion with the help of his master, Frankenstein, and then he would live in seclusion with his partner. This is not only an approach to get rid of loneliness, but also to withdraw from social life.

3.2 Taking Revenge on the Society

This degradation is designed to overcome the sense of isolation by destroying all human beings and things. According to Fromm (1955), "There is another answer to this necessity for transcendence: if I cannot create life, then at least I can destroy it. Because even the destruction of life is a form of transcendence."

This is what controls the Monster's mind. The book *Paradise Lost,* made the Monster identify with Satan. He even thought that "Satan had his companions, fellow devils, to admire and encourage him, but I am solitary and abhorred." This feeling became increasingly evident with his unhappy experiences until he became a real Satan. When Felix struck the Monster out of the house, he felt "I, like the archfend, bore a hell within me", and he even "wished to tear up the trees". After the removal of the family of De Lacey, the Monster felt that it was abandoned by them. So he "placed a variety of combustibles around the cottage; and, after having destroyed every vestige of cultivation in the garden, I waited with forced impatience until the moon had sunk to commence my operations." Then he committed a heinous crime: he directly killed three people, Frankenstein's little brother, his wife and a good friend, also killed Frankenstein's servant indirectly by imputing the death of Williamto her, finally led Frankenstein to death.

3.3 Pursuing for Death

The last and most negative destruction form of the Monster is his pursuit for death. He was dominated by the desire to return to the womb, to earth, darkness,   and death. The monster chose to kill himself because he felt profound loneliness after the death of Frankenstein, the only person he could talk to, even he was the one received his revenge too. As what mentioned above, the Monster preferred the book, *Sorrows of Werter*, which also had a influence on the Monster's acts. Because he thought that "Werter himself a more divine being than I had ever beheld or imagined; his character contained no pretension, but it sank deep. The disquisitions upon death and suicide were calculated to fill me with wonder", and "I did not pretend to enter into the merits of the case, yet I inclined towards the opinions of the hero, whose extinction I wept, without precisely understanding it."

However, the Monster's pursuit for death is not only a degraded life strategy, but also a rational return. Since he finally confessed to Frankenstein's body, "Blasted as thou weft, my agony was still superior to thine; for the bitter sting of remorse will not cease to rankle in my wounds until death shall close them for ever."

Chapter 4   Conclusions

Dinosaurs defeated in the biological evolution, and the Monster failed in his way to spiritual evolution. Moreover, the destruction of the monster due to his failure to identify himself properly.

However, though the Monster failed to really know himself, it is also worthy of respect with his passion and endeavour to understand both himself and the world. What's more, the limitation of the Monster is the same to each other, but not everyone could bear his pain.

References

[1] Erik H. Erikson. Identity Youth and Crisis[M]. New York: W. W. Norton & Company, 1994.

[2] Fromm Erich. Psychoanalysis and Zen Buddhism[M]. New York: Harpercollins, 1970.

[3] Fromm, Erich. The Sane Society[M]. London: Routledge, 2001.

[4] Mary, Shelley. Frankenstein, London: Alma Books, 2014.

[5] 霍晓珊. 弗兰肯斯坦对身份的寻求与认同[D]. 华中师范大学，2006.

[6] 李玲. 论《弗兰肯斯坦》中科学人的身份困惑与伦理选择[D]. 华中师范大学，2015.

[7] 郑峥. 《弗兰肯斯坦》怪物自我寻求中的悲惨命运[D]. 山东大学，2007.

从人物性格分析《理智与情感》中的婚姻观

刘文佳

摘　要：简·奥斯丁是英国文学史上伟大的现实主义女作家。她在创作中，把注意力集中在她那个时代的中产阶级妇女的爱情和婚姻观上。她认为只有获得建立在理智上的情感，才会给予人们真正意义上的幸福和美满的婚姻。在对《情感与理智》进行文本内容分析的过程中，将对书中的两位女主人公埃利诺和玛丽安两姐妹的性格进行重点的研究和分析，通过介绍她们在处世、恋爱中的不同反应以及两个主人公在书中的不同结局分析她们的婚姻观，以《情感与理智》这本小说的主要文本内容为出发点对简·奥斯汀的婚姻观进行了介绍和分析，以帮助读者理解埃莉诺的理智与玛丽安的情感以及玛丽安的新女性形象，同时以此得出对现代女性有启发意义的正确婚姻观。

关键词：理智与情感；婚姻观；人物性格

Abstract: Jane Austen is a great realistic writer in the history of British literature. Jane Austen's novels have a very narrow range of topics and her worksare always centered on middle-class who are either about to be married or ready for it at that time.She believes that only the sensibility based on sense would bring real happiness and perfect marriage. This paper focuses on the analysis of the personalities of Elinor and Marianne in *Sense and Sensibility* and analyzed their views of marriage by their words and behavior in daily life and love relationship, to help readers betterunderstand Eleanor's senses and Marianne's sensibility, as well as Marianne's new female image, and at the same time to get inspirations of right view of marriage for modern women.

Key Words: sense and sensibility，view of marriage, characters' personalities

Chapter 1　Introduction

Jane Austen was the seventh of eight children and she was born in the village of Steventon in Hampshire in 1775. Jane was educated at home and began to write at an early age. In 1793, Jane began to write *Sense and Sensibility*. Three years later, she wrote her masterpiece, *Pride and Prejudice.* Jane Austen's novels have a very narrow range of topics and her stories is always centered on young girls who are either about to be married or ready for it. Big world events do not appear in her novels. On the whole, rank, money and marriage matter greatly in the novels. Skillful use of dialogue and tight plotting are the main features of Jane Austen's style. Although without big events and exciting scene，she thinks it the most trivial accidents that reveal the feelings naturally. She just uses these common things and details to give people the deepest enlightenment.

In *Sense and sensibility*, the story develops around the Dashwood sisters, Elinor and Marianne. While the former is a sensible and rational girl, the younger sister is romantic and emotional—the title Sense and Sensibility is a pair of antonym, symbolizing the two writing characteristics of the novel. As for Edward Ferrars, a potential and suitable man for Elinor, he and she didn't express love to each other and then Elinor finds he has a fiancee secretly when he was young. Meanwhile, Marianne fell in love with a man *"his person and air were equal to her fancy"* (Austen 60): That is Mr. Willoughby, a new neighbor. He is so changeable and selfish that he abandons Marianne later and married another young and wealthy lady. How each of the sisters reacts to their romantic misfortunes and the lesson they learn have finally brought the happy ending.

Experts from home and abroad have done many studies on this novel. They mainly focus on her literary achievements, her feminist view, and her view of marriage displayed in the novel. Before 1980s, the general researchers regarded Austin as a woman against oppression and a fighter for women' marriage Liberation with high political consciousness. Later, most of researchers focused on the objectivity of Austen's minds and her contribution to the life and values of the British middle class. And now in the background of gender equality and the deep development of women's liberation movement, there is a trend to study the view of marriage from the perspective of feminism especially the inspirations for modern women.

From the title Sense and Sensibility, we would take it for granted that the author will portray two characters in opposite personalities, thus constituting the main thread to support the whole frame. However, we can also see a perfect balance of the opposing forces. The characters in the novel have the complementary personalities and different views of marriage, but to some degree it is not totally the opposite aspect that supports the frame. There are opposition and unity between them, and Elinor and Marianne respectively symbolize one personality, sense and sensibility, but in some cases, we can also see Elinor's sensibility and Marianne's sense. What's more, their attitudes toward love have also combined sense and sensibility. Austen has also used romanticism and realism to fulfill the balance of opposition and unity to express Jane Austen's view of marriage and her understanding of the situation of British women at that time.

Chapter 2   View of Marriage Based on the Analysis of Elinor and Marianne's Personality

The character's personality is the core of the literature creation. In the history of literature, some characters' characteristics are so simplified，making the images boring and dull. The diversity of a person's characteristics is to some extent influenced by the external elements. There are oppositions embodied in the two sisters' characters, which made make the characters vivid and full. *"The round characters can be embodied in different forms, such as the inconsistent behavior, the opposition of sense and sensibility and double even multiple characters."* In this novel, Elinor and Marianne show their double characters respectively through their words and behavior, because of their life experiences. Through the analysis of Elinor and Marianne's personality, their views of marriages could be compared and analyzed.

2.1　Elinor's View of Marriage Based on the Analysis of Personality

Elinor, who is the "ideal lady" at Austen's heart, symbolizes the personality of sense. She came on the stage when her mother Mrs Dashwood had quarreled with her brother "*She would have quitted the house for ever, had not the entreaty of her eldest girl, Elinor, induced her first to reflect on the propriety of going.*" (Austen 6) From this, we have the first impression of Elinor's personality: cautious and considerate. The novel directly describes her:

Elinor, this eldest daughter, whose advice was so effectual, possessed a strength of understanding. and coolness of judgment, which qualified her, though only nineteen, to be the counselor of her mother, and enabled her frequently to counteract, to the advantage of them all, that eagerness of mind in Mrs Dashwood which must generally have led to imprudence. She had an excellent heart; her disposition was affectionate, and her feelings were strong; but she knew how to govern them. (Austen 6)

This is the only detailed description of Elinor's personality in concrete words. In the following part, the author depicts her characteristics as well as the view of love and marriage in vivid dialogues and concrete behavior. She is obviously a typical type of character with the sense of responsibility and thoughtfulness. Unlike her irritable mother and emotional sister, she shows great courage in managing their daily life and has become the main support of the family after her father's pass away. She does not easily express her inner thoughts, even if she falls in love with Edward. Although she is attracted by Edward's rich knowledge, keen sight and elegant behavior, she is not totally lost in her affection. Even when facing her rival in love, she still remains graceful and even consider about others. After Lucy tells her about the engagement with Edward, she tries to think and talk in calm, under shock and pain she has ever felt before.

From these analyses, we can decide that Elinor is surely sensible. However, although Elinor shows more calmness and sense than her sister Marianne, she also has romantic feelings and imagination sometimes. When Marianne criticizes Edward about his dull mind and bad paintings, Elinor always defends her lover Edward. When Marianne said, "*What a pity it is that Edward should have no taste for drawing*". (Austen 24) And Elinor said immediately "*He does not draw himself, but he has great pleasure in seeing the performances of other people.*" (Austen 24) She thinks her lover has the ability of appreciation, but does not have chance to improve it.

In *Sense and Sensibility*, obviously, Elinor's marriage views are Jane Austen's ideal marriage views. The author stressed Elinor's character: sensible, calm but enthusiastic in heart. To be worth mentioning, through her, we can find the opposition and harmony of *Sense and sensibility*, that is, on the one hand, supporting for sense and against for sensibility; on the other hand, pursuing true love and against for traditional marriage for money. Elinor is sensible to control herself and to consider for others. When Edward leaves, Elinor thinks "*It was her determination to subdue it, and to prevent herself from appearing to suffer more than what all her family suffered on his going away.*" (Austen 51) She did not try to change his mind. When Elinor hears of Lucy's engagement with Edward, she also controls her emotion and even insists on her promise not to reveal Lucy's secret. "*For four months, I have had all this hanging on my mind, without being at liberty to speak of it to a single creature."* (Austen 87) The phrase "hanging on" gives some indication of Elinor's sense of responsibility towards her behavior. Elinor struggles to control the pain of love so that she can take her obligations as a daughter and a sister. She is rewarded and gets her own happiness. Through the novel, it can be obviously found that Austen is in favor of Elinor's propriety and control of emotion rather than Marianne. Personal feeling for true love is precious but it must be confined to society.

2.2 Marianne's View of Marriage Based on the Analysis of Personality

Marianne symbolizes the personality of sensibility. In the novel, Austen wrote：

"Marianne's abilities were, in many respects, quite equal to Elinor's. She was sensible and clever, but eager in everything: her sorrows, her joys, could have no moderation. She was generous, amiable, interesting: she was everything but prudent. The resemblance between her and her mother is strikingly great." (Austen, 7)

Marianne shows more sensibility than her sister Elinor and never hide her emotion and thoughts. To assess Edward, Marianne holds different views with Elinor. Marianne thinks him lovely but cold, and he lacks the charm which can attach Elinor. In Marianne's view, *"To satisfy me, those characters must be united. I could not be happy with a man whose taste did not in every point coincide with my own. He must enter into all my feelings; the same books, the same music must charm us both."* (Austen, 22) We can see that Marianne holds very strict requirements to her lover and she would not accommodate anyone. However, she is not shallow and ignorant woman with daydream and fancy. She loves reading poems and could play beautiful piano music. When love comes to her, she is brave enough to catch it without hesitation. She falls in love with Willoughby, who saved her from danger on a rainy day. Marianne refuses to conceal her feelings in any way, despite her sister's kind warning. Her strong love and craziness has even blinded her eyes. However, later, Willoughby abandons her and gets married with another young lady.

There is a proverb "a fall into the pit, a gain in your wit". Having suffered great pain of loss, tired Marianne grows mature. She realizes her impulsion and shows regret about her behavior. Then she determines to learn from her sister Elinor and control her temper. In the past, she thought she lived for love, but now, she holds that she must live for her family, for those people who cares about her and become more sensible. Finally, she learns to control her feelings and sensibly accepts the proposal of Colonel Brandon.

To be frank, Marianne is not just for criticism and her view also shows Jane Austen's views on marriage and love. At first, Marianne does not like Brandon very much. She just wants to be a friend of him, not a close friend. He is not active or passionate. After being cheated by Willoughby, Marianne's attitude towards love has changed a lot. She realizes that Willoughby is just a libertine and not loves her as much as she does. This kind of people is changeable because of many factors. Looked after by Brandon carefully, Marianne realizes he is a good and reliable person worth of respect. He has the ability and patience to take good care of her and bring her happiness. Marianne's view of marriage has changed from sensibility to sense. This sensible view of love is pointed by Jane Austen. It seems that she gives her advice to young girls that they should never lose their sense in love and marriage.

So how to understand and appreciate this view of love? Love is not only the affair between the man and woman, but it can reflect some social features. This view of love has its own particular historic and social meaning. First, Austen explains the women' s situation, such as that women cannot go outside to work for money and that they cannot to inherit fortune. In such an environment, if the young girls are lack of sense, they would be easily hurt both in heart and body. Willoughby gives up Marianne, but he was not punished by the society He pursues money and status protected by the society. However, there is no difficulty finding that although Austen is surrender to the reality, she is still influenced by the Romantic Movement at that time. Actually, Marianne's spirit of pursuing the true love is worth praising. But under the pressure of social, she has to acknowledge the importance of it. She discovers that she needs knowledge and the control of emotional impulses. She has to accept the fact that trusting one's intuition of feeling in forming judgments may be unreliable. For Austen, she has no alternative but knows deeply in life both the heart and the mind often come up against all difficulties at that special time.

Chapter 3   Inspiration for Modern Women

Sense and Sensibility are all virtues. People must be thankful if he or she possesses either of them. It is well-known that everything is related with each other and nothing comes united. Sense and Sensibility tells that Elinor is not a girl without sensibility and Marianne also has sense too. The most different point of the sisters exists in how to coordinate sense and sensibility. In other words, only if the people who own it are not excessive, sensibility is a method of strengthening. So appropriate sensibility is the result of coordinating sense. Their combination can bring about happiness marriage. Therefore, only view of marriage based on balanced sense and sensibility can bring about happiness.

It's easy to find that the holders of the three kinds of views of marriage all pursue happiness in their marriages. However, some of them can not properly deal with the relationship between sense and sensibility, which cause them fail to reach happiness. What' s more, they not only destroy their own happiness, but also others. Through the discussions above, it's concluded that the view of marriage based merely on sense is utilitarianism. The holders of this kind consider money and social status as the most important factor to marriage, and no love in marriage at all. While the view of marriage based on excessive sensibility is impractical. Only the view of marriage based on balanced sense and sensibility is the way to get happiness.

The analysis on the views of marriage is certainly helpful to comprehensive of matters around us in nowadays. Sense and sensibility are both virtues of human beings. The key is how to deal with the relationship between sense and sensibility. Only people, who balance them, can achieve their real happiness in marriage. At last, researching on the views of marriage can help to know people's marriage conditions at that time and also give a guide for us on marriage.

References

[1] Gao Feng. Opposition and Harmony of Austen's View on Love in Sense and Sensibility [J]. Journal of Language and Literature, 2011(8): 43-46.

[2] Jane Austen. Sense and Sensibility [M]. Shanghai: Shanghai World Book Publishing Company, 2009.

[3] 简·奥斯汀. 理智与情感[M]. 北京：外语教学与研究出版社，1995.

[4] 张梓煜. 透过理智与情感看简奥斯丁的婚姻观[J]. 读与写杂志，2015（2）：25-26.

[5] 朱虹. 奥斯汀研究[M]. 上海：上海译文出版社，1985.

Feminist Reading of *Heart of Darkness*

冯雨雪

摘 要：《黑暗的心》被称为 "没有女人的男人" 小说。通过从女性主义者西蒙·波伏娃在其著作《第二性》中关于他者的理论出发，深入分析《黑暗的心》中五位女性角色的他者形象，可以得出结论：在父权制下，《黑暗的心》的女性是绝对他者。

关键词：《黑暗的心》；他者；女性角色

Abstract: *Heart of Darkness* are regarded as a male novel without female. From the aspect of theory about otherness in *The Second Sex* written by Simone de Beauvoir, this thesis tries to deeply analyze the otherness image of five women in *Heart of Darkness*. The author found that five women are absolute the Other in patriarchal society.

Key Words: *Heart of Darkness*, otherness, female images

Chapter 1　Introduction

Joseph Conrad (1875—1924), one of the greatest English novelist at the end of the 19th century. In modern British literature, he's rather a special figure. His adult life may be divided into two major stages, during which he leads to different life, one on the sea as a captain, the other as a writer on the land. *Heart of Darkness*, one of his most famous works. This novel was based on Conrad's real experience of Congo. In this novel, Conrad was determined to attain his goal, to be the pioneer explorer and faithful recorder of the human soul—as long as human history, its nature uncannily hidden and veiled, as "inaccessible" and "dark" as primitive African jungle, as "blank" and vast as the mysterious sea. (Daiches, 33)

Ever since its publication in 1899, critical interest in *Heart of Darkness* has been strong. Critics' view cover issues including the theme of the work, the purpose of the frame, the language of the novel and so on. People read it mainly from psychoanalytic perspective and imperialism, colonialism or racism. However, women and gender was few discussed.

Conrad has been regarded as a male-oriented author for long time. This thesis will read *Heart of Darkness* from feminist perspective. The author will analyze the female characters with Simone de Beauvoir's "otherness" theory. This paper concludes that women are absolute Other in patriarchal society.

Chapter 2　Beauvoir and the Other

As one of the French existentialism philosophers in the 20th century, Simone de Beauvoir

(1908—1986) is an important representative figure of modern feminism. Her status in the history of feminist thought is established by *The Second Sex*. Its content includes the description of the female's situation, the relationship between two different genders and relationship between the female, as well as her suggestions on liberal women. Beauvoir was also a famous writer productive of many books, and she described a lot of female figures in them, while demonstrates her concern for female's destiny and embodies her feminist thought.

2.1 Definition of the Other

In the introduction of *The Second Sex*, Beauvoir pointed that women are the Others. She said: "humanity is male and man defines woman not in herself but as relative to him; she is not regarded as an autonomous being. She is defined and differentiated with reference to man and not he with reference to her; she is the incidental, the inessential as opposed to the essential. He is the Subject, he is the Absolute—she is the Other". (Beauvoir, 11) It means that women are affiliation, non-autonomy, secondary as relative to men.

Otherness is a fundamental category of human thought. Thus it is that no group ever sets itself up as the One without at once setting up the Other over against itself. The otherness is not absolute. While one side considers himself as the One, the other side would become the Other. The real gender relationship is mutual: each side is both the Subjecy and the Object, both the One and the Other. However, actually the mutual relationship is denied in the gender relationship. Women are absolute the Other and can't be turned to be the One.

2.2 The Explanation of the Other

Alterity is a feature of women as absolute the Other. "Women" is the sensible symbol of alterity. (Beauvoir, 170) This kind of alterity is passive. When men think that they are the Subject, woman is a kind of threat and danger. Woman is object against subject; she is the diversity against unity; it is material against form; it is chaos against order. Woman is a kind of threat and danger. It is Manichanism. (Beauvoir, 74) In men's view, women's being is to satisfy men's need and desire. The male-centered culture tends to vilify women as representing darkness and chaos.

Women are men's dependants. The reason for this is that women lack concrete means for organizing themselves into a unit which can stand face to face with the correlative unit. They live dispersed among the males, attached to fathers or husbands because of residence, housework, economic condition, and social standing to certain men. Women are willing to accept to receive the benefits from dependant status especially in marriage. Women never create direct autonomous relationship with men.

The other is immance. Beauvoir thought that all existence is immance and transcendence. She said: Husbands are labours. They face with society benefit more than family benefit. They start their future through cooperation while building collective future. Meanwhile, women are doomed to give birth to offspring and care for families. Most of women can't make deep impression on the world. (Beauvoir, 122) Women never dominate the world, on the contrary, they are dominated by the society.

The two sexes have never shared the world in equality. And even today woman is heavily handicapped. Now, what peculiarly signalises the situation of woman is that she—a free and autonomous being like all human creatures – nevertheless finds herself living in a world where men compel her to assume the status of the Other. In patriarchal society, women are marginalized and kept out of mainstream under the rule of men. The ideal place for women is the domestic field.

Chapter 3   Analysis of Female Character

The prejudice against women can be traced back to Aristotle, who said: "The female is a female by virtue of a certain lack of qualities"; "we should regard the female nature as afflicted with a natural defectiveness." And St Thomas for his part pronounced woman to be an "imperfect man", an "incidental" being. This is symbolised in Genesis where Eve is depicted as made from what Bossuet called "a supernumerary bone" of Adam.

There were 5 female characters in this novel: two women/ knitter, Marlow's aunt, the saverage woman, and the intended. All of them didn't have full name. Women's title showed the relationship between them and men. In this way Marlow denied women's identity and consider women as dependant.

3.1   Two Knitting Women

Men want to keep women in the place of mystery to keep her in her place and keep her at a distance. An approach to mystify and distance woman is to rendering them as fearful as serpents.

… She seemed to know all about them and about me, too. An eerie feeling came over me. She seemed uncanny and fateful. Often far away there I thought of these two, guarding the door of Darkness, knitting black wool as for a warm pall, one introducing, introducing continuously to the unknown, the other scrutinizing the cheery and foolish faces with unconcerned old eyes. AVE! Old knitter of black wool. MORITURI TE SALUTANT. Not many of those she looked at ever saw her again-not half, by a long way. (Conrad, 12)

The two old women were dressed in black, knitting black wool silently. They looked like the guardians to the gate of Hell. Marlow felt nervous and thrilled as if he would suffer omniscient Fates. They seemed to know all the secrets about the business of imperial trade and colonization. The old women knew all the comers who would fall into an unknown world where they have attached great dreams and hopes. In ancient Greek myth, there are three goddesses who control the fate of human and gods by spinning, measuring and snipping the thread of life. I think the images of two old women were originated from three goddesses. They can prejudice all fates of the comers.

3.2   Marlow's Aunt

Marlow asked for his aunt's help when he wanted to be employed by African company. The aunt tried her best to offer any help to Marlow kindly and selflessly like a mother seeking for a job for her own son. Without his aunt's help, Marlow couldn't achieve his dream. But he expressed his prejudice and contempt to his aunt. Influenced by domestic mass media, she firmly believed Marlow "like an emissary of light, something like a lower sort of apostle" and "weaning those ignorant millions from their horrid ways". However, actually, the company ran for the profit. At the end of the talk, she reminded Marlow to wear flannel in Africa.

It's queer how out of touch with truth women are. They live in a world of their own, and there has never been anything like it, and never can be. It is too beautiful altogether, and if they were to set it up it would go to pieces before the first sunset. Some confounded fact we men have been living contentedly with ever since the day of creation would start up and knock the whole thing over. (Conrad, 13)

As the Marlow said, Eve was a rib of Adam. Women were men's dependant. Because women were imprisoned in the unreal truth, Marlow mocks their lack of knowledge of the world. When men experienced the outside world, women should guard from all this should be the angel of the house, bringing men comfort, peace, shelter.

3.3 Kurtz's Black Mistress

… bizarre things, charms, gifts of witch-men, that hung about her, glittered and trembled at every step…She was savage and superb, wild-eyed and magnificent; there was something ominous and stately in her deliberate progress. And in the hush that had fallen suddenly upon the whole sorrowful land, the immense wilderness, the colossal body of the fecund and mysterious life seemed to look at her, pensive, as though it had been looking at the image of its own tenebrous and passionate soul… Her face had a tragic and fierce aspect of wild sorrow and of dumb pain mingled with the fear of some struggling, half-shaped re- solve. She stood looking at us without a stir, and like the wilderness itself, with an air of brooding over an inscrutable purpose. (Conrad, 81)

These words "seemed to" "as though" reveal Marlow's subjective expression of the woman and the jungle. His description was elusive and distanced. Kurtz' black mistress stood for the mysterious life of the jungle. She seemed to be Kurtz' subordinate and sexual tool. The woman was seen from outside rather than inside. In Marlow's view, she was devil. Her original desire and the blame on Kurtz were described as greed and evil behavior. The image of cruel vampire would eventually force Kurtz, the symbol of civilization to death. Kurtz' black mistress represented the otherness of African Continent.

3.4 The Intended

She was beautiful and and elegant. Kurtz' Intended was the idol woman. "She struck me as beautiful— I mean she had a beautiful expression. I know that the sunlight ycan be made to lie, too, yet one felt that no manipulation of light and pose could have conveyed the delicate shade of truthfulness upon those features". (Conrad, 98)

"… I had to wait in a lofty drawing- room with three long windows … The tall marble fireplace had a cold and monumental whiteness. A grand piano stood massively in a corner; with dark gleams on the flat surfaces like a sombre and polished sarcophagus. … She came forward, all in black, with a pale head, floating towards me in the dusk. She was in mourning. … The room seemed to have grown darker, as if all the sad light of the cloudy evening had taken refuge on her forehead. This fair hair, this pale visage, this pure brow, seemed surrounded by an ashy halo from which the dark eyes looked out at me." (Conrad, 100)

The background color of the Intended's drawing room mainly consisted of black and white. Her solemn appearance symbolized lifeless. She was a tender, virtuous and devoted housewife. Since she was informed Kurtz had died, her whole world broke down. Marlow showed his sympathy to the Intended. She kept mourning even after more than a year of Kurtz's death. She had "mature capacity for fidelity, for belief, for suffering". She was a self-sacrificing ideal woman.

And you admired him, she said. "It was impossible to know him and not to admire him. Was it?"

"He was a remarkable man," I said, unsteadily. Then before the appealing fixity of her gaze, that seemed to watch for more words on my lips,

Who was not his friend who had heard him speak once?' she was saying. "He drew men towards him by what was best in them." She looked at me with intensity. "It is the gift of the great," "His words will remain," I said.

"And his example," she whispered to herself. "Men looked up to him— his goodness shone in every act. His example—" (Conrad, 101-102)

This woman expressed her deep love to Kurtz and her determination and glory in Kurtz's belief. Marlow lied to the Intended. Concealing Kurtz's cry of "The horror! The horror!" Marlow told the Intended that Kurtz's last words are her name instead. He wanted to protect this lady from dark truth as the men done.

'Girl! What? Did I mention a girl? Oh, she is out of it—completely. They—the women, I mean— are out of it—should be out of it. We must help them to stay in that beautiful world of their own, lest ours gets worse. Oh, she had to be out of it. (Conrad, 64)

This means that history is his story and women have no share in it and therefore should be excluded from men's realm. In this way, men can continue to experience the truth and confine women to the beautiful world of their own in which they can continue to offer powerful ideological support to their menfolk.

What does the title "heart of darkness" refer to? Some take it to be the wilderness of Africa, while others consider it as the symbol of the dark part of human soul. From feminist perspective, "heart of darkness" refer to feminine world. In Marlow's view, women are related to darkness. The two company women "guard the door of darkness." "knitting black wool." The intended "came forward, all in black, with a pale head, floating towards me in the dusk."

Chapter 4   Conclusions

To sum up, the author explains the definition of the Other and its features: alterity, dependence, immance and marginalization. Guided by Beauvoir's the Other theory, this thesis concludes that women are inherently inferior to men in patriarchal society. Influenced by such prejudice against women, the male-dominated society gives some stereotypes of femininity: formlessness, passivity, piety, irrationality, silence, docility, spirituality and confinement. Men tend to divide women into two kinds: devil and angle. Perhaps men have become accustomed to the humble nature of a woman as usual, perhaps they deliberately ignore the existence of women hidden female voice deprived of women's voice. While the latter shows exactly the fear of men's potential for feminine potential for their high male authority. As the feminist pioneer Beauvoir said, "a woman is not born to be a woman but a society that makes her a woman." All female characters in Conrad's writings in literary works are so tame. It is fully displayed by the female center of the whole work by the compromise of the woman and the disposition of the whole work of the deceased. In fact, the images for women are fully exposed to its manipulation to regulate the production of female images.

References

[1] Daiches David. The Novel and the Modern World [M]. Chicago: University of Chicago Press, 1960: 33.

[2] 康拉德. 黑暗的心[M]. 叶雷译. 南京：译林出版社，2016.

[3] 西蒙·德·波伏娃. 第二性[M]. 陶铁柱译. 北京：中国书籍出版社，2004.

"Monster" or "Angel": A Feminist Reading of Lily Bart in *The House of Mirth*

胡希雅

摘　要：伊迪斯·华顿（1862—1937）是 19 世纪末 20 世纪初一位杰出的美国女作家，在美国文学史上有着不可替代的地位，与其他女性作家不同的是，伊迪斯·华顿出生于 "老纽约" 社会中的上流家庭，并且对它有很深的洞察力。小说《欢乐之家》以老纽约上流社会为背景，以女主人公莉莉·巴特为代表揭示了女性的生存状况。基于桑德拉·吉尔伯特和苏珊·古芭在其著作《阁楼上的疯女人》中提出的关于天使形象与恶魔形象的理论，通过深刻分析《欢乐之家》中莉莉·巴特女性形象，可以探究伊迪斯·华顿的女性观，并揭示天使形象和恶魔形象产生的原因。

关键词：天使；魔鬼；女性主义；莉莉·巴特

Abstract： Edith Wharton (1862—1937) was one of the most outstanding American writers at the end of the 19th century and the beginning of the 20th century who took an irreplaceable position in the history of American literature at the turn of the 20th century. Distinguished from other female writers, Edith Wharton was born in an upper-class family in the Old New York society and had deep insight into it.

Her novel, *The House of Mirth*, tried to reveal women's situation under the background of Old New York. Based on the theory of angle and monster put forward by Sandra Gilbert and Susan Gubar in the Madwoman in the Attic, this paper attempts to deeply analyze the female image: Lily Bart in *The House of Mirth* to explore Edith Wharton's view of women and explain the emergence of angle images and monster images.

Key Words: angel, monster, feminist, Lily Bart

Chapter 1　Introduction

Edith Wharton (1862—1937) was one of the most celebrated American writers at the end of the 19th century and the beginning of the 20th century. She is declared to be "one of the most intelligent American women who ever lived" by R. W. Lewis in his monumental Pulitzer Prize-wining biography, Edith Wharton: A Biography, which has been so far viewed as the most authoritative biography of Edith Wharton. Commenting on Wharton's position in literary history, Lewis claims that "Edith Wharton was almost without peer in her American as a judge of achievement in fiction and poetry."

Edith Wharton was so versatile as well as prolific that she published over forty books during her writing career, including some twenty novels, ten collections of short stories, books of verse, a pioneer work in interior design, several books of travel, an autobiography, and books on Italian villas, France and fictional theory. It is by her fiction, however, that her importance as a writer must be judged.

When it comes to Wharton's novels, The House of Mirth must be one of the most famous. It tells the story of Lily Bart, aged 29, beautiful, impoverished and in need of a rich husband to safeguard her place in the social elite, and to support her expensive habits - her clothes, her charities and her gambling. Unwilling to marry without both love and money, Lily becomes vulnerable to the kind of gossip and slander which attach to a girl who has been on the marriage market for too long. Wharton charts the course of Lily's life, providing, along the way, a wider picture of a society in transition, a rapidly changing New York where the old certainties of manners, morals and family have disappeared and the individual has become an expendable commodity.

In Edith Wharton's novel world, she paid close attention to women and their survival conditions, however, Edith Wharton is not a feminist, and her moral outlook also tends to be constructive. That is why Lily Bart, the main character in The House of Mirth appears to have a so complex personality that we sometimes have no idea whether to define her as Angel or Monster.

By taking Lily Bart as examples, we may have a clearer recognition of the female characters built by Edith Wharton and the reasons for her to create those beautiful and unforgettable female characters.

Chapter 2   Female Characters: "Monster" or "Angel"

So far scholars has been interested in categorize female characters appeared in article works including novels, paintings, movies, etc. One of the most popular approaches is to classify female characters into monsters and angels.

In 1979, Sandra Gilbert and Susan Gubar made a breakthrough in feminist criticism with their work The Madwoman in the Attic: The Woman Writer and the Nineteenth-Century Literary Imagination. In this text, Gilbert and Gubar used the figure of Bertha Mason as the so-called "Madwoman in the Attic" to make an argument about perceptions toward female literary characters during the Nineteenth-Century. According to Gilbert and Gubar, all female characters in male-authored works can be categorized as either "angel" or "monster".

The "angel" character was pure, dispassionate, and submissive; in other words, the ideal female figures in a male-dominated society. In sharp contrast to the "angel" figure, the "monster" female character was sensual, passionate, rebellious, and decidedly uncontrollable: all qualities that caused a great deal of anxiety among men during the Victorian period.

Chapter 3   Lily Bart: The Image of Angel

The "angel" character in literature was pure, dispassionate, and submissive; in other words, the ideal female figures in a male-dominated society. There is no denying that Lily is that kind of women that all men have dreamed of because of her attractive beauty. Apart from her appearance, however, there are more factors that make Lily an angel in that male-dominated time. The following part will analyze in detail why Lily can be regarded as an image of angel.

3.1　An unnecessary ornament

Simone de Beauvoir claimed in her book *the second sex* that it is that no group ever sets itself up as the One without at once setting up the Other over against itself. De Beauvoir argued that woman is set up as the Other of man. (Beauvoir, 2010: 7) Lily's identity as the Other in *The House of Mirth* can be proved that not only men but also women in that novel regard her as an ornament to the man.

Lily is smart, beautiful, graceful and good at social intercourse. We can find all the factors leading man to think of a woman as an angel on her. However, they just regard her as an ornament. For example, Gus Trenor, the husband of Lily's best friend, using Lily's crazy need of money, paid Lily a certain amount of money. But it turned out that he just wanted to "enjoy" Lily's beautiful body. Then Mr. Rosedale a plump rosy man of the blond Jewish type asked Lily to marry him. But it turned out that he just wanted Lily to help him be accepted by the upper class. And when Lily was expelled from the house of mirth by Mr. Dorset, she compromised and showed her willingness in marring him. However, he rejected mercilessly as she was useless to him although he loved her beauty in his inner heart at that time. What makes it worse is that women in this novel also treat Lily as an unnecessary ornament. Mrs. Dorset use Lily to hide the relationship between her lover and her. Mattie Gormer and Mrs. Hatch regarded her as a step stone to the upper class.

Ironically, she also believes firmly in this conception that women are ornament to men. "A woman is asked out as much for her clothes as for herself. The clothes are the background, the frame, if you like: they don't make success, but they are a part of it. Who wants a dingy woman? We are expected to be pretty and well-dressed till we drop—and if we can't keep it up alone, we have to go into partnership."

Lily's position in the upper class no longer exists, but she never knows this. The reason for her to stay in the house of mirth is that she has the beauty that men love and value women can make use of.

3.2　Repeated compromise

Lily's position in the upper class is peculiar. She belongs to it in terms of origin and relation. But with the decline of fortune after her father's bankruptcy, she becomes a social parasite living on the rich, with the sole aspiration in her mind that she would be one of them. From the very beginning, she has been bought up in the faith that "to be poor is to live like pigs, is a confession of failure that it amounted to disgrace". (Wharton, 1984:31) And "whatever it cost, one must be decently dressed". (Wharton, 1984: 28) After her father's ruin, her beauty was the "last asset in their fortune" to her mother, as if "it were some weapon to get it all back, with her face". (Wharton, 1984: 26)

To get a rich man to marry, Lily compromised again and again to the men appeared in her life. As has been mentioned above, when Lily was expelled from the house of mirth by Mr. Dorset, she compromised and showed her willingness in marring him. However, he rejected mercilessly as she was useless to him. In addition, even on her train to Trenors' party, she didn't want to miss the chance to know some rich man, so "she glanced about in the hope of seeing some other member of the Trenors' party". (Wharton, 1984: 18) She succeeded in attracting the attention of Mr. Percy Gryce, a rich guy who would be a suitable man to marry. She made a compromise in what she was interested in, just because Mr. Percy Gryce was interested in collecting books. To be a better wife that will be easily accepted by the upper class, she changed herself into a woman who would obey the old traditions and who would take family as the center of her life. Although finally she failed as she found she could not bear the boring life in the rich family, we cannot deny her efforts in marring a rich guy, which can be seen as a proof that she is an image of angel.

Chapter 4　Lily Bart: The Image of Monster

In The House of Mirth, Edith Wharton unfolded before usa vivid panorama of the upper class in New York at the turn of the 20th century against which the rise and fall of the fate of Lily Bart is pathetically depicted. One unique thing about the character of Lily is that, as Showalter pointed out in Sister's Choice, "she is neither the educated, socially conscious, rebellious New Woman, nor the androgynous artist who finds meaning for her life in solitude and creativity. She pursues lady-like manners in the midst of vulgarity, boorishness and malice." (Showalter, 1991: 87) Lily was so complex an image that we can also find she has some characters that make her a monster in that man-centered society. The following part will analyze in detail why Lily can be regarded as an image of angel.

4.1　Lily's two selves

It is very surprising that Lily, who is such a skilled player in the game of market of marriage with her beauty, her grace, her rich knowledge concerning the shades of differences regarding rules and values of her society, would fail again and again. It seems that there are two selves of Lily: her true self, i.e. her impulsive free resistant self and her debased captive self. Each time when the glittering opportunity comes, whether in the case of Gryce, Rosedale or Dorset, her real self would rise up to overthrow or make her shrink from it. This was even discernible to her friend, the sophisticated Mrs. Fish:" she works like a slave preparing the ground and sowing her seed, but the day she ought to be reaping the harvest she oversleeps herself or goes off on a picnic. I suppose she despises the thing she is trying for. It's the difficulty of deciding that makes her such an interesting study." (Wharton, 1984: 179)

Just as what Mrs. Fish said, Lily despises marring a rich guy from her inner heart, which she had always been trying for. She didn't want to have a loveless marriage and sacrifice her freedom in exchange of a rich and comfortable life. This was what most women dared not do in that man-centered society and also what made Lily am image of monster.

4.2　Lily's escape motif

Lily's life in The House of Mirth is filled with various escapes, and every time to escape derives from the depth of her heart, all the experiences have gradually mended her ugly mind and broken soul. Though she does not maintain her position in the upper class and failed to hunt a wealthy husband for the rest of her life, yet she obtained a pure spirit and realized exactly what she want. At last, the life journey brought Lily to her self.

Lily had no choice but to escape if she wanted to rebel against her fate in that man-centered society. Her death, for example, was her last yet greatest escape.

At the end, Lily Bart took an overdose of chloral, cast out by the world and her friends, without money, was not able to find a job that had enough salary to maintain her life. The dominant feeling at the last time is of profound loneliness: "Her eyes sought the faces about her, craving a responsive glance, some sign an intuition of her loneliness." She did not have the energy to continue her life any longer and did not want to give a chance to others and herself to make a difference for her, choosing to escape into death rather than revealing the secrets of her friends for an opportunity to marry into the upper class. Finally, she decided to die in order to escape from the society, which helped to maintain her pureness in her inner heart.

Lily's death is a silent rebellion to the man-centered society and also what makes her an image of monster.

Chapter 5　Conclusions

So far scholars has been interested in categorize female characters appeared in article works including novels, paintings, movies, etc. One of the most popular approaches is to classify female characters into monsters and angels. But we may find it difficult to catalogue Lily. On the one hand, she submitted herself to that man-centered society and tried her best to marry into the upper class. However, on the other hand, she tried to escape from the life she dreamed of and rebel against the society. Here are some reasons that make Lily so complex an image.

The first reason is relevant to the background of the story and her family. Lily lived in the world when the capitalism and the accompanying consumerist drives were in full swing. People were all crazy about ranking among the upper class. This was also a time when women were regarded subordinate to men and the only approach for women to join the upper class was to marry a man from that class. And this was exactly what Lily's mother believed in. She taught Lily to accept the fact that she was a product and she should get all things belonging to her and her family with her beauty. To her mother, Mr. Bart was never mentioned or thought of except for his remittances. After his bankruptcy," to his wife he no longer counted: he had become extinct when he ceased to fulfill his purpose. She sat at his death bed with the provisional air of a traveler who waits for a belated train to start." (Wharton, 1984: 31) Even if Lily pitied her father, for her feelings were softer, her filial instinct was overshadowed by her mother's resentment: "you are sorry for him now, but you will feel differently when you see what he has done to us." (Wharton, 1984: 31) In this environment of money cult, and commodity fetishism, human relations, even those among the beloved ones, are devoid of any tender feeling and become materialized. However, it was Lily's father that led her to explore the mental world. That's why we can feel Lily's two selves are struggling when dealing with choices throughout her life. The two different way of education endowed Lily a complex personality and made her a combination of angel and monster.

Secondly, we always say the character in the novel is a mirror to the author. In Edith Wharton's novel world, she paid close attention to women and their survival conditions, however, Edith Wharton is not a feminist, and her moral outlook also tends to be constructive. That is why Lily Bart, the main character in The House of Mirth appears to have a so complex personality that we sometimes have no idea whether to define her as Angel or Monster.

As has been mentioned above, "she is neither the educated, socially conscious, rebellious New Woman, nor the androgynous artist who finds meaning for her life in solitude and creativity. She pursues lady-like manners in the midst of vulgarity, boorishness and malice". (Showalter, 1991: 87) Lily is more like the combination of angel and monster. And the author believes it is the contradiction that Lily has that leaves her the everlasting lily flower in our heart.

References

[1] Lewis R. W. Edith Wharton: A Biography[M]. New York: Harper & Row Publisher, 1975.

[2] Simone de Beauvoir. The second sex[M]. London: Vintage, 1997.

[3] Wharton Edith. The House of Mirth[M]. New York: Bantam Books, 1984.

[4] 潘建. 献给莉莉·巴特的一朵玫瑰——评伊迪丝·沃顿《欢乐之家》女主角莉莉·巴特[J]. 湛江师范学院学报，1999（2）：130-131.

[5] 桑德拉·吉尔伯特，苏珊·古芭. 阁楼上的疯女人[M]. 杨莉馨译. 上海：上海人民出版社，2015.

[6] 伊迪丝·华顿. 欢乐之家[M]. 赵兴国，刘景堪译. 南京：译林出版社，1995.

翻译篇

Methods and Strategies of Jesuit Translation between Late Ming and Early Qing Dynasty

沈安天　吕　汀

摘　要：明清之际的两百余年时间里，中国历史达到了第二次翻译的高潮，同时也是第一次科学翻译的高潮。以文化适应为原则指导下的西洋耶稣会士来到中国，成为"西学东渐"浪潮中翻译活动的排头兵。他们和与其合作的中国士大夫虽然未能建立起系统的翻译理论，但他们首创了"洋译华述"的翻译方法，对"会通超胜"思想和实用主义翻译进行了初步的探索，至今仍具备强大的借鉴意义。通过结合实际翻译活动案例和时代背景，可以对这段时期耶稣会士的翻译方法和思想策略进行概括。

关键词：耶稣会士；翻译；文化适应

Abstract: Between late Ming and early Qing Dynasty, the two centuries marked the second climax of translation and the first one in science translation in Chinese history. Following the principle of cultural adaptation, Jesuit missionaries played the role of pioneers in "eastward transmission of western sciences". Although Jesuits and Chinese literati they cooperated with did not form systematic translation theory, they initiated "Chinese narration plus Western translation" method and explored "Mastery and Innovation" thought and pragmatic translation strategy. These thoughts and strategies have strong modern significance. This essay summarizes the basic methods and strategies of Jesuit translation, combining practical examples and reflection upon the whole picture.

Key Words: Jesuits, translation, cultural adaptation

Chapter 1　Introduction

1.1　Background Information

During 16th and 18th century, cultural communication between China and the West becomes a major part of the climax of Chinese cultural development. The first encounter and mutual influence between European modern science and Chinese traditional science is an important and outstanding component of this communication. What plays the role of the medium of scientific and cultural encounter is Society of Jesus and Jesuits which came into being during European Protestant Reformation and Humanism ideological trends. From 1582, when Matteo Ricci, an Italian Jesuit, reached in Macao, until 1793, when Jean Joseph-Marie Amiot, a French Jesuit and the last Head of Jesuit Mission, died in Beijing, Society of Jesus survived in China for nearly 200 years. The bicentenary marked a climax in Chinese cultural communication history, in addition, the second climax in translation field after the Buddhist Scriptures translation during Sui and Tang Dynasties. Thus, Jesuits are renowned for the pioneers in translation in the "eastward transmission of western sciences".

1.2　Research Status

Research upon Jesuits is the center of scholars major in religion, culture and linguistics. The majority of the research achievements have come out as monographs and essays.

First of all, most research focus on individual cases of Jesuits, especially on Matteo Ricci.

Prof. Feng Tianyu, in his work "The Historical Functions and Modern Enlightenments of the Modern Terminology for Chinese Characters" gives credit for Matteo Ricci's contribution on translating Western terminology and regards him as the "trailblazer" in this field. It quotes, "Eastward transmission of western sciences originated from late Ming Dynasty, which also marks the beginning of the introduction of Western terminology in masses. Matteo Ricci initiated the trend, therefore, his work was of significance in the history of Chinese and Western communication as well as Chinese academics." (冯天瑜 1)

Associate Professor Chen Deng, in his essay "Matteo Ricci's Influence on Chinese Culture in the translation of Western Works", researches on the perspective of translation of Western sciences and generalizes Ricci's influence on Chinese disciplines, such as mathematics, astronomy, geography, art, philosophy, music and so on. (陈登 70)

Secondly, some researches focus on the contents and thoughts of translation.

Associate Professor Li Xinde, in his work "Jesuits' Translation and Interpretation of *Four Books*", proposes that Jesuits' translation of *Four Books* was based on the need of them learning Chinese language and spreading Catholic doctrine. (李新德 98)

Ms Zeng Jing made an all-around summary of the characteristics and thoughts relating to translation in her essay "On the Thought and Influence of Jesuits' Translation". (曾静 45) Ms Luo Ying began with the translation of a Chinese character "Tian" in order to show the ideological and religious differences, especially the view towards heaven, between Chinese and Western people in her essay "On the Jesuits' Latin Translation of Confucian Concepts in the 17th Century, with 'Tian' as an Example". (罗莹 26)

1.3　Significance of the Research

Firstly, in the aspect of contents, Jesuits took aim at translating natural science works on a large scale, turning the first leaf in Chinese and Western science translation. Meanwhile, Jesuits introduced some results of ancient Chinese culture. Research on the translation text is conducive to improving the knowledge of the origin of "Westward transmission of eastern sciences".

Secondly, in the aspect of methods, Jesuits took "Chinese narration plus Western translation" as their core technique. They "Confucianize" Catholic doctrine, which is their typical strategy. In addition, Jesuits pursued the consistency of spirituality and fluency, plus ideology and literariness. In this way, we can take a glance at the confrontation and compromise between Chinese and Western culture by viewing Jesuits' translation with the restriction in that certain time. In conclusion, Western sciences were introduced into China through translation, which brought both challenge to cultural centralism in ancient China and inspiration to translation strategy in modern China.

Chapter 2　Society of Jesus and Jesuit Mission in China

The Society of Jesus is a Roman Catholic Church religious order whose members are called Jesuits, Soldiers of Christ, and Foot soldiers of the Pope, because the founder, Saint Ignatius of Loyola, was a knight before becoming a priest. Jesuits are the largest male religious order of the Roman Catholic Church with 18 516 members. (Society of Jesus)

The Jesuits first entered China through the Portuguese possession of Macau where they founded St. Paul's College of Macau.

The Jesuit China missions in the 16th and 17th centuries introduced Western science and astronomy and its own revolution to China. The scientific revolution brought by the Jesuits coincided with a time when scientific innovation had declined in China:

"The Jesuits made efforts to translate western mathematical and astronomical works into Chinese and aroused the interest of Chinese scholars in these sciences. They made very extensive astronomical observation and carried out the first modern cartographic work in China. They also learned to appreciate the scientific achievements of this ancient culture and made them known in Europe. Through their correspondence, European scientists first learned about the Chinese science and culture." (Udías 53)

Chapter 3　Translation Method

Most Western sciences books introduced to China during Ming and Qing Dynasties are the results of comprehensive collaboration of Western Jesuits and Chinese officials and literati. At that time, there were few people in China who could speak Western languages, neither could any Jesuit missionaries translate science books independently with such low mastery of Chinese language.

For example, Matteo Ricci had constantly complaint about the obstacles he was faced in translating:

"而才既菲薄，且东西文理，又自绝殊，字义相求，仍多阙略，了然于口，尚可勉图，肆笔为文，便成艰涩矣。嗣是以来，屡逢志士，左提右挈，而每患作辍，三进三止。鸣呼！"（徐宗泽 145）

(I had little talent and less learning. Additionally, grammar and semantics of Chinese and Western languages have tremendous differences. I could barely handle with oral Chinese, but as soon as I try to write them down, I am faced with great obstacles. As a consequence, every time I met with notable literati, I am pleased to accept their aid. But when we have tough issues, we tried and gave them up again and again for several times. Alas!)

For Chinese scholars, they were not familiar with Western languages either. The only exception was Wang Zheng, a Ming scientist. But his ability was not good enough, based on his own account in the preface of *Diagrams and explanations of the wonderful machines of the Far West*, an encyclopedia of Western mechanical devices:

"乃其说则属西文西字，虽余向在里中得金四表先生为余指授西文字母字父二十五号，刻有《西儒耳目资》一书，亦略知其音响乎，顾全文全义则茫然其莫测也，于是恳请译以中字。"（徐宗泽 187）

(Their theory uses Western languages and scripts. Although Mr. Nicolas Trigault has taught me twenty-five Latin alphabets at my home, and I have learnt a bit of their pronunciation from his book *Audio-Video Aid to Western Scholars*, I had zero knowledge of the meaning of the whole passage. So I ask them to translate it into Chinese for me.)

The text above clearly reveals that Wang Zheng, in cooperation with Nicolas Trigault in translating books, learnt some foreign languages.

Therefore, Jesuits came up with a new method to translate the books precisely. Jesuits interpreted or orally translated into rough Chinese in the first place, after that, Chinese scholars put it into written Chinese. Afterwards, Jesuits and Chinese scholars cooperated in polishing, examining and editing the original translation texts and got published.

The most important example of this method is the translation of Euclid's *Elements*. Matteo Ricci and Xu Guangqi, a famous scientist who later received baptism, elaborated the translation for at least three times, according to historical accounts. During the work, Xu coined several geometric terms in Chinese, including parallel lines, triangles, acute/right/obtuse angles, etc.

It is worth mentioning that the process in which the duo reached consensus on the Chinese title of the book. If translated literally, the title would not be accepted as a mathematics-related book. Xu thought over several words, finally, he decided to use "几何" (Pinyin: jǐhé) as the Chinese version of "geometry". This translation is listed as an outstanding attempt in the history of Chinese translation, as *Jihe* has similar sound (as to "geo") and meaning (the original meaning of *Jihe* is "how much" or "size, magnitude") to *geometria* (Latin: geometry). (许文胜 118)

During the process of mutual learning, missionaries and literati reached accordance in translating.

Chapter 4　Translation Strategies

During this period, the translation strategies brought up by Jesuits are highly educational to modern translation.

4.1　Ricci's Rule

Jesuits' translation strategy is closely related to the "cultural adaptation" strategy developed by some Jesuit missionaries, including Alessandro Valignano, Michael Ruggieri and Matteo Ricci, which is called "Ricci's Rule", named by Kangxi Emperor of Qing Dynasty.

The main content of the Rule is listed below.

（1）Make acquaintance with upper-class officials and literati, so that the difficulty in evangelism would be decreased.

（2）Use "practical learning", i.e., Western modern sciences, to arouse interest to Catholic Church in Chinese people.

（3）Combine Catholicism with Confucianism in order to avoid confrontation between two cultures.

（4）Show respect to Chinese traditional customs (朱大锋 38).

These rules motivate Jesuit missionaries to introduce Catholic Church into China smoothly, with a humble and approachable attitude, especially in translating Western books.

4.2 "Mastery and Innovation"

In his work *Complete Catalogue of Calendar* (Chinese: 历书总目表), Xu Guangqi stated, "In my humble opinion, in order to innovate, we need master the whole; before the mastery, we must translate." (曾静 45) Here, he proposed his own idea on translation: "会通超胜" (Pinyin: Huìtōng Chāoshèng, sense-for-sense translation: Mastery and Innovation).

In this term, four Chinese characters have progressive meanings, as shown in Table 1.

Table 1　Explanation of "会通超胜"

Chinese	Meaning	Significance
Hui	Combination and understanding of Chinese and Western cultures	Perceptual basis
Tong	Compare both cultures and search for common ground. Achieve mastery through comprehensive study	
Chaosheng	Surpass the original text and studies. Create new ideas and thoughts based on the knowledge	Practical breakthrough

Talking about the purpose of translating, the "Mastery and Innovation" strategy has a clear vision, that is, to aim at developing China's science and technology, by realizing that developing basic disciplines, including mathematics, is the basis. By combining and renovating Western sciences and Chinese traditions, Xu did a lot of comparative research and tried to introduce mathematical logic into the stumbling traditional Chinese science.

For example, after translating Euclid's *Elements*, Xu was not satisfied with introducing foreign mathematical theory. He tried to prove the Gougu theorem (Pythagorean theorem) by systematically reviewing Euclid's *Elements*. Eventually, he successfully completed the work by drawing lessons from Proposition 47, Book 1, i.e., "In right-angled triangles the square on the side opposite the right angle equals the sum of the squares on the sides containing the right angle". His proof was revealed in his book *Gougu*, published in 1609.

In a modern sense, the "Mastery and Innovation" is an embodiment of target language culture-oriented domestication in translation studies. TL culture-oriented domestication is the translation method which attempts to reach "cultural equity" between source language culture and target language culture. The advocates for the theory argue that, it is dangerous to force source language culture into target language users' mind. Thus, it is translators' responsibility to avoid cultural conflict by balancing ideological factors in target language culture. Xu Guangqi adhered to the idea of developing domestic culture by translating. This is a sublimation to the original theory, especially in his introduction of mathematical logic in the proof of Gougu theorem. This demonstrates his ambition in surpassing Western science, making him a pioneer in domestication of translation.

4.3　Pragmatism and Patriotism

Science translation is of important social function. During late Ming and early Qing, agricultural production and technology had reached climax. For instance, the size of labour force and arable land is unprecedentedly tremendous; plough and harrow were improved and became multi-functional; malleable cast iron was applied in agricultural machinery; Champa rice was introduced into China; agronomy was advanced.These factors have contributed a lot to traditional Chinese agriculture.

As Karl Marx put in *Capital*, "All production of surplus-value, and thus all development of capital, has for its natural basis the productiveness of agricultural labour." (Marx 573)In handicraft industry, The Seeds of Chinese Capitalism was born in Mid-Ming Dynasty based on the development of agriculture. In some workshops of well salt industry, silk industry, porcelain industry, mining industry and smelting industry, hiring labour made its debut in Chinese history (Faure 57). New relations of production called on new tools and technology.

In ideology, Pragmatic School came into being in late Ming Dynasty. Some of the Confucian literati, such as GuYanwu, Huang Zongxi and Wang Fuzhi, opposed to vague and general doctrine like Neo-Confucianism (including School of Principle and School of Mind). They were in favor of "study for practical purposes", (Chinese: 经世致用, Pinyin: jīngshìzhìyòng) which strongly affected the translation of that time.

Based on the circumstances mentioned above, translating science books that benefit people's living condition and productivity was put at the top of the agenda.

Some of the Chinese Jesuits emphasized the urgency of translating Western science books. In a petition to the current emperor, Xu Guangqi argued that mastery of cultures between home and abroad is of great importance; he also felt sorry about the small population of Jesuit missionaries that came to China like Matteo Ricci. So he called on the imperial court to support translating Western science books into Chinese. The following statement reveals his ideas:

"遐方书籍，按其义理与吾中国圣贤可相互发明，但其言语文字绝不相同，非此数人，谁与传译？失今不图，政恐日后无人能解……不以此时翻译来书以广文教，今日何以昭万国车书会同之盛，将来何以显历数与天无极之业哉。"（徐宗泽 195）

(When it comes to Western books, their principles could match up with Chinese sages', but their languages have significant differences. Apart from these people (the Jesuits), who else could interpret the meaning? If we miss this opportunity, I am afraid that nobody could understand later... Unless we translate foreign books at the moment to disseminate knowledge in our country, could we read all the books in the world right now and show our country's power in the future.)

In the book *Diagrams and explanations of the wonderful machines of the Far West*, Jesuit Johann Schreck and Chinese scholar Wang Zheng were the first to attempt to present Western mechanical knowledge to a Chinese audience. In the preface, Wang expressed his opinions on translating pragmatically.

"然图说之中巧器极多，第或不甚关切民生日用，又或非国家工作之急需则不录，特录其最切要者。兹所录者虽属技艺末务，而实有益于民生日用，国家兴作甚急也。"（徐宗泽 233）

(In the diagrams, there are many wonderful machines. Some of them are not relevant to people's daily living, some of them were not in accord with country's development, so we didn't record them but the essential ones. Although what we record are the least respectable techniques, they are really urgent and beneficial to people's living and country's development.)

The opinions above clearly reveal Xu's pragmatic thought in translation. The basic standpoint of Xu's translation is to consider the living standards of ordinary people, which is the practical need of the society. This is of great patriotism and an inspiration to translators nowadays.

4.4　Abridged Translation

As Jesuit missionaries were faced with folks from a special culture which has totally different attitude in spiritual life, they had to shift their language to enable translation texts adjust to the culture.

One of the techniques they use is abridged translation. For example, Matteo Ricci's books are not word-for-word translation in most cases. He tried to omit, supplement or rewrite the original text, in order to adjust Catholic doctrine to Confucian tradition and make Chinese people accept their ideas based on the connectivity and complementarity of the two systems.

This strategy was useful during the specific historical period, so is today. A translator should be conscious of the readers from beginning to the end. If we borrow a concept in computer science, we can say an object-oriented translation is the key to effective communication, because being faced with different clients and readers, translators have to adjust the style, cultural connotation and standard of the translation to reach maximization of comprehension.

Chapter 5　Conclusions

Between late Ming and early Qing Dynasties, Jesuit missionaries' evangelism in China via science and technology actually started the first climax of science translation in China. Their translation reflects characteristics of China in late feudal society. "Chinese narration plus Western translation" technique and cultural adaptation strategy resulted in tremendous Chinese books, which brought a positive impact on Chinese science.

Jesuit translation of Western science and technology, from the perspective of methodology, is neither word-to-word translation nor indiscriminate all-round translation. They took a comprehensive attitude towards the original text, so their translation reflects both the spirit of foreign cultures and the need of domestic readers. "Chinese narration plus Western translation", i.e., the cooperation between Chinese and Western scholars, reveals a simple purpose: translating the most "useful" contents to Chinese science, which bares the translator's subjectivity and cultural self-consciousness.

From the perspective of translation thoughts, Mastery and Innovation was the core. This strategy aimed at comprehensively comprehending the advantages of foreign cultures, combining the essence of domestic and foreign cultures without giving up on domestic one and consequently surpassing foreign cultures. Translators today ought to draw lessons from them and do more than switching the language but initialing cultural dialogues.

From the perspective of culture, Jesuit translation broke the barrier of Chinese ethnocentrism, and improved humanities in China. Nevertheless, we should admit that, apart from these benefits, there existed quite a few failures in their translation. Jesuit translation was fragmentized and unsystematic. For instance, Ricci and Xu only translated the first six chapters of Euclid's *Elements* because of effort limit. They did not agree to a common standard for translation nor form a translation society in global cooperation and communication. Eventually, Catholic Church failed to take a deep root in Chinese traditional culture.

JiXianlin, a notable scholar and translator, once said, "If compared to a river, Chinese culture is a long one. It has gone through ups and downs, but it never dried up. The reason isthat there has always beenfresh water emptied into the river. The most remarkable "flood" was from India and the West, and they all came in via translation." (季羡林 3) In this statement, Mr. Ji compared the translation of Buddhist texts to "flood from India" and that of Western science and technology by Jesuit missionaries to "flood from the West".

Thanks to Jesuit missionaries, modern Chinese translators draw lessons in target language culture-oriented domestication and pragmatic translation. In fact, contemporary translators are endowed with the mission of centralizing audience and contributing to social development, which is the social function of translation in modern times.

References

[1] Faure David. 中国的资本主义萌芽[J]. 中国经济史研究，2002（1）：57-67.

[2] Marx Karl. Capital [M]. New York: International Publishers, 1894.

[3] Society of Jesus. News from the Curia (Vol. XIII, N. 9). The Jesus Curia in Rome. 11 May 2009. http://www.sjweb.info/news/index.cfm? Tab=7&Language=1&PubNumID=15.

[4] Udías Agustín. Searching the Heavens and the Earth: The History of Jesuit Observatories. Astrophysics and Space Science Library. Berlin: Springer, 2003: 645-646.

[5] 陈登. 从西学翻译看利玛窦对中国文化的影响[J]. 湖南大学学报（社会科学版），2002（1）：70-73.

[6] 冯天瑜. 近代新语的历史功能与当代启示[J]. 鄂州大学学报，2002（4）：1-4.

[7] 季羡林. 中国翻译词典序[J]. 中国翻译，1995（4）：4-5.

[8] 李新德. 耶稣会士对《四书》的翻译与阐释[J]. 孔子研究，2011（1）：98-107.

[9] 罗莹. 十七世纪来华耶稣会士对儒学概念的译介——以"天"的翻译为例[J]. 学术研究，2012（11）：26-31.

[10] 谢天振. 中西翻译简史[M]. 北京：外语教学与研究出版社，2009.

[11] 徐宗泽. 明清间耶稣会士译著提要[M]. 上海：上海书店出版社，2010.

[12] 许文胜. 徐光启"会通—超胜"翻译思想例说[J]. 同济大学学报（社会科学版），2016（4）：117-124.

[13] 曾静. 论明末清初耶稣会士的翻译思想及影响[J]. 长春教育学院学报，2014（18）：45.

[14] 朱大锋. "利玛窦规矩"与明末清初的中西文化交流[J]. 兰台世界，2009（7）：38-39.

关于纽马克《翻译方法》的简要介绍与分析

郭　萌

摘　要：彼得·纽马克是著名的翻译家和翻译理论家，提出了许多重要的翻译理论，其中，以语义翻译和交际翻译最为著名。本论文以纽马克《翻译教程》中的第五章"翻译方法"为研究文本，简要介绍纽马克在翻译方法、对等效应方面的观点以及他提出的翻译建议，并结合实例对此进行分析。

关键词：彼得·纽马克；翻译方法；对等效应

Abstract: Peter Newmark is a famous translator and translation theorist, and he put forward a lot of important translation theories. Among these theories, semantic translation and communicative translation are most widely known. This essay will take the fifth chapter "Translation Methods" of Newmark's *A Textbook of Translation* as the research text, and analyze Newmark's opinions about translation methods, equivalent effect and his translation suggestions with examples.

Key Words: Peter Newmark, translation methods, equivalent effect

1　引言

要想成为一名优秀的译员，对于翻译理论的学习是必不可少的。纽马克作为一名著名的翻译家和翻译理论家，在翻译领域具有举足轻重的地位，他的很多理论至今仍具有很大的影响力。本论文主要研究纽马克《翻译教程》中的第五章"翻译方法"，简要介绍并分析了纽马克对翻译方法的分类、各个方法的具体含义，纽马克对于对等效应的观点以及他对译者提出的一些建议，希望能够让读者有所感悟与启发。

2　翻译方法

在《翻译方法》一文中，纽马克将翻译方法分为八种，分别是逐字翻译法、直译法、忠实翻译法、改编法、意译法、习语翻译法、语义翻译法和交际翻译法。

逐字翻译法，顾名思义，就是一个字一个字地翻译，它经常表现为行间翻译，也就是指将目的语直接标在源语言的下方，并保留源语言语序。它的主要作用是帮助译者理解句子结构，或者作为翻译前的一个过程来分析一个较难的文本。因此我们平常翻译之前所做的"查单词"这一工作便属于逐字翻译的一种。

在直译法中，源语言当中的语法结构会被转换成目的语中与之最接近的对等体，不过单词的意义依旧是脱离上下文单独译出的。在这个过程中，源语言的语法结构可能会发生改变，也可能不发生。比如，将 *Pride and Prejudice* 翻译成《傲慢与偏见》，源语言的语法结构就未发生改变，而把 *The Age of Innocence* 翻译成《纯真年代》，源语言的结构就发生了改变。

忠实翻译法是在源语言语法结构的限制下，根据上下文准确地再现原文的意义。在翻译过程中，文化特色词会做相应的转化，在某种程度上保留语法和词汇的"非常规性"，也就是说，可能会偏离源语言的规范。忠实翻译完全忠实于源语言作者的意图及其文本表现方式。

改编法通常运用于戏剧（尤其是喜剧）和诗歌翻译，指在保留主题、人物和情节的基础上，将源语言和目的语的文化背景进行转换，然后将文本进行改写。比如英国汉学家闵福德将"十年一觉扬州梦，赢得青楼薄幸名"翻译成：

"From my Yangzhou Dream I wake at last——Ten years a rake, ten years gone so fast!"

在这一译文中，原诗句的主题得到保留，但其表达方式更加符合西方诗歌的要求。

意译法是指翻译原文的主旨而忽略其风格，或者说仅翻译原文内容而忽略其形式。在纽马克看来，经由意译的文章通常比原文篇幅要长，也就是所谓的"语内翻译"，冗长而做作，全然不是翻译。然而，笔者认为意译法用来翻译一些较短的语句也是不错的选择，比如，将 *Waterloo Bridge* 翻译为《魂断蓝桥》，将 *Up* 翻译为《飞屋环游记》，将《摇啊摇，摇到外婆桥》翻译为 *The Shanghai Triad* 等等，既保留了原标题的主旨，又利于目的语观众理解。

习语翻译法指的是再现原文的"信息"，但偏好采用原文中不存在的口语和表达方式来表现原文的意义的翻译方法。

语义翻译法侧重还原表达源语言作者的情感与目的，但与忠实翻译法不同的是，语义翻译法会更多地考虑文本的美学价值，在必要的时候，可以妥协语义，以便译文在谐音、双关语、反复这些手法方面与原文一致。而且，对于不太重要的文化特色词，语义翻译可能会用与目标语中与文化无关的中性词或是有同等功能的词来翻译，而不用文化对等词。忠实翻译法往往拘泥于原文，不做变通，而语义翻译法更加灵活，除了绝对忠实外也接受创造性，并考虑译者在思想情感上与原作者一致。

交际翻译法是指从内容和语言两方面出发，将原文的准确语境意义译为读者易于接受和理解的文本。

这八种方法各有特点，不过在纽马克看来，只有语义翻译法和交际翻译法能够达到翻译的两个目的：准确和简洁。一般来说，语义翻译法是从作者的角度出发进行翻译，准确再现原文意义，而交际翻译法则是从读者的角度出发，其目的是让读者迅速、方便地去了解文本。比如，对于"谋事在人，成事在天"这句话，现有以下两种翻译版本。

A. Man proposes, Heaven disposes.

B. Man proposes, God disposes.

这两种版本的区别在于对"天"的翻译。"天"在中国古代文化中是自然界的主宰，A 将"天"翻译为 Heaven，忠实地保留了原文的道教概念，而 B 将其翻译为 God，也就是西方基督教徒心目中自然界的主宰，符合西方读者的宗教背景和接受心理，因此，A 为语义翻译，B 为交际翻译。

总之，语义翻译法强调原文再现的准确性，交际翻译法强调译文阅读的流畅性，两者虽在细节方面有着多种区别，但同时也构成一个整体，在翻译过程中运用比较广泛。

3 对等效应

对于翻译，人们经常会有这样的看法：翻译一定要完全准确地去重现原文，也就是说，原文中的每个词语都要在译文中找到对应的词语。这属于"完全对等"观点，纽马克并不赞同。在他看来，对等效应只是一个尽力去追求的结果，而不应该是翻译的目的，尤其是当源语言和目的语有着不同的目标的时候，比如，一方面是侧重于感染性，另一方面侧重于告知性；或者是当源语言和目的语之间存在较为明显的文化鸿沟的时候，完全对等效应也很难实现。

上文已经提到，准确和简洁是翻译的两个目的，虽然完全对等效应很难实现，但翻译还是要尽力去做到准确，因此纽马克提出，对于不同的文本类型，对等效应有着不同的重要程度。

纽马克将文本分为三种类型：表达型文本、信息型文本和号召型文本。

表达型文本的核心是表情达意，强调作者的绝对权威，不会考虑读者的反应，其中，作者独特的语言形式和内容同等重要。典型的表达型文本有私人信件、自传、散文等。因为其原则是作者第一，因此通常用语义翻译法来翻译这类文本。在表达型文本中，如果作品的内涵具有普适性，那么就会达到更为宽泛的对等效应，也就是说，会被更广泛的读者群体接收，比如《哈姆雷特》中"to be or not to be"这一哲理。

信息型文本的核心是语言之外的现实世界，强调"真实性"，多运用第三人称和过去时态，感情不明显。这类文本包括非文学作品、教科书、学术论文和报纸杂志等。语义翻译法和交际翻译法均适用于这类文本的翻译。由于在这类文本中，很多知识都是靠通用术语来解释，因此如果源语言文化和目的语文化相去甚远就很难达成对等效应。然而，对于这类文本中具有号召性质的知识则要尽力在翻译过程中实现与源语言的对等。

号召型文本的核心是号召读者去思考、行动、感受，并做出反应，强调以读者为中心，因此在翻译这类文本时的原则是"读者第一"。这类文本包括产品说明书、告示、指示、宣传广告等，其中最为典型的是那些以取悦读者为目的的通俗小说。翻译号召型文本时，主要运用交际翻译法。在这一过程中，对等效应是基本且必要的。因为它是判断翻译后的号召型文本产生的效果的标准。比如翻译某种商品的广告时，如果忽视对等效应，目的语读者就可能会对产品产生误区，从而影响产品销量。

总的来说，如果一个文本的文化独特性越强，那么在翻译的过程中，对等效应就越难实现，除非读者具有丰富的想象力和强烈的敏感度，并且对源语言文化十分熟悉。比如那些生活在夏天气候炎热难耐地区的人们，就很难去理解莎士比亚的诗句"Shall I compare thee to a summer's day?"的美丽。

因此，纽马克总结说："对等效应是一个重要的翻译学概念，各种文本对其都有着一定程度的应用，只不过重要性不同。"按照纽马克的观点，我们需要明白，在翻译过程中，一定要先分清源语言文本的特点，再对对等效应做出不同程度的处理。

4 翻译建议

经过对翻译方法、文本类型、对等效应的分析，纽马克还提出了一些翻译建议，对于译者有较大启发。

首先，在翻译之前，译者需要做好充分地准备工作，尤其是当原文的文学性或者指向性很强的时候，准备工作就需要准备得更加完善。好的翻译并非一蹴而就，它需要充足的前期积累。比如闵福德在翻译《红楼梦》时，除了理解原文，还花了大量时间学习霍克斯的译文和风格，学习如何写英文小说。正是由于有了大量的积累，他与霍克斯所翻译的英文版《红楼梦》才会如此自然流畅，佳句不断。

而如果准备工作做得不够，译者在翻译过程中就很可能会对文本产生一些误读，尤其是对关键词的误读。文学作品中的关键词往往会起画龙点睛之笔，如果源语言并非译者的母语，那么译者就很可能因为事先没有见过这个词的新奇用法而产生错误的理解，由此还会导致对整个段落甚至整篇文章的内容把握产生偏差，白白浪费时间。

其次，在翻译过程中，如果还未读完两到三个段落就已经翻译了好几个句子，往往会出现很多问题，比如与下文的内容出现偏差等。因此，译者在翻译的时候一定要切忌未读其文，已翻其意，而应该通览全篇，对整篇文章的目的、内容、情感态度等方面有一个大致的把握，这样翻译出来的文章才会逻辑清晰，衔接流畅。

除此之外，对于先翻词还是先翻句的问题，纽马克这样解释：当你弄明白文章的大致含义的时候，先从句子翻起，然后再检查译文里面是否已经包含原文中每个单词的含义，因为实际上有很多词并不需要对等翻译出来，比如语气词、术语、语法词等。然而在现实情况中，如果这些词有着专门含义，则需要去优先对待它们，然后再将其置于上下文之中检查翻译出来的含义是否正确。

5 总结

通过对纽马克关于翻译方法的理论的学习，笔者对于翻译方法和文本类型有了更系统的了解与认识，明白了在翻译之前要先了解文本属于哪类类型，"对症下药"，根据文本特点选用合适的翻译方法，并做好充足的准备工作，力求能够让自己的译文达到准确和简洁这两个标准。

参 考 资 料

彼得·纽马克. 翻译教程[M]. 上海：上海外语教育出版社，2001.

从修辞角度看《荷塘月色》四英译本的结构美与意境美

齐 翔

摘 要：从修辞角度出发，对比《荷塘月色》的四个英译本，分析译本是否传达出原文本的修辞效果，并从句法角度探讨译本的修辞句是否体现出原文本的结构美，从语义和语音角度探讨译本的修辞句是否体现出原文本的意境美。本文将重点从对偶与排比两种修辞方法探讨结构美的实现，从比拟与通感两种修辞方法探讨意境美的实现。

关键词：荷塘月色；修辞；翻译

Abstract: This essay compares four translations of *Moonlight over the Lotus Pond* from the perspective of rhetorical devices, analyzing whether translations have the same effect of source text. Following questions are discussed in the essay: Syntactically, whether the beauty in structure of source text can be reflected in rhetorical sentences in translations; semantically and phonetically, whether the artistic conception of source text can be delivered by translators. This essay focuses on antithesis, parallelism, simile, metaphor, personification and synaesthesia.

Key Words: Moonlight over the Lotus Pond, rhetorical devices, translations

1 引 言

1.1 《荷塘月色》的修辞

朱自清先生是一位善用修辞的高手，在《荷塘月色》中，生动形象的比喻、拟人，对仗工整的对偶句和排比句以及具有诗意的通感等修辞手法的运用使得这篇散文的语言更具艺术魅力。

从句法角度看，《荷塘月色》中有部分句子和段落有着整齐划一的结构美，这主要得益于对偶和排比。例如，"我爱热闹，也爱冷静；爱群居，也爱独处。"再如，"层层的叶子中间，零星地点缀着些白花，有袅娜地开着的，有羞涩地打着朵儿的；正如一粒粒的明珠，又如碧天里的星星。"

从语义角度看，朱自清先生的比拟句具有独创性，但又在情理之中，非常自然。如，"叶子出水很高，像亭亭的舞女的裙"。再如，"月光如流水一般，静静地泻在这一片叶子和花上。"这些比拟句十分生动形象，又不落俗套，很能唤起读者诗意地联想和想象。

通感手法带来的意境之美也是本篇散文的特点之一。例如，"微风过处，送来缕缕清香，仿佛远处高楼上渺茫的歌声似的。"清香可嗅而不可闻，歌声可闻而不可嗅，这句话将读者的听觉与嗅觉打通，让读者体会到这香气的缥缈，新颖却贴切。

总的来说，这篇散文中的比拟与通感带给人一种诗意的意境美，而对偶句和排比句又给人一种整齐划一的结构美，两种美感互为表里。而译者在翻译这些修辞句的过程中也要注意还原原文所带来的美感享受。

1.2 批评赏析的标准

散文翻译的三个要义就是"真""情""美"。既然"真""情""美"乃散文之本色，那么散文翻译之原则应围绕"真""情""美"的传达来进行。所谓"真"就是要求译文在词汇的各种意义、句法信息和各种修辞、语篇与主题等方面力求与原文等质等量。所谓"情"就是要求译文能反映出原文中字、词、句及修辞、逻辑等反映出的整体情感。所谓"美"则是要求散文翻译要以精湛的语言艺术和巧夺天工的语言技巧不仅再现散文的意境和情趣，更再现散文的各种形式，以充分传达出散文之美。

除此之外，语料库的使用也可以在一定程度上检测翻译是否地道。所以本文在进行赏析时，会用到语料库进行辅助检验。笔者根据译者所对应的年代，分别使用了美国当代英语语料库（Corpus of Contemporary American English (COCA)）和英国国家语料库（British National Corpus）。

2 形式美：对偶与排比

2.1 对偶

对偶独具艺术特色，看起来整齐醒目，听起来铿锵悦耳，读起来朗朗上口，便于记忆、传诵，为人们喜闻乐见。散文中出现对偶句，在长短不一的句子中独具一格，更能吸引读者的眼球，给读者留下深刻印象，比如下面这句：

"我爱热闹，也爱冷静；爱群居，也爱独处。"

（朱纯深译本）I like a serene and peaceful life, as much as a busy and active one; I like being in solitude, as much as in company.

（杨宪益、戴乃迭译本）I like both excitement and stillness.

（李明译本）I enjoy atranquil life as well as a bustling one; I enjoy being in solitude as well as being in company.

（David E. Pollard 译本）I like excitement, and also like calm; I like to be in crowds, and also love to be on my own.

四个译本中，只有杨、戴的译本对这一句做了简单的处理，没有还原原文的对偶句式。而其他三个译本都是用分号将两个相似结构的句子连接起来，形成对仗工整的英文句子。这样的结构和中间的分号使译文取得和原文一样的阅读效果，句式整齐、对应，读起来朗朗上口。这种对原文对偶句的处理体现出英语结构对称、句式平衡的特点，即因汉英语音、结构、语法等的差异，英译文没有中文对偶要求的完全字数对等，而是结构、字数大体相似。译文能保留对偶的格式，使得译文在一定程度上也保留了与原文一致的结构美。

在翻译"爱冷静"时，为了追求辞藻的华丽，李明在复译时将朱译本的 peaceful life 改为 tranquil life，笔者通过 COCA 语料库查询两个词组的使用频率，发现前者使用频率更高。（如表 1 所示）中文此处的措辞是简单朴实的常用词，所以笔者认为译文应当符合原文的措辞风格，因此朱译本的 peaceful life 更佳。

表 1

	context	frequency
word1	peaceful life	73
word2	tranquil life	6

2.2 排比

散文中排比句的使用使文章语言充满韵律和节奏感，这亦是《荷塘月色》的文体特色之一。对原文平行结构的翻译处理是译本是否精彩的关键。如：

"层层的叶子中间，零星地点缀着些白花，有袅娜地开着的，有羞涩地打着朵儿的。正如一粒粒的明珠，又如碧天里的星星，又如刚出浴的美人。"

（朱纯深译本）Here and there, layers of leaves are dotted with whitelotus blossoms, some in demure bloom, others in shy bud, like scattering pearls, or twinkling stars, or beauties just out of thebath.

（杨宪益、戴乃选译本）And starring these tiers of leaves were white lotus flowers, alluringly open or bashfully in bud, likeglimmering pearls, stars in an azure sky, or beauties fresh from the bath.

（李明译本）Upon layers of leaves are dotted with shite lotus flowers, some blooming gracefully while others budding bashfully. They are just like pearls shining bright, or stars twinkling high in an azure sky. They are also like fair ladies coming fresh out of a bath.

（David E. Pollard 译本）Here and there among the layers of leaves were sown shining white flowers, some blooming glamorously, some in shy bud, just like unstrung pearls, or stars against a blue sky.

此处朱自清先生用三个比拟句构成排比结构，使读者得到语义和结构美的双重享受。从句法上看，朱译本中，使用"some in... others in..."和"... or... or..."结构，组成了两个平行结构，且比拟句也翻译准确，明喻对明喻，暗喻对暗喻，很好地还原了原文的修辞手法与结构美。这体现了散文翻译原则中的"真"。杨、戴以及李明的译本则是更注重意义的翻译，而忽略形式上的平行结构的修辞。虽然没有在形式上体现"真"，却在内容上忠实原文。Pollard 的译本用"some+非谓语动词... some+介词短语"和"... or..."结构来对应中文的排比句式，虽然不是严格意义上的平行结构，但是也看出译者有意图翻译出原文的修辞格。然而"又如刚出浴的美人"一句译者可能出于文化考量没有翻译，却又没有找到英语中对等的比喻，进而直接省略，使得该句翻译略显失真。

3 意境美：比拟与通感

3.1 比拟

朱自清先生善用比喻，其设喻新颖独特，又非常传神，描写月光的句子最为经典，例如：

"月光如流水一般，静静地泻在这一片叶子和花上。"

（朱纯深译本）The moon sheds her liquid light silently over the leaves and flowers.

（杨宪益、戴乃选译本）Moonlight cascaded like water over the lotus leaves and flowers.

（李明译本）The moonlight, like a cascade, was flowing down quietly to the leaves and flowers.

（David E. Pollard 译本）The moonbeams spilled placidly onto this expanse of leaves and flowers like living water.

朱译本这里的比拟句翻译得很巧妙，原文是"月光如流水"是一个明喻，而朱译本却说是"liquid light"，也就是用形容水的"liquid"来形容光，虽然作喻的方式改变了，但喻体和本体却没有改变，保留了原文中的意境美，即美好的月色与静谧的夜晚。其他三人的译本皆是保留了明喻的修辞格，其中杨、戴和李明都对流水般的月光给了具象化的描写，用了"cascade"一词，直译"瀑布"之意，这种译法在笔者看来有点用力过度，因为"瀑布"不仅给人以视觉上的直观感受，也给人以听觉上的感受，显然与原文的"静静地"不符，打破了月色下夜晚的静谧，没有做到散文翻译原则之"情"。

拟人修辞格的使用也在本文中出现，其中描写荷塘四周树荫之时很是出彩，用"没精打采"来形容灯光，生动地写出了灯光之昏暗。

"树缝里也漏着一两点路灯光，没精打采的，是瞌睡人的眼。"

（朱纯深译本）Through the branches are also a couple of lamps, as listless as sleepy eyes.

（杨宪益、戴乃迭译本）And between the trees appeared one or two street lamps, listless as the eyes of someone drowsy.

（李明译本）Through the branches could be seen some light from a couple of street –lamps, which was as listless as the eyes of someone who is drowsy.

（David E. Pollard 译本）A few gleams from streets lights also leaked through the interstices of the trees, but they were wan and lifeless, eyes heavy with sleep.

前三个译本用明喻来表现原文拟人的修辞格，用了"as… as…"或直接用"as"连接，最后一个译本则是直接把"streets lights"当成人去描写，更加与中文中"拟人"的修辞格对等，但美中不足的是，最后一个译本将"没精打采"翻译成"lifeless（死气沉沉）"和"wan（病态的，苍白的）"，其意境与原文本已经相去甚远。

3.2 通感

朱自清先生对《荷塘月色》中所描写对象有着非常细致的观察和深刻的体会。因此，他突破人们平常的经验，采用"通感"这种奇特而新颖的修辞手法，将作品的语言表达推向炉火纯青、出神入化的艺术境界。

所谓"通感"，就是在描写客观事象时，利用人们各种感觉之间的息息相通，进而运用形象化的语言把某一种感观上的感受移接到另一种感观上。钱钟书先生也曾指出，巧妙地运用"通感"的手法能使读者在不知不觉中产生"一种感觉超越了本身的局限，而领会到属于另一种感觉"的印象。"通感"修辞方法的运用，在现代散文创作中并不多见，但朱自清先生却能将这种手法运用得如此自然而娴熟，并且恰到好处，实在令人击掌称奇，如：

"微风过处，送来缕缕清香，仿佛远处高楼上渺茫的歌声似的。"

（朱纯深译本）A breeze stirs, sending over breaths of fragrance, like faint singing drifting from a distant building.

（杨宪益、戴乃迭译本）The breeze carried past gusts of fragrance, like the strains of a song faintly heard from a far-off tower.

（李明译本）When a breeze passes, it wafts breaths of fragrance, which are like faint singing drifting from a far-away building.

（David E. Pollard 译本）Their fresh fragrance wafted on the faint breeze, like snatches of song from some distant tower.

从句法角度看，四个译本都是用了"... like..."的结构，都成功地将嗅觉转化成了听觉。具体看词汇，前三个译本都用了"faint（微弱的）"一词来形容歌声；而第四个译本用了"snatches（一阵阵）"，与前面的"缕缕"形成对应，不失为一种更好的选择。从语音角度看，朱纯深和李明的译本更为出彩。原文中"缕缕"为叠词，"仿佛"和"渺茫"都是双声词，在描写声音的句子里出现这种汉语独有的表现音韵美的词，会更能体现出原文想要表达的意境。在朱、李的译本中，分别用"breeze""stirs/ passes""breaths"和"fragrance"押尾韵，再用"singing""drifting""building"一组词押尾韵。在音韵方面贴近原文的意境，在结构和意境上都做到了散文翻译之"美"。

在 COCA 语料库中，breaths of fragrance 表达的使用率为 0，可见母语者很少用 breaths 做量化词去限定"香气"。Pollard 作为母语者显然意识到了这点，所以决定省译"缕缕"这样的量词。而"清香"一词译作"fresh fragrance"在语料库中有 4 条引用，证明这样的表达是可以被母语者接受的（如表 2 所示）。

表　2

	context	frequency
word1	fresh fragrance	4

4　结　语

以上是笔者在对比《荷塘月色》四个英译本关于修辞句翻译时的所思所想。笔者进行翻译批评与赏析的原则，主要是按"真""情""美"三个原则。通过句法、语义和语音三个角度分析，以对偶、排比、比拟（比喻和拟人）以及通感四个修辞格为例，对比分析四个英译本的出彩和不尽如人意之处。

不难看出，译者在还原原文的结构美和意境美方面用了不少心思，力求在句法、语义等方面与原文保持一致，如果有可能，译者也追求语音方面还原原文的意境。翻译的过程中语言、文化、受众等因素会限制译者的发挥，每个译者在翻译的过程中侧重不同，会有不同的考量，自然会有不同的译本出现。因此不能绝对化的批判某个译本的省译或改译之处。

参 考 资 料

[1] 何荷. 朱纯深《荷塘月色》译文的美学价值——以修辞句的英译为例[J]. 郑州航空工业管理学院学报（社会科学版），2016，35（2）：128-130.

[2] 李明. 翻译批评与赏析（第二版）[M]. 武汉：武汉大学出版社，2006.

[3] 刘慧群. 《荷塘月色》修辞翻译管窥[J]. 语文学刊：外语教育教学，2015（10）：54-55.

[4] 潘聪聪. 从《荷塘月色》探析修辞之美[J]. 潍坊工程职业学院学报，2013，26（2）：37-38.

[5] 乔彩霞，张凌. 从美学视角探讨汉英散文翻译——以朱自清《荷塘月色》为例[J]. 语文学刊：外语教育教学，2015（8）.

[6] 吴崇新."淡淡"月色"泻"荷塘——朱自清《荷塘月色》的修辞艺术品析[J]. 广西青年干部学院学报，2014，24（3）：82-84.

[7] 杨昊. 从翻译审美主客体看《荷塘月色》英译本[J]. 语文建设，2015（12）：61-62.

[8] 杨金艳. 散文翻译如何在语音层面再现"真"——以《荷塘月色》的四种英译本为例[J]. 海外英语，2014（13）：149-150.

[9] 朱沛杰. 从修辞翻译看《荷塘月色》的三个译本[J]. 海外英语，2011（14）：205-207.

[10] http://corpus.byu.edu/coca/.

[11] http://corpus.byu.edu/bnc/.

《母鸡》翻译习作

迟姗姗

原文本分析

1 外文本分析

老舍先生的创作风格一直被众人所熟知，其土生土长的北京人，他一生的大部分时间都是在北京度过的，深刻地影响他的写作特点。老舍主张用方言写作，带有地方色彩，生动具体。他还应用口语写作，这使得他的作品读来轻快幽默，所以他的文字也被誉为最活泼、最俏皮、最上口的优美文字。他从小与母亲生活在穷人杂居的小胡同里，对贫民生活非常熟悉，所以他的作品又具有悲剧倾向的特点，取材也是贫民化的。

以上写作特点均在本篇选文中得以体现，该短篇小说语言的地域风味极浓，且俗白，简练，纯净，生动，又风趣幽默。文章通过描写了作者对母鸡看法的变化，表达了对母爱的赞颂之情。文章以情感变化为线索，对母鸡的情感由"讨厌"转变为尊敬，前后形成了鲜明的对比，塑造了一位"伟大的鸡母亲"的形象。本文的语言风格比较口语化，直白自然，散发着浓郁的生活气息，读起来令人感到亲切舒服。

2 内文本分析

2.1 词法

词语方面，作者多用形容词语描绘其前后形象，并表达自己感情。比如"如怨如诉"形容没完没了地抱怨、诉说。本文用拟人化的手法来形容母鸡拉长音的叫声影响人的情绪，令人讨厌。"乘其不备"来形容母鸡在欺负自己的同类时是出其不意地下毒手，非常凶狠，让人厌恶。后用"警戒"指母鸡为了保护小鸡的安全，一直保持着高度的警惕，并不畏任何强敌，随时准备作战，更表现了这位鸡母亲的负责、慈爱、勇敢与辛苦，也表达了作者的敬意。作者的用词极具生动性，也是翻译的着重点。

2.2 句法

句子方面，通篇短句，简洁凝练，紧扣中心，生动形象。比如，"恨不能让全世界都知道它这点儿成绩；就是聋子也会被它吵得受不了"。作者用分句表达，加以强调与修饰，讽刺了母鸡的炫耀，淋漓尽致地表达了讨厌母鸡的情绪。"它负责、慈爱、勇敢、辛苦，因为它有了一群鸡雏。"此句由词语构成，并直接表达其原因，对母亲的赞颂之情在逐句加深。结尾一句"我不敢再讨厌母鸡。"来表明自己对母鸡情感的变化。他此时已不是简单的喜欢，而是对母爱的一种纯洁、神圣的尊敬，是情感的升华。更可以体现出其用句之简短，不多做修饰，却仍能给读者留以无限遐想的空间。

2.3 修辞

即使老舍先生一贯用词直接，但也从没忽略过修辞的运用，语言的打磨。该篇文章多处用修辞来描述母鸡性格，从一开始的拟人化修饰到最后以母亲来比喻，处处包含着隐喻、拟人等手法。

2.4 篇章结构

篇章结构方面，作者采用一贯先抑后扬的方法，表达厌恶，而后通过描述一瞬转变其态度，不拖泥带水，由于短篇小说的原因，结构也相对较为紧凑，无其他明显特征。

原文

《母　鸡》
老　舍

　　我一向讨厌母鸡，不知怎样受了一点惊恐，听吧，它由前院咕咕到后院，由后院咕咕到前院，没完没了，并且没有什么理由。有的时候，它不这样乱叫，可是细声细气的，有什么心事似的，颤颤巍巍的，顺着墙根，或沿着田坝，那么扯长了声如泣如诉，使人心中立刻结起个小疙瘩来。

　　它永远不反抗公鸡。可是，有时候却欺侮那最忠厚的鸭子。更可恶的是，当它遇到另一只母鸡的时候，会下毒手乘其不备，狠狠地咬一口，咬下一撮儿毛来。

　　到下蛋的时候，它差不多是发了狂，恨不得让全世界都知道它这点成绩，就是聋子也会被它吵得受不了。

　　可是，现在我改变了想法，我认识了一只孵出一群小雏鸡的母鸡。

　　不论是在院里，还是在院外，它总是挺着脖儿，表示出世界上并没有可怕的东西。一个鸟儿飞过，或是什么东西响了一声，它立刻警戒起来，歪着头听，挺替身预备作战，看看前，看看后，咕咕地警告鸡雏要马上集合到它身边来。

　　当它发现了一点可吃的东西，它咕咕地紧叫，啄一啄那个东西，马上便放下，教它的儿女吃。结果，每一只鸡雏的肚子都圆圆地下垂，像刚装了一两个汤圆儿似的，它自己却削瘦了许多。假若有别的大鸡来抢食，它一定出击，把它们赶出老远，就连大公鸡也怕它三分。

　　它教给鸡雏们啄食，掘地，用土洗澡；一天教多少多少次。它还半蹲着。教它们挤在它的翅下、胸下，得一点儿温暖。它若伏在地上，鸡雏们有的便爬在它的背上，啄它的头或别的地方，它一声也不哼。

　　在夜间若有什么动静，它便放声啼叫，顶尖锐、顶凄惨，使任何贪睡的人也得起来看看，是不是有了黄鼠狼！

　　它负责、慈爱、勇敢、辛苦，因为它有了一群鸡雏。它伟大，因为它是鸡母亲。一个母亲必定是一位英雄。

　　我不敢再讨厌母鸡了。

译文：

The Hen

Translated by Chi Shanshan

　　I abhor the hen all the time. Listen! It clucks from front yard to back yard and then backs to front yard without end, and there is no reason to the whole process. What a nuisance that the hen is.Sometimes it does not cluck insanely,while mumble in a soft vice as if something is on it mind.The tremulous voice spread along the foot of the wall or the field dam. The long low lonesome murmur seems to express sadness, bring knot on your heart,which makes you feel uncomfortable.

It never stands against a rooster, but bully the daffy duck.More abhorrent sometimes is to hurts another passing female chicken deliberately by pecking off a pinch of its feather while others unprepared.

It was almost go mad at egg-laying time as if it wants the whole world to know his little bit merit and contribution. You can't stand this noise even though you are a deaf.

But I have changed my view point until I witnessed a hen hatching a brood of chicks. The hen always hold it head high to show nothing in this world could make it afraid whether in the yard or outside yard.It would beinstantly on guard and listen with with tilting its headonce a bird flew over or a sound was heard.Straightening back to prepare for battle,it was aware of going on around it sand cautioned the chicks to gather around it.

When it found something edible, it made short "coo-coo" sounds immediately.And then it pecked at what it found and laid it down right away to let its children eat.This means that the tummy of every chick was hanging down like a little having a rice dumpling, but the mother hen became thinner significantly. If other big chicken came to rob the food, the mother hen would attack and drive the intruder far away. Even big rooster fear it somewhat.

It taughtchicks to peck at food, dig into ground and bath with dirtmany times a day.Sometimes it squatted down so that the chicks could squeeze underneath its wings and breasts to get a little warm.If it was lying on the ground, the chicks would climb to its back and peck at its head or other places. Not a word falls from her lips.

It was all ready to flap and squawk shrilly,miserably at the slightest move anybody makes,and any person in deep sleep would get up to check if a weasel come.

The mother was responsible, loving, courageous, and hard-working as a brood of little chicks' mother. It was mighty because it was a mother.A mother must be a hero.

From now on,I do not hold the hen in awe and veneration.

译后记:

译时，觉得原文章的语言相对简洁凝练，但符合作者一贯的稳准、精确风格，因此该篇文章翻译时，我格外注重词汇的选择。

原文简单叙述原作者从一开始对母鸡的厌恶、恐惧到后期生出的敬佩之情，大量运用形容词来描述其情感以及母鸡形象的变化，语言朴实，处处留心适用平常用语，突显短篇习作风格。通过分析文章的词法、句法、修辞、篇章后，发现这篇文章不能过分地追求以往译时的句式之繁杂、多变，翻译时更多地需要按照原文本的写作风格来构句对我而言是一次全新的接触。

全篇更是多有拟声词、衍生词、内涵词等需要采用多种不同的翻译方法才能更好地体现原作者的根本出发点，例如，"daffy duck"原文为忠厚的鸭子，在此我认为直译忠厚略显欠缺，可以融入一些西方元素，此时我想起了小时候看的西方动画片 Daffy Duck 其最早作为专有出现于《波基猎鸭》中，当时被认为成为"那只蠢笨的鸭子"。但后来达菲鸭作为固定的动画角色再次出现时，便形成一种虽然脑筋不够好使，但对朋友（兔八哥等）真诚的形象。时时给人笨笨的形象，所以这里我选择 daffy 更好给译文读者直接感受。再比如，"go mad" 这里是指母鸡生产时的发狂，go mad 通常用于女人发狂，但这里我又认为这种发狂来源于生产的疼痛，想换有类似词语时，有想到原文作者老舍当时对母鸡心存芥蒂，他可能看到该场景时没有想到生产疼痛并对其产生怜悯，而是仍觉得母鸡烦，所以我按原文意思译为 go mad。

除词汇外，另有一些连接句式更应被注意，根据原文本我们可以看出，作者惯用短句，因此翻译时更要考虑到怎么译可以显示出原文本的风格并不让文章显得过于单调，于是，句式的选择也一定程度上成为我翻译的重心。在句式的选择上我多用、分句、条件句、状语、不定式等讲句子时时刻意拆分成块来符合原文的构句，以显原文。

翻译后进行修改，仍觉得自己翻译时，过于注重词汇的解析，没有注意到整体的文章结构和感情色彩，并意识到我对英文修辞的写作手法不熟练、不会运用，导致我部分翻译纠结，很久也没体现出作者想表达的含义，在用英文表达时觉得过于简朴直述，不能体现出原文想表达的情感，我的表达手法只能意译其本意而无法深刻直观，仍需积累。

《红鬃马》翻译习作

李金慧

1 外文本分析

申平（1955—）笔名灵羊，男，汉族，内蒙古赤峰人。中共党员。1982 年毕业于辽宁师范大学中文系。中国作家协会会员、惠州市作家协会副主席、惠州市小小说学会会长、国家一级作家。迄今已发表作品 230 多万字，出版中短篇小说集和小小说作品集 6 部，尤以小小说创作见长，其动物小小说更是脍炙人口。单篇作品《头羊》获 2001—2002 年全国优秀小小说作品奖；《猎豹》获 2005—2006 全国小小说佳作奖；《红鬃马》《猫王》等多篇作品被选入《中国小小说 300 篇》等文集、权威选本中。《红鬃马》一文收录于《申平动物小小说名篇欣赏》中。

2 内文本分析

小小说是介于边缘短篇小说和散文之间的一种边缘性的现代新兴文学体裁，字数少于 1000 字。阿•托尔斯泰认为："小小说是训练作家最好的学校。"以微知著，以近知远；短小精悍，却意味深长，发人深省。申平的《红鬃马》，讴歌马的旺盛的生命力，流溢出浑厚、悲壮的风格。作品篇幅短小精悍，但表现出丰富的思想容量，使读者回味再三。同时，作品的切入点以及切入角度十分独特，往往将笔锋聚焦于一个情节或一个核心道具，然后层层展开，并从中挖掘主题、刻画人物。申平在草原上生活过多年，有着浓重的草原情结。因此，他泼洒大量的笔墨去描绘草原，对草原上的动植物进行讴歌和赞美。而充满野性和执着的生命力的马，自然而然成为申平所讴歌的草原上的动植物不可缺少的一部分。倘若从创作冲动的角度去考察《红鬃马》，它的成功离不开作者的草原情结。

《红鬃马》成功的第一个因素得益于作者对"红鬃马"形象的塑造。作者用极致的方式塑造红鬃马，让红鬃马的悲剧是其以大无畏的精神主动铸就的。由此，一匹刚烈、倔强、顽强的马的形象跃然纸上。《红鬃马》成功的第二个因素是其强烈的画面感和紧凑的情节。短短的千余字篇幅中，至少有两幅画面能让读者的眼睛久久停驻。第一幅是红鬃马的剪影，"它的身子如锦缎一样闪闪发光""那顺着脖子拖下来的长长的鬃毛一跳一跳，正如一团火焰在燃烧"；第二幅是红鬃马与狼激战的场景，激烈，生动，层次分明。可见作者深厚的语言功底和白描水平。情节安排上，按照时间顺序，先是找马、观战，接着拴马、拘马、揍马，最后又是找马。环环相扣、层层递进，迅速将读者带入故事之中。

全篇无冗词冗句，以养马人的视角所观，进行了景物描写和大量的对红鬃马的动作、神态描写以及在描写中间掺杂了养马人的心理活动，语句多短小，动词使用频繁，多次出现惊叹词。比如，"危险！""啊，马鬃！""两只狼"等等。一个句子里包含多个连续动作前后或者并列发生，同时与描述动作的形容词和副词紧密衔接。作者在描写红鬃马时，巧用比喻，比如，"它的身子如锦缎一样闪闪发光；夕阳也照着它的红鬃，那顺着脖子拖下来的长长的鬃毛一跳一跳，正如一团火焰在燃烧""长鬃啪的一下，宛如一条巨鞭""它那长长的鬃毛现在竖起来了，在脖子上轻轻晃动，正像一面战旗在飘扬"等；巧用拟人，比如，"儿马子平安地回来了，它如凯旋的将军""草原沉默，冷冷地把他的声音抛掷回来"；以及渲染动作生动性的拟声词，比如，"啪的一下""咔嚓咔嚓"等。全篇通过描写养马人的动作和语言来展现主人的心理活动，其中主人的话语十分鲜活、接地气，民俗气息浓重，比如，"全是这鬃把你烧的！""逞能的东西，找死的东西""看你他妈再去惹事"等等。因此，在翻译此文时，需注意篇幅，不能过长；用词需鲜活而不失凝练，将儿马子的倔强、刚毅、悲壮一丝不落地描绘出来；比喻及拟人修辞部分需着重考虑形容词和副词的选择；动词部分则要选择最为传神精炼的；关于语言描写则需先弄清俗语的深层含义，接着转译为与目标语最为贴切的语句；时态上以一般过去式、过去进行时和过去完成时和过去完成进行时为主。

《红鬃马》中英文对照

（1）一连几日，红鬃儿马子老不按时回来，回来时全身便如水里捞出来的。	（1）The red colt had been late for home several days. Everytime it came back, its body was drenched with sweat as if dragged out of the water.
（2）那天，红鬃儿马子索性一夜未归，主人一早骑马去找，却见它正站在一座山头上，冲着东方红日嘶鸣，那剪影极为精彩。主人策马驰去，看见儿马子又是全身湿透。疑疑惑惑把它赶回马群，套住它用马鞭子揍它一顿，可是这天晚上，儿马子挣断缰绳又跑了。主人不得不留心到底怎么回事。	（2）One day, the colt unexpectedly stayed out for a whole night. Early morning the raiser rode to look for it, a spectacular silhouette registering on his eyes. The red colt, whinnying towards the sun, was standing loftily as a giant on the hilltop. Near to him, the colt was found to be drenched again. Being kept in suspense, the raiser had to drive it back to horses, then roped it up and lashed with a whip. However, the colt split the rein and ran away once again, which alarmed the raiser what had really happened.
（3）太阳偏西，红鬃儿马子独自离开马群朝着草滩那边的山上跑去。夕阳射在它的身上，它的身子如锦缎一样闪闪发光；夕阳也照着它的红鬃，那顺着脖子拖下来的长长的鬃毛一跳一跳，正如一团火焰在燃烧。	（3）Now was afternoon, the red colt departed alone for the mountain, there lying a grass pool at the skirt of it. The setting sunlights fell on its body, glistening as smoothly as silks on every inch of its skin, and along his neck was long red horsehair, dancing like burning flame.
（4）主人骑着马，远远跟在后面。他的头颅刚跃出山岗，立刻使劲勒住马，他被眼前的情景惊呆了。	（4）The raiser on the horse, followed far away the colt. The moment he reached the hilltop, he immediately reined in and was shocked by what he saw.
（5）两只狼！	（5）Two wolves!
（6）这是两只狡猾的狼。它们一前一后把红鬃儿马子夹在中间，转着圈子寻找攻击机会。儿马子却毫无惧色。它那长长的鬃毛现在竖起来了，在脖子上轻轻晃动，正像一面战旗在飘扬。它谨慎小心地踏着步子，移动着身子，不断破坏着狼的进攻角度。	（6）These coony wolves sandwiched the colt by front and back, circling around for seizing any attack points. The red colt, even without giving an air of horror, but cocked his long swaying horsehair,waving slightly like a battleflag. It tried to defend against every possible attack by meticulously pacing and moving.

（7）半空里黑影一闪，一只狼斜刺里闪电般向儿马子的脖子扑去。另一条紧跟着跃起，冲向儿马子腹部，危险！儿马子不慌不忙，身子微微一侧，长鬃啪的一下，宛如一条巨鞭，把第一只狼抽得在地上连翻了几个跟头，紧跟着后蹄腾空，把第二只狼踢出数丈。两只狼沮丧地爬起来，又开始组织进攻。主人勒马回逃。只在心里祝愿儿马子可别打败。

（8）儿马子平安地回来了，它如凯旋的将军，跑进马群里左冲右撞，和母马亲热地嬉戏，像在夸耀自己保卫马群的赫赫战功。

（9）主人却又把它套住，又用马鞭子揍了它一顿，边打边骂："逞能的东西，找死的东西！"打完了，又喂了它点料。

（10）这一天，儿马子被拴在圈里，不许出场。天傍黑，远处传来狼嗥，儿马子暴躁不安，它吼、它踢马槽，简直疯了一样，在屋里喝酒的主人气冲冲出来，拿鞭要打，儿马子前趴后踢，根本不让近前，主人只好隔着马槽揍它两鞭子，想不到儿马子长鬃一竖，身子一侧，"啪"地一下，把主人抽了个跟头。啊，马鬃！全是这鬃把你烧的！主人恼羞成怒地从地上爬起来，跑回屋，拿出一把锋利的剪刀，跑到马槽上去，"咔嚓咔嚓"，马鬃纷纷落地。他得意地骂："看你他妈再去惹事！"

（11）这一夜，主人不断听到狼嗥和马嘶声。但他不敢出来，他相信儿马子没了鬃也不敢出去。天亮了，主人出去一看，惊呆了：槽头只剩下半截咬断的缰绳。

（7）Suddenly, a black shape flashed before his eyes. It was a wolf, springing at the colt's neck as a bolt of lighting from an oblique direction and the other one closely followed, throwing itself at the colt's abdomen. How dangerous! However, the colt showed his poise and tilted slightly to fly his horsehair like a heavy whip, lashing one wolf with such a hard splat that it was bumped backwards for several somersaults. The colt's hindlegs jumped to the air and kicked the other one far away. Two wolves picked themselves up disappointedly, starting to organise a new attack for secong time. The raiser fled the fierce scene, what he could only do was to pray for the colt.

（8）To his surprise, the colt came back without any injury. As a triumphal general, it ran into horses and joslted by companions and flirted with mares as if flaunting its great contributions to protecting everyone from danger.

（9）But the raiser lassoed him again, whipping while scolded, "Badass, you arecourting death!" After the punishment, the raiser still gave it some forage crops.

（10）That day, the colt was chained down in the stable. Night fell. Somewhere distant came the howl of wolves. The colt had been roaring and crazily kicking the manger when the raiser was drinking in the house. Hearing the noise, he stormed out of the room and intended to whip the colt. But he failed because the colt gave no approchable chance, kicking up and down all the time. The raiser had to lash him over the manger,but tumbled and only to be whipped by his powerful horsehair. Oh! Horsehair! Damn it makes you vain and foolish! Enraged, the red-faced raiser rose up to his feet and fetched a scissor from the room, then he jumped on the manger and cut the horsehair. He cursed with satisfaction,"Wanna go out? No way!"

（11）That night, howls and whinnies had been continuously impacted the raiser's ears. But he daren't go out, for he betted, without horsehair, the colt had no courage to fight. Day broke. The raiser came out and astonished. There left nothing in manger but a half-bited rein.

（12）主人骑马去找，他走过山头，希望再看到儿马子对着红日嘶鸣；他走过山冈，希望再看到儿马子和野狼搏斗，然而他只在草地上发现了血迹……主人对着草原呼喊，草原沉默，冷冷地把他的声音抛掷回来。主人不由浑身发抖。	（12）He drove his horse to look for the colt. After crossing the mountain, he expected to see the colt fighting against those wolves, while he just found the blood on the grass. He yelled at the land, but it kept silent, casting back his voice mercilessly. A thrill of horror overwhelming his body.
（13）远处，传来得意的狼嗥。	（13）Far came the exultation of howls.

3 译者后记

在翻译本文时，我尽量采取与原文相一致的叙述方式即"白描"进行操作，但是译文不可避免地会多过原文，原文语言精练，但译文在最大化程度上与原文保持相近文体的同时，最重要的是保证译文的通顺、翔实和准确。国外的小小说即便很短，但是若做到内容通顺弄懂，字数也会超过1000词；而中国方块字有些就可以省略不说，也不会影响内容的通顺性，所以更加凝练传神。因此，在许多细节上，为了保证"信"，我做了略微详细地解释。

关于选词。这篇小小说的精彩之处就是在于描绘红鬃马与狼群搏斗的精彩过程，所以使用了大量的动词，充满了动感和画面感，因此译文也选用了较多的动词，直接将红鬃马的动态跃然纸上，并且这些词十分常见，较为短小，读起来也更加朗朗上口。关于描写静态画面的形容词，我个人认为在译文中可以表达得更为美观，但碍于思索时间有限，所以没有做到美之极致，还有更多提升完善的空间。关于构句，我将简单句与复杂句交替使用，避免单调或者晦涩。

以上是我的译后心得，翻译是一种美学，更是精巧的学问，只有在不断的实践中，才能慢慢领悟翻译的真谛，发现美，寻找美，创造美是一位译者所应该具备的起码的素养。